St. John's
Halifax
Ottawa
Montreal
Toronto

A GREENER THUMB

PENGUIN BOOKS

Mark Cullen is Canada's leading garden expert. His education in horticulture began as a child in the family garden business; he is now President of Weall & Cullen Garden Centres throughout Southern Ontario. He is the resident garden expert on CFRB Radio and for *Canadian Living* magazine, and the author of a syndicated garden column for newspapers throughout Canada. He is also the author of *The All Seasons Gardener* and co-author of *The Real Dirt*.

Contributing Editors: Clifford Maynes and Kathy Woodcock
Horticultural Editor: Russ Gomme
Copy Editor: Christopher Blackburn
Jacket Design: Monique Oyagi
Book Design and Art Direction: Andrew Smith
Layout: Annabelle Stanley
Art Production: Nancy Knox
Illustrator: Wallace Edwards
Map Artist: Donna Gordon
Studio Photography: Dieter Hessel
Line Illustrations: Lynn McIlvride Evans
Section Illustrations: Paul Zwolak
Typesetting: Q Composition

Lawn Boy power mower and roto-tiller
provided courtesy of Outboard Marine Canada.

A Greener Thumb

THE COMPLETE GUIDE TO GARDENING IN CANADA

MARK CULLEN

Penguin Books

PENGUIN BOOKS
Published by the Penguin Group
Penguin Books Canada Ltd, 10 Alcorn Avenue, Toronto, Ontario, Canada M4V 3B2
Penguin Books Ltd, 27 Wrights Lane, London W8 5TZ, England
Penguin Putnam Inc., 375 Hudson Street, New York, New York, 10014, U.S.A.
Penguin Books Australia Ltd, Ringwood, Victoria, Australia
Penguin Books (NZ) Ltd, cnr Rosedale and Airborne Roads, Albany, Auckland 1310, New Zealand

Penguin Books Ltd, Registered Offices:
Harmondsworth, Middlesex, England

First published in Viking by Penguin Books Canada Limited, 1990
Published in Penguin Books, 1998

3 5 7 9 10 8 6 4

Manufactured in China.

Canadian Cataloguing in Publication Data

Cullen, Mark, 1956-
A greener thumb

ISBN 0-14-027307-7

1. Gardening - Canada. I. Title.

SB453.3.C2C84 1998 635.9'0971 C97-932097-6

Visiti Penguin Canada's web site at **www.penguin.ca**

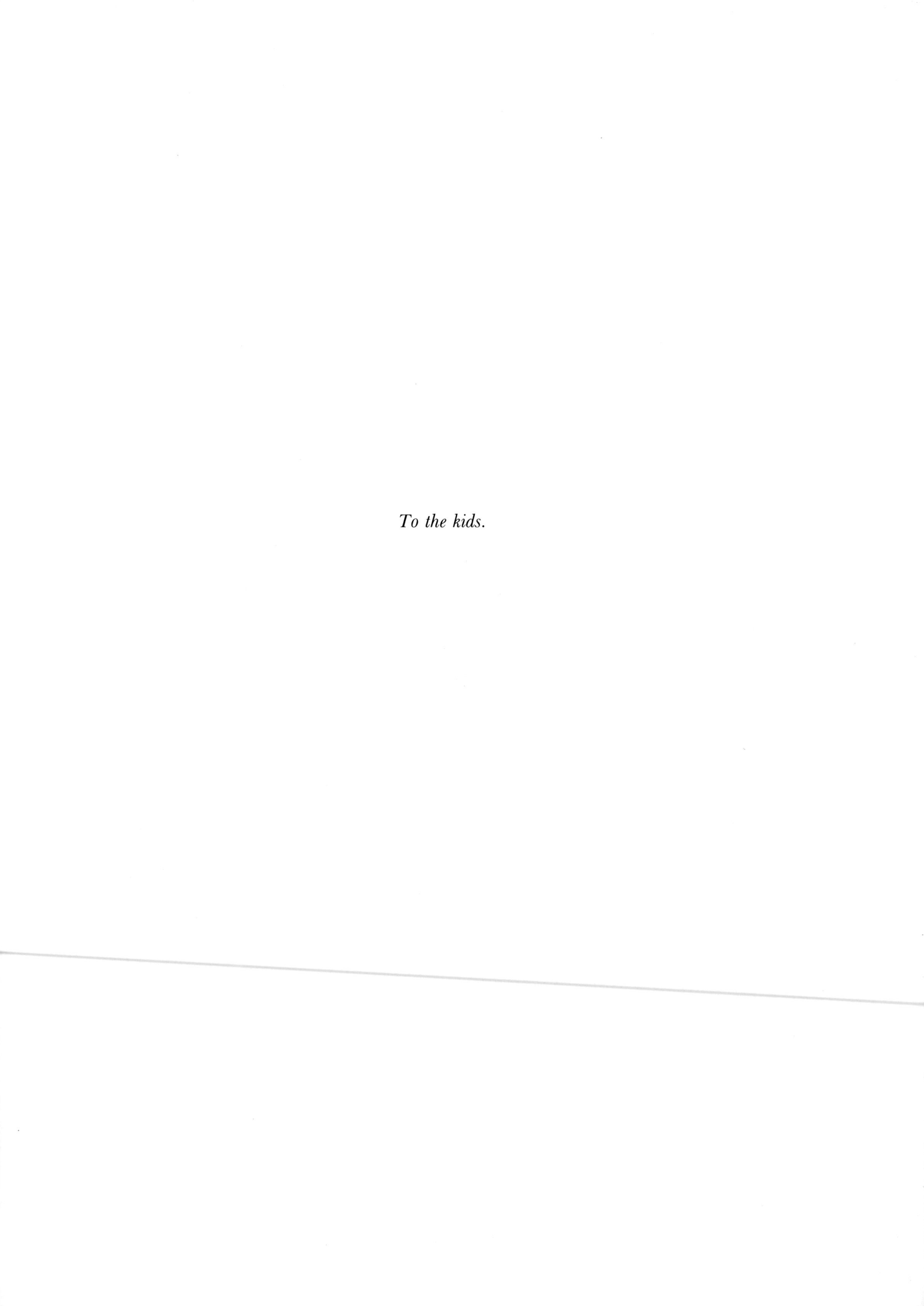

To the kids.

TABLE OF CONTENTS

SECTION III

SECTION IV

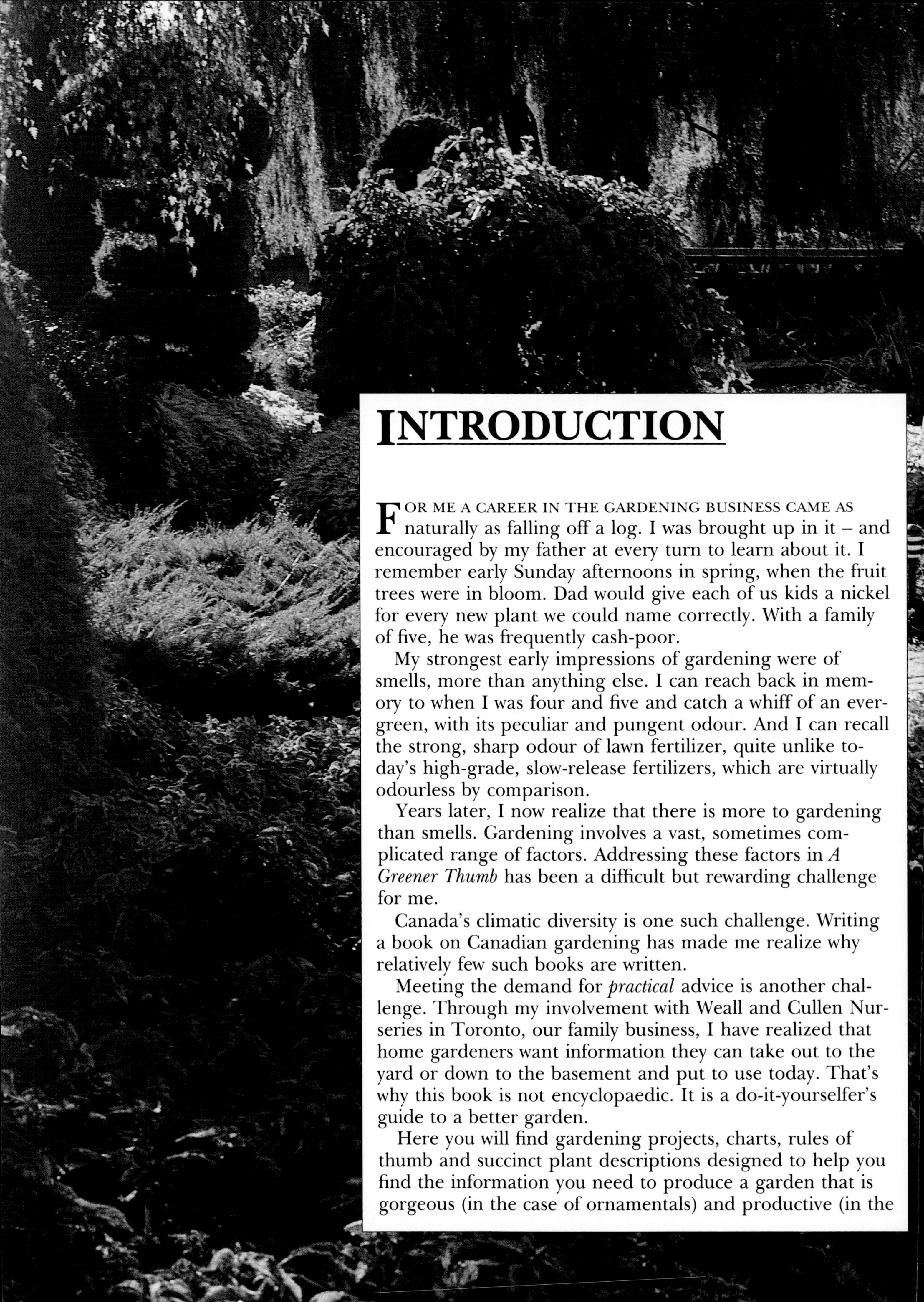

INTRODUCTION

FOR ME A CAREER IN THE GARDENING BUSINESS CAME AS naturally as falling off a log. I was brought up in it – and encouraged by my father at every turn to learn about it. I remember early Sunday afternoons in spring, when the fruit trees were in bloom. Dad would give each of us kids a nickel for every new plant we could name correctly. With a family of five, he was frequently cash-poor.

My strongest early impressions of gardening were of smells, more than anything else. I can reach back in memory to when I was four and five and catch a whiff of an evergreen, with its peculiar and pungent odour. And I can recall the strong, sharp odour of lawn fertilizer, quite unlike today's high-grade, slow-release fertilizers, which are virtually odourless by comparison.

Years later, I now realize that there is more to gardening than smells. Gardening involves a vast, sometimes complicated range of factors. Addressing these factors in *A Greener Thumb* has been a difficult but rewarding challenge for me.

Canada's climatic diversity is one such challenge. Writing a book on Canadian gardening has made me realize why relatively few such books are written.

Meeting the demand for *practical* advice is another challenge. Through my involvement with Weall and Cullen Nurseries in Toronto, our family business, I have realized that home gardeners want information they can take out to the yard or down to the basement and put to use today. That's why this book is not encyclopaedic. It is a do-it-yourselfer's guide to a better garden.

Here you will find gardening projects, charts, rules of thumb and succinct plant descriptions designed to help you find the information you need to produce a garden that is gorgeous (in the case of ornamentals) and productive (in the

case of vegetables and fruits).

This book also includes many of my personal garden experiences. Gardening, I have found, is a personal thing. Although technical advice is often useful, there is no substitute for the knowledge that comes from your own trials and errors over a lifetime of gardening. So *A Greener Thumb* is often the equivalent in book form of the personal experiences gardeners share with one another over the back fence, in the back seat of a car pool, in the cafeteria at work, or on the sidelines at their kids' soccer games.

The diversity of gardeners is another challenge for the author of a gardening book. Gardening is Canada's most popular outdoor activity – and it sometimes seems that every Canadian has his or her own vision of an ideal garden. Thus, *A Greener Thumb* describes a large sample of the vast selection of plants now available, including some gourmet and unusual vegetable varieties. And the book surveys the incredible variety of different gardening techniques, from portable rooftop containers to raised bed vegetable gardeners. If you are a novice gardener, *A Greener Thumb* will help you to determine your own special vision of a dream garden.

Gardeners also vary in their commitment to their gardens. Low-maintenance gardening and gardening for the lazy gardener are popular topics today, as well as perennial flower gardening (the fastest growing segment of gardening and *not* for lazy gardeners), annual flower and vegetable gardening and, of course, gardening in containers. Your property size, soil and weather conditions have little to do with your commitment to the aforementioned vision you have of an ideal garden. *A Greener Thumb* addresses every level of commitment to this particular pastime in an organized and easy to understand format.

Spend some time with *A Greener Thumb* and I believe you will find your gardening experiences more successful. Armed with new knowledge of how to save time and money *and* produce a beautiful garden, your attraction to gardening will grow as naturally as rolling off a log.

SECTION I

Making the Garden

THE KEY TO LASTING SATISFACTION from your garden is preparation. Just as a building requires a solid foundation, your garden requires solid groundwork. This section deals with the techniques and skills you'll need to produce a good-looking and productive garden.

Plant hardiness is one major factor. Familiarize yourself with the zone map on the inside cover to ensure that the plants you use can thrive in your climate.

Soil is another major factor. The information outlined below will help you understand the soil-conditioning methods and amendments needed to make your soil rich and friable.

This section on Making a Garden removes the hocus-pocus of gardening, with an emphasis on non-chemical organic approaches. Read it as necessary background to the advice offered for the individual plants, shrubs, vines, and trees listed in the chapters that follow.

Gardening may seem complicated to the novice, but it's not really. Instead of all the technical mumbo-jumbo, I find that it's easier to rely on some simple rules of nature. My Rules of Thumb should help you dig into your garden with confidence and, ultimately, the satisfaction of doing it right.

CHAPTER 1
LANDSCAPING

Landscaping – the process by which we shape our environment – is an art, a science, and a craft. And, unless you can afford to hire an army of designers, horticulturists, soil scientists, and labourers to landscape your own yard, it's also a lot of hard work.

Fortunately, it's all worthwhile – for the aesthetic enjoyment, the creative satisfaction, and the economic benefits of a landscaping job well done.

This chapter provides a brief overview of the numerous considerations involved in planning your own landscape. These range from the inspirational to the mundane, the fanciful to the practical. In the end you must determine the appropriate compromise between what you want from your landscape and the options you have to work with.

Above all, don't be intimidated. Nobody is better qualified to determine the style and shape of your yard. Be creative. Think of it as an opportunity to put your personal stamp on a small corner of the world. If you run into problems, help is as close as the nearest garden centre or library. Most nurseries willingly offer planting advice and landscape services. There are also horticultural societies, garden clubs and other local organizations that may have the answers to your questions, and that welcome as members anyone interested in horticulture.

A garden (right) and the garden plan from which it was developed (below). Your garden plan must integrate a variety of factors, including intended uses, aesthetic preferences, financial resources, and the characteristics of the site.

DECIDING WHAT YOU WANT

There are many different schools of landscaping. The naturalist school favours a minimalist approach. Naturalists believe that landscaping should reflect rather than alter what is found in nature. On the other extreme, the conventional suburban school of landscaping demands that every lot in a new subdivision be planted uniformly according to strict rules. In some cases, developers actually restrict home owners in their selection of plants.

There is no right or wrong style when it comes to landscaping, just different tastes and philosophies. You have to decide for yourself what you want: an austere, pristine Japanese garden, an immaculately manicured and symmetrical garden in the classical French style, or a colourfully disordered English cottage garden – what my wife Mary calls "a messy garden", a style she favours.

Inspiration

If you are not sure what you want, take a look at what others have done. Winter is a good time to browse through the pages of this book, studying the illustrations and the descriptions. While you're at it, check out a good sampling of gardening magazines and books. Summer is a good time to tour your neighbourhood, public gardens, local parks, nurseries – even shopping malls – for a firsthand look at a variety of landscape treatments. This will help you decide which plants and planting techniques you like best. You will acquire an educated eye without spending a dime. You'll also learn to

Your choice of plants must correspond to factors such as available light. Here, shade-loving Impatiens have been used to good effect on a shady site.

identify new plants, and develop a working knowledge of what plants grow well in your area.

Talk to friends and neighbours about *their* gardens. It always amazes me how the topic of gardening induces even the shyest of people to volunteer information, enthusiastically, about their gardening experiences. Fact is, most "experienced" gardeners (myself included) learn far more by asking questions and listening carefully to the gardening experiences of other gardeners than through practical gardening experience.

A few pertinent questions

Good landscape architects, like good interior decorators, consult at length with clients about how they want to use their property. But you don't need professional help to determine your own priorities and intentions. Anyone with a long-term interest in a property should do this. It will save you time and money, and help you to avoid grief in the long run.

Take several blank sheets of paper, then jot down your thoughts on each question:

* How does your family want to make use of this landscape? (Consider such uses as a flower garden, vegetable garden, play area, barbecue, patio, swimming pool, swing set, or sand box.)
* How will your yard look from indoors (especially the room you intend to use most)?
* How will it look throughout the year? (Include evergreens for year-round colour.)
* Do you want to attract birds?
* Do you want shady spots and wind breaks?
* What about the future? Are the children who need an enclosed play area today desperately going to want a swimming pool five years from now?
* Do the family cooks yearn for an herb garden by the kitchen door?
* How are pets going to be restrained?
* Is mowing the lawn a favourite pastime, or should your lawn area be reduced?
* Do you have the space for both flower and vegetable gardens? Do you have the time to tend them in addition to your regular property maintenance tasks? Do you want a low-maintenance landscape or can you afford to put some work into it?
* Is there adequate storage space?
* Where do you gain the best view of your landscape?
* Do you want to highlight certain sections of your property?
* Is there a landscape style that appeals to you?
* Would your family prefer a naturalized wildflower meadow to a formal Rose garden?
* How will your landscape design complement the architectural style of your home?
* Are there natural features of the landscape that need to be accented, minimized or eliminated?
* What materials and patterns do you favour for paths and driveways?
* Is the entrance to your home welcoming?
* Do you want to emphasize privacy, using plants as screens?

RULE OF THUMB

Plants come in every conceivable shade and hue. If you're unsure of how to best combine colour in the garden, use a colour wheel. Each colour on the wheel harmonizes with the one beside it. Dramatic contrast is obtained by combining colours opposite one another. For instance, yellow blooms complement blue or violet shades.

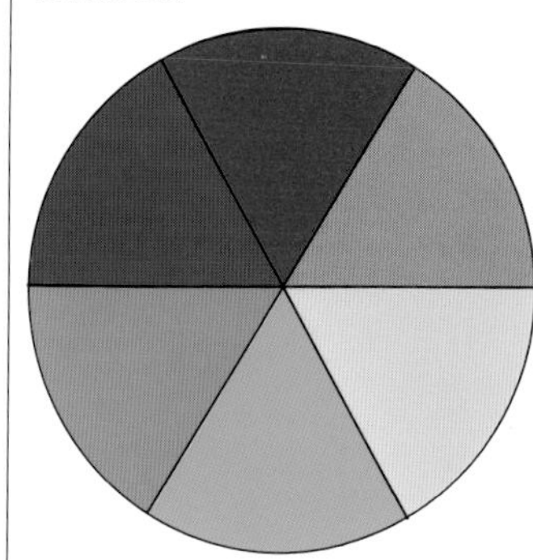

TAKING STOCK

Like any renovation, landscaping begins by taking stock of what raw materials you've got to work with. This includes physical features, like the size and shape of your property, soil type, drainage and slope. It also includes climatic factors, like wind, temperature and average rainfall. We gardeners like to think we are the masters of our own backyards, but we ignore nature at our peril.

Get to know your soil characteristics during the planning stages so you can choose appropriate plants, plan for the necessary soil amendments, etc. See Chapter 2 for details.

Climate

Every Canadian gardener has lost at least one plant to the dreaded "winter-kill". Climate can be ruthless, and it pays to know your enemy. Don't buy a single plant until you are familiar with the "plant hardiness designation" of your region. Major nursery plants are sold with notes indicating the zones in which they are most likely to survive. See the inside cover of this book for a climate zone map of Canada.

More detailed maps are available from government agricultural offices that indicate climatic zones and general weather histories, including frost dates, precipitation levels, and general wind conditions.

However, climate zone maps won't tell you exactly what's going to happen in your backyard. They won't prophesy extreme departures from the average, such as unusually severe winters, mild winters, floods, droughts or hail-storms – all of which could devastate long-established plants. They will only tell what sort of weather you can generally expect within your region.

Nor will climate zone maps tell you the microclimate of your immediate area, which may differ considerably from the climate of your region. Microclimate is a function of topography and siting, which affect the amount of shelter, sun, and drainage your garden provides. It generally requires a few seasons and a few lost plants to gain a working knowledge of your microclimate, and to determine which plants will adapt well to localized weather conditions.

Site

Prepare a scale drawing of your property, including boundaries, paths or driveways, and significant objects like trees and storage sheds. How do these features affect your landscape plan? You will want to incorporate some of them, perhaps with amendments; you will want to eliminate others altogether.

Is your site exposed or sheltered? Some plants, like Delphinium, need to be staked if they are exposed to winds. Many plants need lots of sunlight, and won't do well on a shaded site. Others need shade, which you will have to provide if it is not naturally available. See Chapter 2 for a further discussion of sun and shade tolerance. See the individual plant descriptions for the sun and shade tolerance of each.

Soil

Like people, plants need food to live (consumed in a liquid form in the case of plants). And, like people, they have varied nutritional requirements. A soil bed which produces a carpet of Primrose will not sustain Portulaca or Poppies. Read Chapter 2 for information about different soil types and the amendments which are available to improve or adapt the soil to suit the plants you want to grow. Read the plant descriptions throughout this book for the requirements of each.

Resources

List the resources you will need to realize your desires, including money, time, equipment, and skills. In one sense, landscaping pays for itself – it improves your property value while increasing your enjoyment of your home. But most people want to do more than they can afford, at least in the short term.The costs involved may include excavation, soil amendments, tools, containers, lawn furniture, nursery stock, gazebos, fencing, patios or pools. It adds up pretty quickly.

Fortunately, you don't have to buy all of this in one year. You can stage your landscaping over several seasons.

Many gardeners, especially new gardeners, plan bigger plots than they can comfortably or efficiently maintain. If you're a novice, decide what size of garden you want and then reduce that estimate by half.

Starting out with a garden of modest proportions has several advantages. It is easier to focus your energy and attention. Weeding doesn't become an awesome chore and, where vegetables are involved, harvests are manageable. You'll also gain practical experience in

gardening techniques, like succession planting or interplanting, without becoming frustrated by your own ambition. Once your gardening skills are well honed you can enlarge your plot as your budget permits.

Landscaping over a period of several years requires patience and compromise, virtues well understood by experienced gardeners. It will also require some long-term scheduling. Make sure there's access for heavy equipment if you plan to install a pool three years from now. Delay planting trees or laying paths that would be demolished by a back hoe. And if you are developing a foundation planting surrounding your house, begin by planting tall specimens or shrubs adjacent to the dwelling. Add plants of medium and then low height as you want to extend the border. Planning minimizes work and trauma to plants.

To all things there is a season . . .

Gardeners share a common interest with bees – both work to maximize bloom. Bees do it by transferring pollen; people do it through plant breeding and plant culture. People tend to be rather more deliberate about the process.

If you can co-ordinate the succession of blooms so that it is both harmonious and continuous, spring through summer, you have achieved real landscaping success. Learn the seasonal history of the plants that interest you. Each plant has its own characteristics. Some plants, especially annuals, are very accommodating and provide bloom over the course of several months. Others, like many of the best-loved bulbs and perennials, may only flower a few days.

Form

Shape is a major consideration when spacing plants. Healthy plants increase in size and bulk, spreading out as their roots and foliage expand. They will compete with the surrounding vegetation for moisture and nutrients. The shape of your landscape is bound to alter over the course of time. Plan accordingly by giving plants, particularly large ones like Hosta, room to spread out.

Plants grow up as well as out. If you're working with ornamental plants, stagger them according to height. Generally speaking, place tall plants like Rudbeckia at the back of a border, medium-size plants like Iris in the middle, and low or ground-hugging plants like Dianthus at the front. Narrow shrub and flower borders appear deeper if you place darker-coloured plants at the back and lighter-coloured ones up front.

Other large items in the landscape like trees and hedges form a backdrop against which borders will be viewed. If you view a rectangular border from a distance, put tall flowers at the far end.

Texture

Successful landscapes are rhythmical. The eye should travel with ease from one section to another. Accents like curved borders, plants of different height and varying foliage, ornaments and ground covers provide points of interest throughout your landscape. Ground covers, including turfgrass, are especially important in this regard. They are like the threads of a landscape; they fill in the bald spots and tie it all together.

Make imaginative use of contrasting form and texture to create a striking overall impression.

Use low-voltage lighting to show off your home and landscape after dark.

Shaping the Space

By now, you have thoroughly studied your property, analyzed your own practical and aesthetic concerns, and learned quite a bit about gardens and gardening. Shaping the space is the next logical step. It is time to begin making adjustments to your terrain – on paper, at least. Using photocopies of the scale drawing you prepared, pencil-in various alternative treatments for your landscape.

Landscape architects have developed standard treatments for dealing with problems of shape and form. Some of them may suit your purpose:

- Trees and other big items tend to dominate. If that's not what you want, find ways of redirecting attention elsewhere. Statuary or benches draw the eye from a large tree.
- Place specimen trees off centre in your yard – preferably toward a corner, to avoid making your yard look small.
- Break the line imposed by a long fence with shrubbery and vines.
- Retain mature plants whenever possible. Established plants are already a proven success in your microclimate, and they are able to provide a finished effect which new nursery stock can't provide for several years.
- Pools are much better integrated into a landscape if they are combined with container gardens. Consider the addition of a small fountainhead and leave room for colourful annuals or perennials.
- Long or very narrow lots can be made less awkward by introducing visual distractions. A path that curves off centre, an elaborate bird bath, or an assortment of brightly coloured plants arranged at different heights will reduce the tunnel effect. A bench offers a logical resting place for your body as well as your eyes.
- Square lots offer the interesting design possibilities of symmetrical and island beds. I always avoid straight line beds on a square lot. Curved beds are more interesting, and help to enhance the illusion of space.
- Terraces or rock gardens are both highly favoured treatments for slopes or hillside lots. The stairs and retaining walls that connect levels can themselves become focal points in your design.
- Where lots are very steep, extended decks or multi-tiered decks joined by stairs are often the most appropriate means of obtaining usable outdoor living space. Flagstone or pre-cast concrete steps can also be used.

- Consider the other significant elements of your landscape: paths, fences, patios or porches. These extras could make or break your design. Select materials for their durability and the ease of maintenance.
- Don't neglect decorative finishing touches, such as containers, outdoor lighting, garden furniture, and ornaments. Containers can be used for a tremendous variety of plants, both large and small, and can often be placed in sites otherwise inappropriate for plants. Window boxes, hanging baskets and terracotta planters welcome visitors and, by repeating colour and pattern, they reinforce your design intentions.
- Good landscape plans, like the gardeners who design them, must be flexible. Plans should be capable of change to reflect changes in personal preferences and material costs, or the failure of plants to grow in your environment as intended.

Decorative finishes such as containers, outdoor lighting, and garden furniture can be used to reinforce your landscape design intentions.

If you have a long, narrow lot, avoid a tunnel effect by using a curved walkway and visual distractions to interrupt the view.

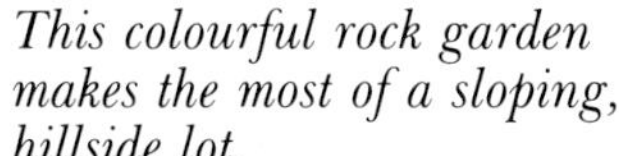

This colourful rock garden makes the most of a sloping, hillside lot.

CHAPTER 2

GARDEN PREPARATION AND MAINTENANCE

Dirty knees. They distinguish the gardener from the casual putterer, who cuts the grass and occasionally spares some token time to keep the yard respectable.

Gardeners wear their dirt proudly, mainly because they are proud of what their "dirt" produces. They understand something about the soil and have a respect and appreciation for it that further distinguishes them from their neighbour.

This chapter will explain some important things about your soil, and about the relative importance of your garden soil to plants. I'll explain how to improve your soil, how to plant in containers, the importance of light, how to winterize your garden and (this is my favourite part) how to build and produce your own compost. I'm sharing my passion for compost in this chapter in the hopes that you will indulge yourself in the exercise of composting and, in time, experience the satisfaction of producing your own beautiful garden from yard waste and kitchen scraps.

So take your time. The next few pages lay the groundwork for your most successful garden ever!

SOIL

If gardeners had commandments the first would be: Know Thy Soil. Understanding soil composition is the important first step in creating a bountiful garden.

Soil, the gardener's essential medium, is more than just dirt. At its best, it contains all the mineral and organic material necessary for healthy plant growth. Soil does more than provide support for plant roots – it is a community of living, breathing organisms. Every handful.

Soils differ, and plants differ in their soil requirements. Successful gardening depends on correctly matching plants with their preferred soils. This doesn't require a degree in chemistry or soil science. All you need is a working knowledge of soil and plant preferences. And planning.

Organics – the soul of soil

Poor soil can sometimes be made more workable if it is augmented with an alternate soil type. Adding sand to clay will improve its texture, for example, but adding complementary soils is usually not adequate by itself. The environmental conditions that created your soil type in the first place – lack of moisture, erosion, and nutrient depletion – are likely to reassert themselves. The only way to achieve enduring improvements in soil quality is with regular supplements of organic material, such as *mature* compost from plant material, rotted manures, peat or green crops.

Continuing organic supplements are necessary regardless of the quality of soil you begin with. You can bring in truckloads of rich topsoil, but even it will eventually need to be replaced unless it is cared for.

Organic material creates air pockets, counteracting the soil's natural, gravity-induced tendency to pack down. These air pockets help soil to absorb and retain water and oxygen, and allow growing roots to penetrate the soil easily.

Organic material also acts like a slow-release vitamin for your garden. As it decomposes, it gradually discharges the mineral elements essential to plant growth.

In nature, soil contains only 1 to 5 per cent organic material. It is in a constant process of decomposition, and the nutrients it produces are depleted by plants and aeration. To encourage continuing good performance, gardens need to be supplemented with organic material at least once a year. While there is varied opinion on the nutrient needs of plants, soil which is 20 per cent organic is sure to sustain plants very well indeed. Horticulturists suggest that higher levels of organic matter can result in excessively moist soil and nutrient imbalances. Soils that are 30 per cent organic are essentially acidic, unoxygenated muck.

Nutrients

Plant soil should provide a diet of 13 elements to promote growth and vigour. Most of these elements, such as calcium, copper and iron, are required in only small amounts. These are often referred to as "trace elements". But three – nitrogen (N), phosphorus (P), and potassium (K) – are required in much larger quantities. Nitrogen is needed for good colour and most aspects of growth. Nitrogen-deficient soils produce pale, stunted plants. Phosphorus, plentiful in seeds, is associated with blossom and root development. Potassium enhances plant respiration, stem growth and gen-

(Opposite) Plants may differ considerably in their soil requirements, depending on conditions in their native habitat. These Rhododendrons need acid, rich damp soil of the type common to shade woodlands.

Adding organic soil amendments is the best way to achieve better soil quality.

1. Crumble in alternative soil types to improve the consistency.

2. Add soil amendment such as manure, peat, or aged plant material compost.

3. Dig in well with a spade.

Digging in manure or compost to your soil bed provides early season nutrients and improves water retention capability.

eral health.

The element nutrients act together – too much or too little of any one can affect the ability of the others to function properly. Plants may be damaged as a result. Too much phosphorous will affect plant uptake of zinc and iron, resulting in retardation of growth and *chlorosis*, a common affliction of plants in which leaves turn yellow. Plants oversupplied with nitrogen at the expense of phosphorous will develop lush green stems and leaves but may fail to produce flowers.

Organics vs chemicals

Organic material is increasingly favoured by gardeners as the ideal nutrient source because it normally contains all the elements. A growing number of organic gardeners eschew all use of chemicals, some with spectacular results. The nutrients in organic material are discharged gradually, eliminating the danger of a burst of chemical action which may occur with chemical fertilizers. Inorganic fertilizers may supply the same nutrients but they do so without improving soil moisture or oxygen levels. Chemical fertilizers must also be measured and carefully applied to avoid overdoses which kill plant roots and foliage.

On the other hand, synthetic chemical fertilizers continue to find favour in some circles. When properly used, they are like blood transfusions for plants. Unlike slow-acting composts, they release nutrients into the soil rapidly and in known quantities. Many gardeners also find chemicals are less fuss, bother, and expense than compost or manures. A common mistake, however, is to assume that chemical fertilizers are complete substitutes for stable, organically rich soil. They aren't.

The most successful chemical gardeners are those who use chemicals to supplement an ongoing organic programme, for situations such as new plantings or a lawn that needs a quick fix.

Inorganic fertilizers are available in powder, liquid, granular, stick or spike forms. Instructions for application and coverage should be followed carefully. Always avoid direct contact with plant roots or crowns during application.

Ratings for the chief required elements – nitrogen, phosphorus, and potassium – are given in that order and as a percentage of weight. The amount of each will vary according to intended use. A typical lawn fertilizer formula, like 21-7-7, is higher in nitrogen than phosphorus because most gardeners prefer a green lawn to one which self-seeds. Conversely, a formula intended for flower borders or new tree plantings, like 6-12-12, contains more phosphorus to promote maturity and blossom development.

Slow-release spikes are popular for individual plants, particularly heavy-feeders. They discharge according to moisture and heat levels. They are less likely to leach or cause damage because they liberate elements into the soil very gradually. Synthetic organics such as urea formaldehyde are a main ingredient in most plant spikes.

THE ELEMENT NUTRIENTS

Macronutrient Elements

Nitrogen
Phosphorus
Potassium
Sulphur
Calcium
Magnesium

(Also, Carbon, Hydrogen, and Oxygen are macronutrient elements immediately available from air which don't require soil or bacteria to be converted to a usable form.)

Micronutrient Elements

Iron
Boron
Zinc
Manganese
Copper
Molybdenum
Chlorine

Fertilizing tips

- Always water well before you fertilize. Plant roots saturated with water are less likely to burn if a chemical is over-applied. Besides, when a plant is watered it is stimulated and better equipped to make use of the fertilizer.
- Fertilizers are most effective when applied during periods of peak growth. Elements that are not absorbed when they are discharged will simply leach away.
- Plants fertilized late in the growing season may produce new growth which doesn't adequately 'harden' in preparation for cold weather. Fertilize only with slow-release formulas in the late autumn to avoid excess winter-kill. Do not fertilize winter hardy plants from August 1 through October 15, with the exception of your lawn, which should receive an application of extra slow-release fertilizer between September and late November.
- Fill fertilizer applicators on a hard surface or over a piece of canvas cloth to avoid spills on your lawn or garden. If concentrated fertilizer spills unintentionally on vegetation, pick up what you can and then flood the area with water to prevent plants from burning.
- When spreading fertilizer, keep moving. Stop the flow of fertilizer every time you turn or a couple of steps before you stop.
- Fertilizers which contain broadleaf herbicides for killing weeds are intended for lawn use only. Gardens and trees (especially small ones) can be severely damaged if unintentional run-off, flooding or leaching occurs.

You can buy a backyard composter, or make your own. The composter should have spaces or holes to provide ventilation, which is necessary for the rotting process to work efficiently. Add alternating layers of kitchen scraps and yard wastes, and turn periodically.

COMPOST

Compost is a general term for plant material which has broken down into crumbly tilth. Compost aerates, provides nutrients and generally enriches the soil by providing plentiful organic matter. It has been called "brown gold" and "the cadillac of soil amendments" for those reasons. It can be purchased commercially or produced easily at home by using kitchen and garden scraps that would otherwise go to waste.

Good maintenance of your compost heap is the trick to reducing disagreeable odours and maximizing nutrient potential. A compost heap can smell pleasantly like a hardwood forest after a spring rain if properly constructed.

Collect organic household waste in a bin or composter. Exclude any animal products that would attract flies or your neighbour's dog. This includes fats, even milk and oils.

In 5-6 in. (12.5-15 cm) layers, alternate kitchen scraps with a mixed layer of grass clippings and leaves. Material from the garden should be chopped into smaller pieces. The collection will need to be aerated or mixed together with a spade every 3 weeks or so.

You can cut leaves and pulled weeds into a fine mulch for the compost heap by running your lawn mower over them.

If you notice a bad odour, add extra organic material, like leaves or grass clippings. Aerate by stirring or turning with a garden fork.

When the bin is full the mixture may need to be stored until fully mature. Compost takes an average about 3 months to reach the point where it can be worked into your garden soil. Less time may be required in hot weather, which aids decomposition. Heat also helps to eradicate harmful bacteria and weed seeds.

Composters work best in a sunny location. Water during hot spells but in heavy rains apply a plastic cover. In cold periods a sheet of clear plastic will trap heat and keep the compost working.

SOIL TYPES

Soil consists primarily of minerals which fall into three main particle groups: sand, silt and clay. Sand particles are the largest, clay particles are the smallest. These particles combine in varying proportions with organic material to produce topsoil, the 8 in. (20 cm) crust of the earth's surface which sustains all plant life.

Soil is classified according to its primary constituents:

* Sandy soil contains mostly particles of sand. It attracts heat but leaches water and nutrients rapidly.
* Clay soil consists of minute, densely packed particles. Clay soil holds little oxygen but retains water well.
* Silty soil shares characteristics of both sandy and clay soil.
* Loam – what I often refer to as sandy loam – is optimal gardening soil. It is composed of nearly equal parts coarse sand, fine sand, silt and clay. True loam contains plentiful organic material and is "friable" – it breaks up in clumps. Loam can be easily recognized by its dark colour and tendency to crumble or smear when squeezed in the palm of your hand.

If you're unsure of your soil type, have it tested. Government agricultural offices often do the job at minimal cost. Testing kits are sold by garden supply companies, but unless you use the kit very accurately you could make an error.

Tests are conducted by gathering soil from different sites on your property. It's then mixed together and tested for general characteristics, including acidity.

If time is short, drop by a full-service garden centre with a soil sample. With one good look, an experienced horticulturist can determine the basic characteristics of your soil. Don't be surprised if he or she gives it a good smell and taste.

Once you know your soil type and characteristics it's time to decide what plants are best suited to it, or what amendments may be required to grow the garden you want.

Rocky Soil

The amount of rocks and stones will affect the fertility of your soil. It is easily drained, but needs frequent applications of bulky nutrients such as manure and peat moss, to improve fertility and water retention.

Silt

This soil type has small, fine particles, which compact easily when wet, causing poor drainage. Silt needs to be amended with compost.

Limestone

A pale, light coloured soil characterized by a high proportion of calcareous matter. It is free draining, and highly alkaline. Limestone needs to be amended with topsoil and frequent application of organic matter to improve water retention and Ph balance.

Clay

Clay (left and lower left) is a heavy, compact soil composed of fine particles which causes poor drainage. It is one of the most common soils in Canada, and while generally good for growing plants, needs the addition of sand to make it more friable.

For a wide variety of plant types in your garden, loam is an optimum soil type to have.

Sandy Loam

Similar to Loam but with more silicates, or sand particles in the mix. It therefore draws more easily, losing its nutrients quicker. It will need to be fertilized more frequently than loam, but is generally a good soil for growing.

Loam

Loam is the ideal soil type for growing. It is dark loosely compacted and contains small stones and pebbles. It has a high quantity of humus or organic matter and has good water retention.

Soil pH (acidity) should match plant requirements. Test the pH with a home test kit, or send a soil sample to a testing laboratory. Add amendments such as lime and sulphur to adjust pH.

Soil acidity

If you can grow berries and Lily-of-the-Valley but fail at Clematis or Cabbages, the problem is too much acidity. Soil acidity affects plant growth by affecting the bacterial and mineral interaction required to produce nutrients. Acidity also encourages or discourages fungal disorders of plants.

Soil is either acidic, alkaline or neutral. The pH scale measures hydrogen ion concentrations in graduations from 0 to 14: 0 is pure acid, 7 is neutral, and 14 is completely alkaline or basic. Most vegetation (certainly not all) thrives in slightly acid soil with a pH of 6.5. Little plant life survives at a pH of less than 3.5 or greater than 7.5.

Plants which prefer strongly acid soils grow naturally in moist, even bog-like conditions, or in shaded forests where pH levels range between 3.5 to 5.5. They include most evergreens, wild berries, Azaleas, true alpines like Primula and Gentian, certain Iris and numerous other species. Potatoes thrive in acid soil. The scab organism which often afflicts them is unable to survive under acidic conditions. Acid soils boast plentiful humus content with high levels of iron, manganese and aluminum.

Bloom colour can be affected by the presence of aluminum. Common Hydrangea is blue in acid soil but pink in alkaline or neutral soil. (Aluminum nitrate is often used as a soil amendment to turn Hydrangea blue.)

Alkaline soils are generally drier and feature high levels of calcium and magnesium. Plants that tolerate alkaline soils include Lilac, Delphinium, Baby's Breath and many vegetables, particularly members of the Cabbage family. Broccoli, Brussels Sprout, Cauliflower and other Cabbage cousins are often attacked by a fungus called clubroot disease if they're planted in acid conditions. However, Cabbage is one of the few domestic plants that will survive at a high pH level.

Altering acidity

Acidity increases with additions of organic material and fertilizers. You can hurry the process with additives such as peat moss (my favourite and least risky), sulphur, or sulphates of ammonium, iron or aluminum.

Acidity is reduced by increasing the lime content of the soil. Calcitic or dolomitic limestone, available in finely crushed form, will do the job.

Altering acidity can be a tricky, expensive business. It may be too costly to try to change acidity over a large area. Strongly alkaline soils have immense buffering capacity, and it is unlikely that you will be able to transform the acidity of soil with a pH of more than 7, except temporarily.

Attempts to change pH are most successful when applied to an entire bed rather than isolated plants.

Attempts to increase alkalinity are best carried out at the end of the growing season to avoid harming those plants – the majority – which favour slight acidity.

Drainage

Plants need water to survive. As hydroponics has proven, plants are more dependent on water than soil. Many plants are 95 per cent water by weight.

Water is absorbed through roots at soil level and drawn up through a system of vessels analogous to the human circulatory system. Water dissolves and transfers otherwise inaccessible mineral elements within plants.

Plants actually use and retain a remarkably tiny fraction of the water they consume – about 2 per cent. The rest of the water absorbed by the roots is transpired, or eliminated, into the atmosphere. In a single growing season, a healthy Corn plant will transpire more than 100 gal. (450 L) of water. A mature

Maple absorbs and transpires close to 80 gal. (360 L) of water daily.

Water is naturally obtained by plants from three sources: rain, dew and the water table. The water table is like an underground lake which normally rests well below the earth's surface. Some gardens rest too far above the water table while others rest too close to it, or to underground streams feeding into it. In either case, drainage will be a problem.

When drainage is excessive water sinks rapidly to the water table, depriving large trees and other vegetation of needed moisture. Nutrients may also leach off more easily. When drainage is inadequate, bog-like conditions can result. Soil becomes "anaerobic" – lacking in oxygen.

If you suspect you have a drainage problem, dig a hole big enough to hold a large shrub, about 2-ft. (60-cm), and fill it with water. If it drains in less than 2 hours you've got a problem with excessive drainage. If it takes over a day, you've got a problem with inadequate drainage.

A common remedy is sometimes available for both problems: amend the soil – with sand for poorly drained soil, and with top soil for soil which is too well drained.

However, if your soil is water-logged, amending it might not be adequate. You may need to dig a trench between the high and low points of your property to encourage run-off. This method is commonly used in Canadian gardens to divert excessive run-off in spring when snow is melting. Plants may survive winter only to be killed off by spring flooding. They either drown or are washed away.

If your drainage problem is severe, combine trenching with drainage pipes. Dry wells of gravel and sand also work well to collect water from isolated low spots. They are especially recommended for shrubs and trees located wherever drainage is a problem.

Gardeners sometimes circumvent the problem of drainage by using raised beds. Still others solve the dilemma by accommodating nature and planting according to existing conditions. Many beautiful marsh and water garden plants are genetically adapted to wet conditions and survive in no other.

ROTATION OF PLANT FAMILIES

Soil-borne diseases and insect infestations can be reduced by rotating susceptible plants to new locations each season. Vegetables from the Cabbage and Potato families require rotation. They should be isolated from other members of the same family in adjoining locations in the same or succeeding seasons. Related flower species and bulbs can be afflicted by soil-borne pests and will also benefit from rotation.

Plant families can be very large, and contain both flowers and vegetable members distinguished by their shared requirements and enemies. Threats can be reduced by isolating family members from one another and practising rotation planting.

Cabbage is a *Brassica*, or a member of the prolific Mustard family, known to horticulturists as *Cruciferae*. Its vegetable members include Broccoli, Brussels Sprout, Cabbage, Cauliflower, Kale, Rape and Turnip. The flowering members of the family are Arabis, Aubrieta, Aurinia, Ornamental Kale and Cabbage, Evening Stock, Virginia Stock, Iberis or Candytuft, Sweet Alyssum, Lunaria and Wallflower.

Potato, officially known as *Solanaceae*, has more relatives than most people realize. Its vegetable relatives include Tomato, Eggplant and Pepper. Flowering cousins include Petunia, Nicotiana, Schizanthus, Nierembergia and Physalis or Chinese Lantern.

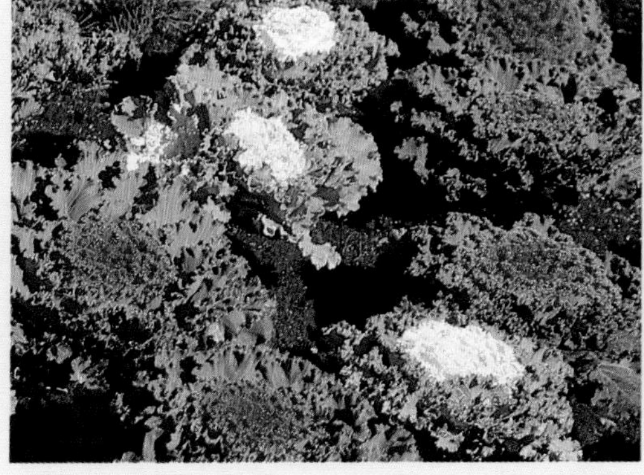

Ornamental Kale (far left) and Sweet Alyssum (left) are both members of the Cabbage family. Plants within the same family tend to suffer from the same insects and diseases. To minimize infestations, related plants should be kept separate in the same and succeeding seasons.

SOIL AMENDMENTS

Shown here are some of the more common soil amendments used to improve soil structure. Some are useful for moisture retention, some for fertilization, and others for breaking down clay soils. To select the proper amendment for your conditions, read the descriptions of soil amendments in the text.

Bark Mulch

Peat moss

Redwood chips

Straw

Composted Manure

Mature Compost

Soil amendments

Ashes: Wood ashes are a good source of lime and potassium, and they reduce acidity. Apply to root crops and plants like Roses or Peony at the rate of 4 lbs./10 sq. yd. (2 kg/9 m^2). Do not combine ashes with fresh manure. This will stimulate the rapid breakdown of nitrogen. Coal ashes have little nutrient value, but small particles of coal are useful as a soil conditioner for heavy clay.

Bark: Pine and cedar chips are attractive and practical as mulches. They're long-lasting, good soil conditioners and they temporarily increase acidity. They outlast most other organic mulches. I have found Canadian Pine bark mulch especially useful for reducing weed problems and retaining soil moisture.

Bonemeal: Finely ground bonemeal is rich in phosphorous and contains some nitrogen. It has little effect on soil acidity and is popular for use with large bloomers like Roses and Dahlia.

Fishmeals: Fish emulsions are a by-product of seafood production often sold as complete and all-purpose fertilizers with varying nutrient content. They can contain crabmeal and are a good source of micro-nutrients.

Gypsum: Calcium-deficient soils that require no pH alteration are best treated with land plaster, or gypsum. Gypsum is a sulphate of lime which provides additional sulphur to soil but has little impact on acidity. It is used chiefly on block alkali soils or on saline soils in coastal regions. Gypsum or calcium sulphate is often a component of superphosphate fertilizers.

Limestone: Calcitic or dolomitic limestone counter the acidifying effects of aluminum and manganese by introducing calcium carbonate to soil. Dolomitic limestone also increases magnesium content. Both are available in finely ground powders. Quicklimes or slaked limes are calcitic limestone which has been combined with wood or coal ash and treated.

Manures: Composted animal wastes have sustained human food production from the beginning of time. They are highly valued as nutrient sources and soil conditioners. Cow manure is most frequently available and usually cheapest. Horse, sheep and chicken manures are richer in nutrient content but are not produced in the same quantity, so they are less accessible and more expensive. The bulk of cow manure also makes it a better soil conditioner. Goats and pigs are good sources of manure. But pig manure is unstable, and is often best mixed with water as a manure tea.

Some thrifty gardeners also make use of droppings from grain-fed household pets such as hamsters, birds or rabbits in their composts. This practice is not without risk. Animal waste, especially from meat-eating pets or humans, may be contaminated with harmful bacteria or parasites. Unless carefully treated they are potentially quite dangerous.

Fresh manure should never be applied to growing plants. Its high ammonia content can damage tender, new roots. Allowing manure to mature prevents nitrogen burns and improves overall nutrient content. Mineral elements also become more available as decomposition progresses. Finally, well-composted manures are less likely to contain either viable weed seeds or pathogens.

Paper: Some city gardeners who lack a good supply of organic material use shredded paper as a garden mulch.

The majority of plants prefer moderately acidic soil (pH 6.5). Lilac is among the minority which tolerates neutral to slightly alkaline soils.

Clean straw makes a good soil mulch. But watch for weed seeds.

While it is very good for retaining moisture, shredded paper may increase slug problems. Printers' ink, especially coloured inks, may pose health risks.

Peat Moss: Peat, which is harvested from ancient bogs, is sphagnum moss which has begun to decompose. It aids water retention, increases acidity, and improves soil tilth. Peat moss can hold 20 times its weight in water, which is why gardeners use it with moisture-loving plants. However, it often needs to be watered before it is worked into the soil. Peat bogs are drained before they're mined, and the peat is dried further in order to reduce shipping weight. By the time it reaches the gardener it's often quite dehydrated. If you work dry peat into the soil it will simply steal available moisture from plants, defeating the purpose and sometimes damaging plants seriously.

Perlite: Perlite is a long-lasting and porous amendment consisting of volcanic rock which has been heated and granulated. It's used often in potting soils or as a sterile medium for storing or packing bulbs and plants. Like vermiculite, perlite is used as a water retaining soil-conditioner, but it lasts longer.

Sawdust or Woodchips: Wood shavings have minimal nutrient value,and should be applied thinly. They're sometimes used as a light mulch or as a soil conditioner. Use with caution. Wood chips can rob the soil of nitrogen.

Seaweed: If you live close to water, seaweeds are a cheap and readily available soil conditioner that rivals manure in nutrient content. In fact, some varieties are harvested specifically for use in cattle feed. While they vary in their nutrient make-up, fresh or salt water weeds are often rich in both micro- and macro- elements. Use them directly as green manures, as mulches, or combine with compost.

Straw: Straw is most often used in combination with manure, or as a mulch. When clean, straw is ideal for keeping down weeds and improving soil texture. However, in my experience straw inevitably introduces a host of weed seeds.

Sphagnum Moss: Often used in planters and for new seedlings, Sphagnum, like peat, has tremendous water retention ability. Sphagnum Moss was commonly used in Europe as an antiseptic dressing during the Great War. It uses those same anti-bacterial properties in combating fungal growths in soil. Sphagnum is especially useful in preventing damp-off mould of new seedlings, and for lining fern baskets.

Sulphur: Used mainly to increase soil acidity, sulphur can be purchased in bulk for use over large areas. Soil organisms must convert sulphur to sulphuric acid before it can be used by plants. The process takes several weeks. One part sulphur produces 3 parts sulphuric acid. Recommended application rates vary according to soil condition, area and pH level. Sulphur may be ineffective on strongly alkaline soils.

Vermiculite: Like perlite, vermiculite is used most often for water retention in potting mixtures. Derived from mica, vermiculite is porous and sterile but it does contain some trace elements. It's distinguished from perlite by its larger granule size, higher nutrient content, greater water-retention and lower cost. Unlike perlite, it does not produce a dust, which can be a real health hazard. However, vermiculite doesn't last as long.

Worms and worm castings: Ordinary earthworms are a gardener's best guarantee of good soil. Worms aerate the soil as they move through it, digesting and refining decaying vegetation. Their castings, or manure, contain rich concentrations of mineral elements. If you don't have a cheap source of worms, create the kind of garden environment they like. Use mulch to keep the ground moist and dark and supplement the soil with compost or manure. Worm castings are available through commercial bait suppliers, but they're not cheap. Worm castings are the black gold of soil amendments, an ideal food for tender young seedlings. I recommend that you toss a few earthworms on your mature compost.

Light

Some plants enjoy intense sunlight while others blossom only in shade. Still others can withstand a range of light conditions. Read the information on sun and shade requirements accompanying your nursery purchases.

Light requirements often coincide with water and nutrient needs. As a rule, plants which like shade also like moisture and acidity. Plants that like strong sun can often withstand drier conditions and more alkaline soil.

It is said that light intensity affects bloom colours. To the extent that it affects the soil and your perception of shade, that is true. But light intensity has a far greater effect on overall plant growth, especially the quantity and quality of blossoms.

It pays to experiment. Gardeners can often restrain rampant growers like perennial herbs and rockery plants by restricting the amount of light they receive. By the same token, certain plants listed as shade-tolerant will perform adequately without direct sunlight, but are more likely to bloom profusely when planted in sun. *Hemerocallis*, commonly known as Daylily, is a good example. It fares well under deciduous trees, where the light is strong in spring before leaves emerge. Depending on the variety, *Hemerocallis* may not bloom at all without some direct sunlight during the course of a day.

Roses, particularly those with recurring blooms, require good light conditions. They may leaf and appear to thrive in partially shaded conditions, but if they flower and infrequently it is a good bet that they have inadequate light.

Then again, many plants emphatically prefer shade. Impatiens, Lungwort and Begonia, for example, are likely to wither away if placed in direct, uninterrupted light. They cannot withstand the heat associated with strong sun unless they are watered continually.

Food plants require maximum sun for growth. A minimum of 6 hours sunlight daily is recommended for vegetable gardens.

Roses may grow well in partially shaded conditions, but they always do best in full sun.

RULE OF THUMB

When constructing a curved or sweeping bed around a house, use a garden hose to lay out a pleasing shape.

DIGGING THE GARDEN

The growth of root systems is linked to the level of available oxygen in the soil. To increase soil oxygen levels, add organic matter and use good cultivation techniques.

Soil becomes hard and oxygen-deprived when it compacts under the weight of rain, plants, or people. New gardeners are often surprised to learn their physical presence can be bad for the soil.

Hoeing breaks surface crust and helps aerate and moisturize the soil surface. But hoeing is not enough. Garden beds need deep spading or ploughing to a depth of at least 12 in. (30 cm) annually. This is best done in the fall, with a rotary tiller or spade, when fresh manure, lime, and other necessary amendments can be worked into the soil.

A motorized rotary tiller can help to take the drudgery out of keeping your garden well dug.

Marking out beds

Once you've selected the site, shape, and appropriate amendments for your garden, mark the edges using stakes and twine.

When marking out beds, leave ample space for paths. Walking space is needed in every garden, whether beds are raised, squared or set out in traditional rows. Paths allow you to tend the garden without compacting the soil around growing plants. Even gardens that abut on fences or stone walls are easier to maintain if a walking space is incorporated at the perimeter.

Paths should be a comfortable width, at least 15 in. (37.5 cm). Some gardeners keep soil compaction to a minimum by laying planks across flat stones or bricks where they wish to walk. Others tend flower borders and rockeries from strategically placed stones.

How to dig

Whichever digging method you use, work routinely, taking care to maintain good posture. Lever a full spade upward with both knees bent, and gradually straighten as each shovelful is lifted clear. Reject the temptation to overload your spade and you'll avoid premature fatigue and the curse of back strain.

The trench method

The trench method is recommended where existing soil quality is reasonably good (i.e. the soil is *not* heavy clay). Divide your plot in half and dig to a depth of at least 10 in. (25 cm) systematically in a straight line down one side. Soil from the first area dug will be used in the last trench excavated. Soil from the second trench can be mixed with manure or compost and placed in the first trench and so on, in succession. The manure or compost should be mixed with existing soil in roughly equal proportions – a shovelful of compost or manure to a shovelful of soil.

Double-digging or deep-bed

The double-digging or deep-bed method is carried out the same way but extended to a depth of 20 in. (50 cm). As soil is removed, a garden fork is used to break up the trench bottom. Manure or compost is added and worked in evenly with the aid of a fork. Soil from the succeeding trench is then placed in the first, as described above. Deep-digging is required wherever soil is heavily compacted or to benefit deep-rooted plants like many perennials, or root crop vegetables such as Carrots, Asparagus, and Potatoes. It is also sometimes used to assist drainage. There isn't a garden that wouldn't benefit from deep-digging every few years.

Bed styles

Like any other human pursuit, gardening is subject to trends. Even the shape of beds has become the focus of fashion in recent years, with the popular revival of intensive gardening. The traditional farm-style row bed remains the most popular simply because it offers easy, straightforward maintenance. But gardeners with the limited space offered by most urban lots can realize greater returns by experimenting a little.

(Opposite) The wide row method of planting flowers results in a very colourful display. Shown here are Snapdragons, Fibrous Begonias, and Dusty Miller.

The wide row method

Many gardeners adopt a more intensive version of the traditional row bed by simply increasing the width of rows. Rather than plant a single row, they plant seedlings 3 or 4 deep, spaced according to the recommendation of the seed companies. The midpoint of each row should be easily accessible from either side. The wide row method, as it is called, increases yields and reduces the space needed for walks. It's great for vegetables and flowers grown for cutting, and it also reduces weeds.

Gardening in blocks

Another intensive option, gardening in blocks, as in the square-foot method, also increases yields while reducing space requirements. All intensive methods make extra demands on soil nutrients, and require some extra compost and mulching.

Raised beds

Raised beds can be constructed in any of the above shapes or styles. They're often framed with cedar, which is long-lasting and free of chemical treatment, and then filled with a mixture of equal parts good topsoil, sand (for drainage), vermiculite, compost, and well-moistened peat moss. Raised beds can also be constructed from a variety of other materials and filled with different soil mixtures suited to your choice of plants.

Gardeners often use raised beds to accommodate plants with special soil requirements. It's less effort and expense to build an island of acidic soil somewhere in your landscape than to attempt to alter pH over a wide area.

Raised beds have other advantages as well. Where topsoil is shallow or substandard, they provide the soil depth plants need to root properly. They discourage weeds. They can also eliminate the need for bending or kneeling, which makes them ideal for elderly or disabled gardeners who may not be able to maintain an ordinary garden.

Raised beds should be built up to a minimum of 10 in. (25 cm) above ground level for most plants, deeper for long-rooted vegetables, perennials or shrubs. Natural aeration, organic decomposition and plant growth will deplete soil in raised beds, so you have to supplement with nutrients at least once a year. Mulching also helps to slow the loss of friable soil.

Situating plants

Orient plants to maximize light. Plant tall specimens and climbers on the north and east sides of your garden so they don't shade shorter plants and can supply them with some protection. For example, a row of Nasturtium planted along the north edge of a garden catches the sun and protects other plants from cool north winds later in the season. Nasturtium also has insecticidal properties that may aid other plants.

Succession planting

Increase the yield from your garden by planting in succession. Herbs or ornamentals can effectively cover declining bulbs that bloom early in the season. Fall-harvested vegetables, like Brussels Sprout and Broccoli, are ideal replacements for vegetables that decline at the height of summer, like Spinach, Pea, Lettuce and Radish.

Succession planting requires a little study and a planning calendar. Determine the frost dates for your area and plant varieties that will bloom or come to maturity before that day. Seed companies will tell you how many days it takes for plants to mature.

Interplanting

You can also improve yields by companion planting. Seed quick-growing plants among those that mature slowly. Radish can be interspersed with Carrot, Spinach with Cauliflower. Summer-flowering bulbs, like Anemone or Lily, combine nicely with mass plantings of Forget-Me-Not or Lily-of-the-Valley.

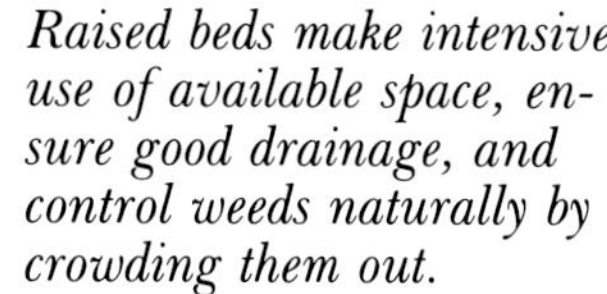

Raised beds make intensive use of available space, ensure good drainage, and control weeds naturally by crowding them out.

CONTAINERS

It is possible to garden without ground or a shovel. Many prolific gardeners produce only from containers. Except for the largest trees, there are few plants that cannot be adapted to a container of some sort.

Containers have much to recommend them. Like raised beds, they make gardening possible for some people with mobility problems. They're also well-appreciated by those with limited space. Because they're portable, containers allow gardeners to decorate and alter their surroundings on impulse.

Containers are available in a vast array of shapes and sizes. They are made primarily from three main materials: clay, wood and plastic. Each has its merits.

Plastics are generally inexpensive, light, colourful and easy to clean. But, because they're non-porous, plastic containers don't breathe and they must have adequate drainage to prevent overwatering.

Wood containers are porous and easy to make. But they are heavy to move, and they deteriorate. They may also harbour insects and diseases.

Clay pots, also porous, absorb insoluble salts along with water and oxygen. They require occasional scrubbing. They also need to be watered often to prevent drying. Clay pots come in some extremely attractive designs and shapes but they can be expensive. Protect your investment. Don't subject them to freezing temperatures or other hazards, like paths with heavy traffic.

The best dirt

Containers are only as good as the dirt you put in them. Use potting mixtures appropriate to the plants you want to grow. Container soil should include sand for drainage, porous material like vermiculite or perlite for moisture retention, and peat or compost for aeration and good tilth.

Bryan Green, who has mixed potting soils for our nurseries for years, devised a recipe consisting of equal parts perlite or fine grade vermiculite, sharp sand, sterile, composted manure, and sterilized top soil. These ingredients can be purchased separately or pre-mixed.

When mixing up your own soil mixtures for containers and seedlings, sterilize top soil by spreading it on a cookie sheet and baking it in a 160°F (71°C) oven for 45 minutes. This kills weed seeds, fungus spores and insects. To sterilize your soil in a microwave, set the dial on high for 3 minutes and cover the soil with transparent wrap.

Watering Containers

It is essential to water containers frequently. For many plants, once a day is not enough when summer heat is intense, especially for hanging baskets which dry out rapidly. Whenever you can, choose containers which will hold enough water for a full day. Very shallow containers dry up quickly. If containers must be exposed to sun for long periods of time insulate them from heat with a lining of foam, vermiculite or wet sphagnum moss. Containers on cement patios should be slightly elevated to prevent them from overheating.

They should be heavy enough to withstand prevailing winds. Support heavy window boxes with brackets.

Balcony containers and window boxes should be designed to be watered without showering neighbours or other plants below.

ROOF GARDENS

Roof gardens take advantage of unused space and the absence of shade. But before you build one, make sure the roof is strong enough to take the weight of large containers full of soil and water. Place containers on or near over load-bearing walls.

If your roof is asphalt and gravel, don't use containers with sharp or square surfaces that could cut and pierce the roof.

(Opposite) Containers, like this wooden barrel planted with Ivy, Begonia, and Ornamental Grass, provide a flexible gardening medium which is more accessible to gardeners with mobility problems.

Planting a container

1. Add a base layer of sterilized top soil, sterilized manure, sharp sand, and perlite or vermiculite.

2. Lower plant into container on top of soil layer.

3. Fill in the sides around to plant and press down lightly.

4. Water frequently – as often as once a day or more.

GROWING FROM SEED

Germinating indoors

There's nothing more satisfying for people with a green thumb than to raise a mature plant from a tiny seed, observing its progress at every stage.

Germinating seeds indoors has several advantages. It allows gardeners to extend the growing season by starting early, and it provides seeds with better odds for survival. This enables better planning, lower costs, less frustration, a great opportunity for your children to get involved in gardening, and a very special sense of personal satisfaction. Starting seeds indoors protects young plants when they're most vulnerable to the elements and predators. The exceptions are plants like Poppy or leafy vegetables which do not transplant well and are best sown directly in your garden.

The process of starting seeds indoors involves several stages: germination in a seed tray, transplanting to transplant pots, "hardening-off" or acclimatizing seedlings to the out-of-doors, and then finally transplanting to your garden.

Use fresh, good quality seeds. Seed catalogues and garden centre racks are reliable sources. Unless you're experienced at cross-pollination techniques you're better off buying than harvesting your own. Although you might wish you could save seeds from a prize-winning Butternut Squash, these seeds may have been sidetracked by an attractive Pumpkin pollen, and the resulting Squashkin will not be to your liking.

Before you open a seed packet read the directions. Most seeds are easy to germinate – they will perform beautifully if lightly covered with prepared soil and kept moist at a temperature of 61 to 86°F (16 to 30°C). But other seeds have rather fussy requirements. Some won't germinate unless exposed to light and heat, while some refuse to germinate unless kept cool and dark. Some, like Delphinium, require the shock of freezing before they are sown. Still others, particularly perennials, take months to germinate. Woodland species, such as Trillium and Helleborus, may not germinate for up to 18 months, while the humble Radish or Marigold reach the 2-leaf (or seed leaf) stage within a week. The length of time required to raise slow-germinating plants is usually reflected in the cost of adult plants.

There are tricks to starting off seeds. Many – especially hard-shelled seeds like Morning Glories and Beans – benefit from a pre-germination soak in water. Some gardeners extend this process to nearly all their seeds, soaking them in a shallow tray lined with paper towels, covered in plastic and placed on a warm surface.

Once the seeds split and extend fine roots they're ready to be transplanted to a growing medium. Some gardeners nick hard shells with a knife to assist the emergence of shoots.

Harden-off seedlings outdoors during the heat of day, and bring back indoors before the temperature cools down, before transplanting them.

Seeds are dormant embryos. Add moisture and warmth and they will germinate. Since seeds are self-sufficient until they have grown to the 2-leaf (cotyledon) stage, most will germinate in a saucer of water, or other infertile medium like peat moss or vermiculite, placed in a warm location. But seed or starter trays are the most popular medium.

Seed trays

Use wide, shallow containers with good drainage. Wide containers filled with two inches (5 cm) of soil provide space to spread out seeds, decreasing the chance of damping-off fungus. Wider containers also make it easier to get at seedlings when transplanting, minimizing root damage and shock. Clear plastic lids, a sheet of glass or an inflated plastic bag will keep seeds warm and moist until germination.

The soil mixture must be light, fluffy and sterile to reduce the potential for weeds or fungus spores. Light soil mixtures are easy on fragile young roots and allow air to penetrate. Many good commercial mixtures are available but you can mix your own with equal parts of vermiculite, fine peat moss and sand.

Have labels ready to use as you sow. Unless you grow only one variety, you will need some way of distinguishing among seedlings. No matter how carefully you try to remember that the Plum Tomatoes are on the left, Beefsteak in the middle and Cherry on the right, there will come a day when you're not sure, especially if the tray is inadvertently moved. Use plastic or wooden labels, which can be cleaned and reused. Unlike paper, they won't deteriorate with watering.

For most varieties, speed germination by keeping seeds warm, at temperatures of 61 to 86°F (16 to 30°C) You can put them close to a window, or an operating appliance, like a refrigerator or stove. But don't let them get too hot. Excess heat can dry out the soil. In combination with plastic covers or unventilated containers, excess heat can also contribute to humidity and mould. A waterproof heating cable which warms the soil to approximately 64°F (18°C) provides consistent, regulated warmth.

Once seeds have sprouted, transfer them to a well-lit location and use protective coverings or heat sources cautiously. Seedlings rapidly deteriorate if you continue to subject them to the temperature they need to germinate.

Damp-off, the plague of young seedlings and gardeners everywhere, is an insidious disease which attacks stems, causing them to rot. Commercial growers and many home gardeners use fungicides to prevent damp-off. Organic gardeners depend on Sphagnum Moss and medicinal sprays of water flavoured with Garlic. But whatever you do, keep germinating seeds warm and moist, not wringing wet.

RULE OF THUMB

To tell if seeds are viable, soak them in water overnight. The poor seeds will rise to the surface and should be discarded.

Planting seeds in seed trays

Fill the starter tray close to the top with soil mixture. Sow seeds, leaving a finger width between each for good circulation, reduced damping-off, sturdier growth and easier transplanting. Very small seeds, such as Campanula, and others, like Flax, don't want any soil covering. But, unless you're otherwise directed by the seed company, give small seeds a bare sifting of soil, and cover larger seeds with up to 1/2 in. (13 mm) of soil to prevent them from drying out. The general rule is to cover seeds by twice the diameter of their smallest part.

Seedlings can never be allowed to dry out. Water by setting individual flats in a few inches (centimetres) of water. When the soil surface is damp, remove the flat and drain. This method is quicker and more effective than a mister but won't dislodge or crush seedlings as often happens when watering with a can.

As your seedlings emerge, remove their protective cover and gradually introduce them to light. Young seedlings will wither if they are exposed to too much sun before their roots have developed adequately. If seedlings begin to topple over or mould, treat them immediately for damp-off as prescribed above. Long, spindly seedlings need to be thinned.

Seed leaves, which are smooth and without markings or serrations, are the first two leaves that appear following germination. Once true leaves begin to form above seed leaves your plants are ready to be transplanted into transplant pots.

Transplanting seedlings into transplant pots

When transplanting seedlings to transplant pots, minimize root trauma. Careless handling tears tiny root hairs which act as water collectors for plants. Without adequate root support seedlings dry up quickly.

Consider using transplant pots made of peat or paper. Because roots can grow right through them, they don't have to be removed when planting in the ground, which reduces the potential for root trauma. In time they gradually decompose.

Before you begin to transplant have all the necessary materials at hand:
sharp stick such as a tongue depressor or blunt tweezers;
clean sterile containers filled with a moist and light potting mixture;
mister;
clear plastic bags or other covers;
trowel;
fertilizer, if desired.

Grasp the plant by a seed leaf – never the stem or true leaves, which are fragile. Lift from the starting tray with blunt stick or tweezers, being careful not to tear the roots. Insert in a transplant pot to the level of seed leaves and firm soil.

Allow seedlings a few days of recovery time to get over the shock of being transplanted to the peat pots. Move the transplant pots gradually into the sunlight. If they become overly-long or leggy, increase their light. Apply a weak water-soluble fertilizer like 20-20-20 weekly until seedlings are ready to be planted.

Cold frames range in size and sophistication from used vinegar bottles to plastic stretched over a metal frame, as pictured here. Cold frames help to protect young seedlings grown indoors by hardening them to the cold before transplanting them to the ground.

Hardening-off

Two to three weeks before you intend to plant seedlings into the earth they need to be "hardened-off" or prepared for colder outdoor weather. Many home gardeners do this simply by carrying seed trays in and out daily, gradually extending the time during which seedlings are exposed to the elements.

Cold-frames provide an easier way of hardening-off plants. They're often a simple wooden frame, with one raised, angled edge covered by a window or piece of plastic. Like a greenhouse, they should face south to trap solar heat. Plants placed in a cold-frame are protected from cold and gain the advantages of increased light and warmth. Lids are normally hinged and propped open except when inclement weather threatens.

Transplanting into the garden

Since seedlings are vulnerable to wilting from heat, transplant from the cold-frame late in the day or when it is cloudy. Garden soil should be watered and dug in advance. Place seedlings in prepared holes, back-filling gently around the rootball. A drink of weak plant-start fertilizer, a watered down 5-15-5 formula, can be applied if desired.

If using peat pots, completely cover rims when transplanting. Otherwise, they act like wicks, drawing moisture from plant roots. Ensure that water or transplant solution actually reaches plant roots by constructing a well-like effect around peat pots. If they dry out, your seedlings are unlikely to recover.

Sowing directly

Precision is important when sowing seeds directly in the garden. Many seeds are warm weather crops and require heat for germination. Otherwise, they may be subject to moulds associated with cold and dampness, and rot. Or they may simply grow poorly. Indiscriminate sowing that neglects these factors will net you few results.

Prepare soil in advance, marking beds and row sites. Plant seeds according to the recommended depth and width. When planting late season crops at the height of summer bury seeds deeper to prevent scorching.

It's a good idea to cover seeds with a soil supplement like vermiculite or worm castings. No crusts will form to hinder the development of newly germinated sprouts. Whatever covering you use, firm it over the seed to ensure that neither seed nor soil will dry out or become easily dislodged. Apply only a fine mist or spray when watering and never allow seedlings to dehydrate.

When sprouts have grown 2 in. (5 cm) or so, thin them according to directions. Many gardeners are reluctant to thin but it is a necessary evil. Sprouts that don't have adequate room will become stunted and thoroughly disappointing. It is sometimes a delicate procedure, especially since some seeds – Beets, for instance – produce more than a single sprout. Thin by extracting the least-developed seedlings, spacing as directed by the seed producer. Disturb the remaining crop as little as possible. For sprouts that are very thick, shearing with scissors may be safer than pulling. Once thinning is complete many gardeners apply a plant-start formula to promote strong root growth.

Caring for young seedlings in the ground

For several days after transplanting, watch seedlings for symptoms of stress. If wilting occurs, shade them with a newspaper or spray them with a fine mist.

Protect transplants and direct-seeded

Harden-off seedlings before transplanting them to the ground, in soil which has been well prepared and watered.

RULE OF THUMB

Allow the surface of the soil to dry between waterings of young seedlings. Too much water is the number one reason for failure.

Landscape fabric or row cover allows sun and moisture to enter but keeps out pests and provides some frost protection.

plants from cold or frost with covers, or cloches. Converted bleach or vinegar bottles work well. So does clear plastic raised over a frame. Clear plastic cloches do not, however, provide indefinite protection. They can stimulate weed growth if left in place too long.

There are also several commercial products available for use as cloches. Waterwells, plastic teepees and corrugat-

POISONOUS PLANTS

The stems, leaves, bark or roots of many garden plants can have toxic effects when ingested. Gardeners should label plants that are potentially poisonous, and never add them to composts. Following is a list of common outdoor plants which may induce reactions including vomiting, diarrhoea, headaches, respiratory difficulty and even death in susceptible individuals, particularly children. Those with potentially fatal or very serious effects are marked with an asterisk.

Crocus *
Daffodil
Hyacinth
Mistletoe
Foxglove *
Lily-of-the-Valley
Tomato leaves and vines
Potato vines, leaves, sprouts and green tubers
Rhubarb leaves

English Ivy
English Holly
Privet *
Daphne *
Rhododendron *
Azalea *
Wisteria
Yew *
Apple seeds ingested in great quantity *
Black Locust
Wild Black Cherry or

Rhododendron and Crocus are among those common garden plants which, though beautiful, can cause serious health effects, and possibly death, if ingested. Keep them out of compost to be used on vegetable gardens.

ed plastic hot caps can be set directly on plants and function like individual coldframes.

Row covers or floating horticultural fabrics allow sun and moisture to enter, and offer some frost protection while excluding pests. They cover plants without crushing them and can be held in place with stakes or weights. They increase yields, reduce erosion and eliminate bug-related losses and damage. However, many brands break down over time when they are exposed to the sun and they will eventually need replacing. Clean and store them when not in use to promote durability.

Row covers should not be confused with landscape fabric, which is meant to suppress plant growth. They are often made from similar material but row covers are white, while landscape fabric is black.

Landscape fabric is often used to cover soils to keep weeds to a minimum. Simply lay it where you need it, weight it down with soil or staples and cut holes for plants. Landscape fabric is great for use around pools, under decks and paths or anywhere else weeds encroach.

Remember that even low-light plants like Impatiens and Begonias need light through late winter and early spring, when the sun is at a low angle.

Support

Plants that need staking should be staked at an early stage to reduce damage to expanding root systems and maximize healthy growth. Install support hoops, trellis, wire baskets, and wooden stakes when plants are still quite young. Many gardeners set supports in place while transplanting.

- *Choke Cherry* *
- *Elderberry stems and uncooked berries* *
- *Horse Chestnut*
- *Oak acorns (raw) or young sprouts*
- *Baneberry*
- *Jack-in-the-Pulpit*
- *Water Hemlock* (root resembles parsnip) *
- *Wild mushrooms* (many harmful types are difficult to distinguish from edible ones) *
- *Jimson or Thorn Apple weed*
- *Death Camas* (bulb resembles onion) *
- *Nightshade* *
- *Poison Hemlock* (root resembles wild carrot) *
- *Rose, Apple and Walnut leaves.*

Don't be alarmed if you realize reading through the list that your garden contains poisonous species. Many plants contain some known toxin but they are rarely consumed in enough quantity to warrant serious concern. Reactions are seldom severe enough to require extended medical treatment. Teach your children by example. Never chew or suck on ornamental plants. Follow standard first aid procedures if you suspect a poisonous plant has been consumed. Call a physician, poison control centre or local hospital promptly and be prepared to supply the name of the plant, quantity and time of ingestion, and the age and symptoms of the victim.

MAINTAINING AND CARING FOR PLANTS

Watering

Most plants need a thorough, deep watering once a week during the growing season. More frequent watering, as often as once a day, may be needed for new seedlings, container plants, and vegetable or fruit crops. Foundation plants located below the eaves of your house may also need extra watering.

Make sure your plants need water *before* you turn on the tap. Push your finger into the soil. If it is dry 1 in. (2.5 cm) below the surface, it's time for a good watering.

Generally it is adequate to apply 1 in. (2.5 cm) of water, or enough to moisten the soil to a depth of 1 ft. (30 cm). Plants that receive frequent but shallow waterings tend to develop shallow roots that are more susceptible to scorching under drought conditions. Less frequent, long soaks will promote deeper root development and healthier plants.

Soils vary in their capacity to hold water. Sandy soil needs to be watered more frequently than loam. Bare soil loses more moisture than covered soil, which is one reason for covering gardens with mulches.

Experienced gardeners can tell when their soil needs watering just by looking at it. Soil becomes lighter in colour as it dries out and begins to lose organic matter. Soil that can't hold shape when compressed in your palm needs water.

Plants often differ in their moisture requirements, as noted in the plant descriptions throughout this book. They give very obvious signals when they need additional moisture. Many wilt when transpiration begins to outstrip water absorption. This is a natural biological response to the need to conserve moisture, and not necessarily cause for panic. As leaves wilt, they roll up, reducing surface exposure, thereby limiting transpiration. they recover independently overnight the problem is not serious.

RULE OF THUMB

Always water your plants thoroughly before applying fertilizer to avoid possible root burn.

Proper watering is essential for a healthy garden. Check the moisture requirements under the plant descriptions to ensure your plants receive the right amount of water.

When to water

There is an age-old debate about the best time of day for watering. Let common sense be your guide. Though many people advise against watering at night, it's clear that Mother Nature has never heard this advice. It rains frequently at night and dew also collects once the sun goes down. The best reason to avoid night watering is to reduce the potential of pests associated with excess moisture: slugs and fungus. On the other hand, watering in the heat of mid-day is really a hapless exercise. Much of what's applied will evaporate. For these reasons early morning waterings are best.

Take the weather into account. Heat reduces water absorption through evaporation and by stimulating transpiration. Wind also encourages water loss through transpiration. Cold weather retards root acquisition of water. Watering in cool temperatures is ill-advised anyway. Shallow roots and plant stems can be killed when surface water freezes.

Is there such a thing as overwatering? Generally, no. For most gardeners, the problem is inadequate watering. But too much water is definitely bad news for plants. Excess water fills up available air pockets in the soil, reducing oxygen levels. Plants die from lack of oxygen. Nutrient run-off and leaching can also be a problem.

See the appendix on tools for a description of hoses, sprinklers, and other tools used for watering.

WINTER-PROOFING PLANTS

Gardeners can become adept at dealing with the vagaries of climate. There are several tried and true methods of protecting against the double threat of cold and wind:

* Maximize whatever site advantages you possess. Situate gardens in spots with maximum sun exposure and the best drainage possible. Consider where spring run-off is likely to occur. If drainage is poor, try to improve it.
* Reduce the effect of prevailing winds with fencing, shrubs, tree lines, or hedges. New seedlings, tall perennials and young trees or shrubs are particularly vulnerable to wind. Incorporating a wind screen in your landscape can reduce home heating costs as well, as cold winter winds are diverted away from your home.
* Use covers, wraps and mulches routinely to extend the growing season and to protect ornamental plants and overwintering crops from frost and wind damage. Apply them carefully to avoid damaging growth tips. If protective coverings are used in winter it is important to remove them once spring has arrived. Otherwise they'll continue to provide an insulating effect, blocking both warmth and moisture and delaying new growth. They may also force new growth, which will be soft and susceptible to wind, sun, and frost damage.
* Site vulnerable individual plants carefully to help them survive harsh winters. They can be planted next to a house foundation for the additional shelter and warmth this provides. Sometimes, however, just the opposite is required. A more exposed and shaded site can delay premature growth of blossoms of early-flowering trees and plants, helping to protect against damage from late frosts. This is a calculated risk, but it has paid off for many a gardener.

In Canada, gardeners must protect their gardens against winter damage. Protective techniques include defensive measures such as careful siting, and insulating coverings such as mulch.

SECTION II

Flowers in the Garden

MOTHER NATURE IS A SHOW-OFF, AND flower gardening is simply a matter of putting this boastful side of her on display in your own yard. The vast selection of colourful plants from which Canadians may choose is truly limitless and mind-boggling. This section attempts to simplify the selection process by narrowing down the selection to those plants that: (a) have proven to be outstanding performers in Canadian gardens, and (b) are generally available at retail nurseries, mail order houses and, in some cases, in the wild, from seed.

This section acknowledges that every garden demands different qualities and virtues from the flowering plants that each gardener may choose to grow there. It also helps you to zoom in on the plants best suited to your situation and desire.

Every plant description includes symbols for quick and easy reference to *light, soil,* and *climate* zone requirements. Not all so-called flowering plants are grown for their flowers, of course. The many herbs discussed in this section are grown more often than not for their seeds or foliage.

Whatever your interest in flower gardens, this section of *A Greener Thumb* will give you a solid understanding of Mother Nature's world of flowers and how to work *with* her to your mutual advantage.

CHAPTER 3

ANNUALS

I love gardening, but I don't love all kinds of gardening equally. I have to admit a perennial weakness for annual flowers. I inherited this affliction from my father, who instructed me at the tender age of 15 to plant up the 200-foot cedar rail fence at the cottage in Petunias and Zinnias.

I rototilled. I added peat moss, composted cattle manure, and the recommended dose of 6-12-12. And then I got down on my knees and planted for four solid days.

Then Dad said, "Nice job. Now why don't you take the weekend off." Which was a smart move. Another day of it and I would have lost any spark of inspiration to take up gardening as an occupation.

But it was my job to water my mass planting of Petunias, to pinch them back and weed them. As it turned out, the planting was so beautiful a picture of it was used the following year on the cover of our company catalogue – a coveted spot indeed.

So I was proud and more than satisfied. And I was hooked on annuals.

Some years later, my experience with this class of plants is somewhat greater. I have favoured the extensive use of annuals in every yard and patio we have ever owned.

Based on my experience, I feel qualified to give you my personal rating of each annual flower species listed in this chapter. You will find a rating on a scale of one to ten at the beginning of each plant description. This rating is by no means a scientific or definitive grade, but it is intended to guide you to the plants with which I have enjoyed substantial success. I have considered the following factors (not necessarily in this order): maintenance requirements, profusion of blossoms, length of blossom period, fragrance, insect and disease resistance, versatility, and reliability (i.e. ability to perform as expected).

If you are a novice gardener, I hope you find this rating useful. It may draw your attention to some annuals you haven't considered growing.

As for my father. Well, he went on to dig up and rototill quite a few

Impatiens provide a thick carpet of colour for large areas.

more acres – with little help from me, I might add. Now he plants this massive area with over 100,000 annual plants every spring, and opens this show garden to the public for their pleasure. He calls his masterpiece of colour Cullen Gardens and Miniature Village, located in Whitby, Ontario.

CONTINUAL OR REPEAT BLOOMERS

Ageratum, Alyssum, Wax Begonia, Browallia, Calendula, Celosia, Cleome, Gazania, Geranium, Impatiens, Lavatera, Lobelia, Marigold, Nicotiana, Pansies, Petunia, Portulaca, Salvia, Snapdragon, Zinnia, Phlox, Ornamental Kale, Ornamental Grasses.

An interesting blend of pink, blue, and white annuals, combined with foundation plantings of evergreens.

CARE AND MAINTENANCE OF ANNUALS

Hardiness

Annuals germinate, bloom, disperse seed and die, all within a single season. They are often used in flower beds on their own, or in combination with bulbs and perennials in a mixed border. Their prolific blooms mask the foliage of plants in decline. They continue blooming through August and often into September (or even later in southwestern Ontario), providing colour long after the most popular bulbs and perennials have blossomed and withered.

While perennial roots survive the winter, sending up new stems each year, annuals die and must reproduce by growing new plants from seed. In order to maximize seed production, many annuals have evolved into veritable flower machines. These annuals – Petunia is the best example – bloom profusely and continuously so long as they are blessed with favourable weather and satisfactory care.

Annuals can be divided into three major categories: hardy, half-hardy, and tender. At the end of each plant description below you will find a symbol noting the hardiness.

Some of the best-loved continuous bloomers are tender annuals native to the tropics and sub-tropics. They adapt well to Canada's warm summers, but both plants and seeds are usually killed by the first light frost. They won't bloom if air or soil temperatures are unsuitable. Young plants must be protected from any hint of frost, and their seeds are killed outright by cold. In climates harsher than Zone 8, most annuals are unlikely to self-sow. Tender annuals include Begonia, Dahlia, Everlastings, Impatiens, Geranium, Petunia, Nicotiana, Ageratum, Browallia, Nasturtium, Celosia, Zinnia, and Mesembryanthemum.

Half-hardy annuals can tolerate a light frost but are killed by the first heavy frost. These include Cleome, Salvia, Swan River Daisy, Nirembergia, Chrysanthemum, and Mexican Tulip Poppy.

Hardy annuals tend to bloom for a limited period, but they can produce winter hardy seeds. Hardy annuals include Bachelor's Button, Pinks, Dianthus, Stock (Malcomia and Matthiola), Evening Primrose, Nemophila, Nigella, Viola, California Poppy, Iceland Poppy, Shirley Poppy, Opium Poppy, and Phlox.

Sun and soil requirements

Most annuals grow well in full or lightly filtered sun, and require a minimum of six hours light daily to bloom to their potential. Only a few prefer shady growing conditions.

In most cases, soil should be well drained and slightly acid, with a pH of 6.5. Prepare soil by amending it generously with compost and moistened peat moss.

The exceptions to this general rule include certain types of Poppies, Baby's Breath, Virginia Stock, and Everlasting flowers, all of which prefer dry, even sandy, conditions often associated with alkaline soils. They tend to do particularly well in sunny coastal regions. Ensure that their soil is not too rich. Do not water excessively and avoid fertilizing. If you have drainage problems where you would like to grow Stock or Poppies, amend the soil with sand rather than peat moss to improve drainage.

A smaller minority of annuals prefer moist, shaded conditions. In their natural habitats, often equatorial jungles, these plants are sometimes perennial. They require rich, humid soil and do best with filtered light. Annuals in this category include Balsam, Wax Begonia, Browallia, Coleus, and Impatiens.

Planting

Annuals can be sown directly in a garden or grown as potted seedlings. Sowing directly is best for Morning Glory, annual Sweet Peas, annual Poppies and a host of others which are difficult to transplant. But some, like Petunia, transplant well and require as long as 90 days to reach the flowering stage. With these you are better off using potted seedlings.

If you decide to raise annual seedlings indoors, review the section on raising seedlings. Home-grown transplants bring a special sense of achievement to gardening with annuals, and starting seeds indoors is a great way to get kids involved in gardening.

If you don't have the room or the patience to raise your own annuals, get bedding plants from a quality nursery source. This ensures healthy, pest-free plants, ready to bloom.

Seeds of hardy annuals withstand light frost. Plant Godetia, Pansies, Poppies, Virginia Stock and other hardy annuals in very early spring, as soon as the ground can be worked. In Zones 8 and 9, sow hardy annuals in fall to get a head start on spring. Protect young seedlings from frost with light mulches of fallen leaves or peat moss.

Delay sowing half-hardy or tender an-

RULE OF THUMB

The fastest germinating annual flower seeds are best sown directly in a well-prepared garden. Try Nasturtiums, Zinnias and Morning Glories.

Planting an annual

1. Plant annual in a well-prepared bed.

2. Place root-ball into holes placed well enough apart to provide room for growth.

3. Fill in with soil and press down firmly.

4. Water generously and frequently to give plant a good start.

RULE OF THUMB

Never cut flowers in the heat of mid-day except Roses which keep quite well if cut in the afternoon.

nuals outside until after the last predicted frost date. The seeds of many are susceptible to frost damage. Wet, cold conditions are fatal to young seedlings. Wait until the earth has warmed to the touch and sow, according to directions, in well-raked earth that has been suitably amended with peat moss and compost or composted cattle manure. Keep mulch (e.g. straw or evergreen boughs) or other protective covering at hand in case of a late frost.

All newly sown seed and seedlings must be gently watered to prevent erosion. Use only a fine spray. Mulch to help retain moisture and protect from weather during this stage.

As plants grow, water regularly, allowing only the surface soil to dry between waterings. A good moisture balance is important. Most annuals cannot tolerate excessively wet soil but, with a few exceptions, neither do they like to be parched. Frequent drying out is particularly damaging for large-leafed, half-hardy and tender annuals. Your safest compromise is to provide well-drained soil and water routinely.

Encouraging maximum bloom

Careful maintenance reinforces the natural tendency of annuals to flower prolifically. Plants always prefer to invest energy in seed production rather than develop new blooms. Maximize flower production by removing or "dead-heading" seed heads or pods. Don't just remove the flower bract – cut them right back to the stem.

Shear back repeat bloomers, like Ageratum and Alyssum, after their initial flowering period. This retards straggly or leggy growth and, more often than not, encourages a second round of blooms. When bud development peters out, trim extensively. Shearing-back also helps plants to spread by stimulating side-shoot development. Side growth can be further encouraged by "pinching-out" buds attached to leaders or central stems.

To encourage bushy growth from the start, particularly with continual bloomers like Petunia and Marigold, some gardeners sacrifice the first blooms of central leaders in this manner. This can be a very painful prospect after a long winter of waiting for a little colour in your garden. But experienced gardeners learn the value of "pinching".

Fertilize after shearing back to ensure successive blooms, using a formula that emphasizes phosphorus (the second number of the formula) rather than nitrogen (the first number (e.g. 6-12-12)). Regular applications of fertilizer or compost, along with dead-heading (pinching), will ensure continuity of bloom in long-flowering annuals.

Avoid fertilizing more often than once every three weeks. Some gardeners fertilize only during their initial planting and then again at mid-season on the assumption that very occasional applications are less likely to injure plants. They're right. Moderation is best. Avoid touching live plant tissue with soluble granular fertilizer, or it may burn. Compost-amended soil, combined with an organic mulch, will satisfy the requirements of most annuals.

CUTTING AND DRYING ANNUALS

Sweet Pea, Cleome, Strawflower, Phlox, and Zinnia are among the many annuals which make excellent, long-lasting cut flowers. Annuals also make up the vast majority of plants used for dried flower arrangements. Baby's Breath, Statice, Everlastings, Nigella and Xeranthemum can all be easily air-dried. Simply hang them by their rootstalks in a spot where they'll remain undisturbed. You may need to use silica gel to maintain colour while drying plants with more delicate blooms.

ANNUALS

Descriptions and requirements

At the end of each description symbols have been included to indicate sun and shade tolerance, hardiness, moisture requirements, and pH requirements.

LIGHT REQUIREMENTS

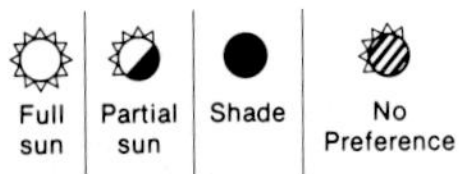

PLANT HARDINESS

Tender: tropical origin killed by first frosts.
Half-Hardy: robust enough to withstand light frosts. Killed by heavy frosts.
Hardy: tolerant of successive frosts; seedlings may even overwinter. Poppies and Dianthus.

MOISTURE REQUIREMENTS

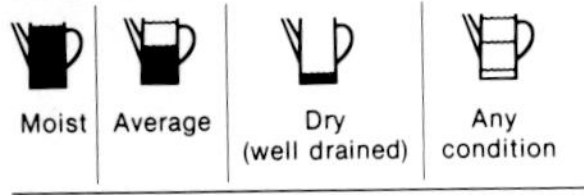

SOIL REQUIREMENTS

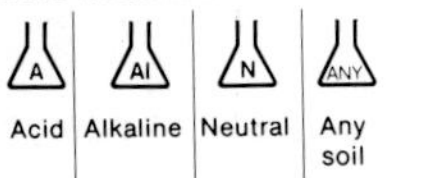

Mark's rating

The number at the beginning of each description indicates my personal rating of this flower on a scale of one to ten. (See the chapter introduction for details.)

(Previous page) This annual flowerbed next to a patio achieves a pleasant mix of height, depth, and colour.

Ageratum

(Ageratum houstonianum)

Mark's rating: **7.5**

This low-growing plant, also known as Flossflower, comes originally from Mexico. Its compact, somewhat feathery, powder-puff flowers provide a carpeted mass in sunny borders, rock gardens and containers, all summer long. Blue is the most popular colour, but you can also get species in pink, purple and white.

Ageratum is slow to germinate, so you should buy bedding plants. Set out plants 9 in. (22.5 cm) apart and water thoroughly.

With proper attention Ageratum blooms well into autumn. The plants grow to a height of 4 to 12 in. (10 to 30 cm), with a similar spread. Increase bushiness by pinching out growing tips early on.

Water regularly. Never let leaves wilt. Fertilize once a month or less often, using a low-nitrogen mixture. Over-fertilizing will encourage too many leaves and not enough flowers.

Ageratum combines well with Petunia, Pinks (Dianthus), and Wax Begonia. Try blue Ageratum with orange or gold French Marigold for dramatic colour at the front of a border.

Alyssum, Sweet

(Lobularia maritima)

Mark's rating: **8.0**

The delicate fragrance of this low-growing, spreading plant gave it the name "sweet". Irregular stalks, growing from 2 to 6 in. (5 to 15 cm) in height, bear intricate green leaves and clusters of small flowers in white, purple or pink. The plants grow quickly and bloom well past the first autumn frost.

If you buy bedding plants, set them out about 1 ft. (30 cm) apart. It's also easy to sow Alyssum directly into the ground. Sprinkle seed into raked earth, cover lightly with fine soil, and tamp down gently. Water gently until the seedlings sprout, then water regularly. Alyssum is fairly hardy, but it likes a drink every once in a while.

Because it's so easy to cultivate, Alyssum is excellent for beginning gardeners, including children. It grows to full maturity in about six weeks, and is easy to maintain.

If blooms fade in midsummer or the plants begin to look a bit scraggly, cut back extensively and apply 20-20-20 fertilizer, according to directions. A fresh second growth will emerge and last well into the fall.

Alyssum is a wonderful ground cover, and good too for awkward spots like driveway strips. Plant it at nose level in hanging baskets to enjoy the fragrance.

Aster, China

(Callistephus chinensis)

Mark's rating: **8.0**

Asters were introduced to the Western world in the eighteenth century when a Jesuit missionary in China sent seeds home to Paris. By the early 1900s the double Aster was hybridized, and today there are over 200 different varieties available. Asters come in a fantastic array of heights, forms and colours. They range from the Dwarf Queen Mix at 10 in. (25 cm) to the Perfection Mix at 30 in. (75 cm), in shades of white rose, blue, pink and scarlet. The flowers can be ribboned, rayed, ribbed or curled, in varieties like pom-pom, peony, and feathered. All make excellent cut flowers, especially taller forms.

Buy bedding plants or, better still, sow directly. Plant seeds in warm, well-drained soil and water regularly until they sprout.

Position tall Asters at the back of a border. Their tendency to become leggy can be disguised by surrounding them with other flowers.

Asters may need more care than some other annuals. They are naturally susceptible to fusarium wilt, root rot, and viruses. Look for modern disease-resistant strains.

Water from underneath so leaves don't get wet. Rotate annually. Weed out sick plants and put them in a plastic garbage bag – not the compost pile.

Baby's Breath

(Gypsophila elegans)

Mark's rating: **6.5**

Baby's Breath is a graceful flower also known as Gypsophila. Its delicate stalks, which grow to a height of 18 in. (45 cm), support masses of small star-shaped flowers, usually white but also available in red, pink, and lavender.

Plant Cosmos where they will receive plenty of sunlight.

Gypsophila softens and fills in a border. It can also be planted between dry-set stones or around a patio. It is a wonderful picking flower, popular with florists for use in flower arrangements and bridal bouquets. It lasts a long time, and dries instead of wilting.

Root disturbance disrupts growth and spread. It's best to sow seeds directly where the plants are to grow. Gypsophila likes dry, alkaline soil. Add lime if needed. Sow in drifts as soon as the earth is warm, rake soil, and gently firm. Each plant blooms only for a short time, so seed every two weeks until the end of June or mid-July for a full summer display.

Seedlings need very little maintenance. Don't over-water or add fertilizer. Help plants stand upright by putting chicken wire over young plants. Baby's Breath will grow through the wire, eventually covering it. This provides support without sacrificing the look of grace and airiness.

Bachelor's Button

(Centaurea cyanus)

Mark's rating: **6.8**

This spritely, hardy annual also goes by the name of Cornflower. Its multi-petalled flowers appear like small puffballs of colour in blue, pink, lavender and white. If planted at two-week intervals, it provides excellent, long-lasting colour. Bachelor's Button also dries well. Both 30-inch (75-cm) and dwarf strains are sold widely. Foliage is narrow and reedy, and silver-grey in colour.

Bachelor's Button is extremely easy to grow by direct sowing, beginning in early spring. This is fortunate since it does not transplant well. Seed requires pre-chilling for germination. Refrigerate for five days and keep dark for seven days. Seed may winter over in climates warmer than Zone 5, in which case seed can be sown in fall.

This plant is not fussy about soil conditions but requires full sun and good drainage. It prefers dryness over damp. Cover seed lightly and thin to 8 in.

(20 cm) between plants.

Balsam

(Impatiens Balsamina)

Mark's rating: **6.2**

This pretty plant is also called Touch-Me-Not because its seed pods burst emphatically when touched. Balsam has an erect single stem growing from 10 to 30 in. (25 to 75 cm). Flowers like tiny Roses or Camellias surround the stem at intervals. Colours are white, pink, salmon and deep red.

Balsam, which originates from tropical regions of India and China, has adapted to warm and even slightly cool summer weather, but it still likes moist soil.

Plant seedlings 10 in. (25 cm) apart, or sow seeds directly into warm, moist soil amended with peat moss. Balsam seeds sprout quickly, usually within seven days. Feed seedlings monthly with a high nitrogen fertilizer like 20-20-20. Provide plenty of water to maintain green colour.

Make sure the flowers get plenty of sun and room to grow. Pinch back leaves which shade their own flowers.

Balsam was very popular in Victorian gardens and is enjoying a comeback today. The plants are delightful massed, or planted with low-growing, colourful annuals like Impatiens (a not-too-distant cousin) and Ageratum.

Begonia, Wax

(Begonia semperflorens)

Mark's rating: **9.2**

Wax Begonia got its name from its flat, waxy leaves, which surround spreading mounds of delicate flowers. Flowers are usually in shades of pink, but white and red are also common.

Thanks to its stunning appearance when massed, and its ease of care, reliability, and versatility, Begonia has regained popularity and is widely used in parks and public places. Try it as a companion for taller plants, or with other low-growing flowers like Ageratum.

In early spring, buy good young plants and set out 1 ft. (30 cm) apart when soil is warm to the touch. Dig in a substantial amount of peat moss or other organic material. Begonia can also be sown from seed indoors in January.

With minimal care, Begonia blooms all summer and into autumn. Water well, but let the earth surface dry out a bit between waterings. Feed every three weeks with a half-strength solution of 20-

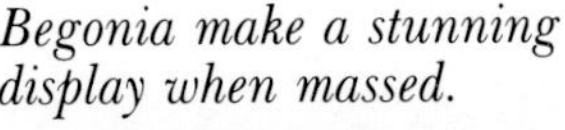

Begonia make a stunning display when massed.

20-20 or other fertilizer. Dead blooms fall off by themselves, but if green seed pods form, pick them off or they will compete with flowers. In fall, pot the plants and bring them indoors for the winter.

Browallia

(Browallia speciosa)

Mark's rating: **9.0**

Browallia, also called the Amethyst flower, is a great shade lover for people who are looking for something other than Impatiens to provide colour in the shade. Browallia is a 1 ft. (30 cm) plant with graceful trumpet-shaped flowers. Flowers come in shades of blue with a white eye, or in pure white.

Browallia should be set into the garden as plants. Grow seedlings indoors or buy bedding plants. They prefer warm soil, so don't set them out too soon. Space 10 in. (25 cm) apart.

Browallia flowers best in partial shade. Ideally, plant where it will receive sun in the morning and shade in the afternoon. When plants are 4 in. (10 cm) high, pinch out growing tips to increase side growth and bushiness.

Water frequently. Feed every 2 weeks with a solution of 20-20-20 or other fertilizer. Cut back in late summer and fertilize again for good new growth. Pot and bring Browallia indoors over winter. Keep them in bright but indirect light.

Browallia is good massed or in borders. It is also an excellent container plant, particularly combined with other semi-shade plants like Impatiens.

Calendula, or Pot Marigold

(Calendula officinalis)

Mark's rating: **7.8**

Calendula grows up to 2 ft. (60 cm) high, with single or double flowers in white, golds and yellows. The flowers, which are 2 to 4 in. (5 to 10 cm) across, resemble Daisies when they're single and Marigolds when double – hence their common name, Pot Marigold. "Pot" was added to the name because the leaves can be cooked as a vegetable and a flavouring in stews, though I have never tried this. Calendula has been grown for centuries, and was popular in Europe and Britain during the Middle Ages.

Pot Marigold likes moist, well-drained soil. When the earth is warm, sow the seeds directly in the garden. Add a second planting in late summer for fall bloom. Calendula is hardy enough to withstand light frost and stay in flower until winter begins. Full sun is best for a second sowing.

To keep the plants bushy, pinch out growing tips regularly. Remove old flower heads for continuous bloom. Cut back if stems become leggy. Remove old flowerheads for continuous flowering. Watch for mildew and slugs. Water occasionally, and only early in the day.

Calendula can easily be dried for arrangements. Tie cut flowers together and hang them upside down in a cool dry place.

Sow in awkward spots like parking strips and side walkways for hardy growth and sunny colour.

Canna

(Canna)

Mark's rating: **8.2**

This is a stunning tropical and subtropical plant which adapts well to life in temperate climes, so long as the soil is right. The leaves range in colour from green to bronze, resembling Bananas. The flowers, which resemble Lilies, are held on long stalks and come in a variety of colours, including whites, pinks, oranges and reds.

Canna grows as high as 6 ft. (1.8 m). A dwarf cultivar, Phitzer Dwarf, reaches only 3 ft. (90 cm), and is good for containers.

Rich, well-drained soil is preferred. Amend it with finely composted humus from your own compost bin or a nursery. Plant the tuberous rootstalks 5 in. (12.5 cm) deep and 10 in. (25 cm) apart as soon as the earth is warm in the spring. Choose an area where the plants will get maximum sunlight.

Canna is spectacular in borders, and wonderful around a pool where the ground isn't soggy. The flowers are best left on the plant, but the colourful leaves can be cut and used in arrangements.

When the foliage begins to fade, dig up the rootstalks and store them for the winter in a cool dry place. Plant again the following year.

RULE OF THUMB

Bend the rules and experiment with annual flowers in various situations. As the years pass, you will develop a list of your own favourites.

Carnation or Dianthus

(Dianthus caryophyllus)

Mark's rating: **7.2**

Border Carnation, often called Pinks, is smaller and bushier than the florists' variety. Plants grow from 4 to 18 in. (10 to 45 cm) high, and bear fragrant flowers, 2 to 3 in. (5 to 7.5 cm) across, in white, pink, purple, red and salmon.

Carnation grows best in alkaline soil. Add lime until the pH is at least 7.0. When soil is warm, plant 10 in. (25 cm) apart in full sun. Pinch terminal buds to encourage bushiness. Stake tall varieties to prevent from drooping. Even short forms of Carnation have a tendency to sprawl.

Water occasionally, but not too much. Good drainage is important. Carnation may be subject to rust. Spray with garden sulphur if this occurs.

Carnation does nicely in borders and containers with other alkaline-loving plants like Baby's Breath and Cosmos. It is an excellent cut flower.

Celosia,or Cockscomb

(Celosia argentea)

Mark's rating: **8.5**

Celosia produce tall erect spires whose flowers resemble a rooster's comb. Of the many different types, the Plume Cockscomb has feathery flowers, the Chinese Woolflower has flowers like tangled wool, and the Crested Cockscomb has velvety flower clusters. The flowers of all are long-lasting.

Vivid colours range from yellows and golds to deep oranges and scarlets. Dwarf Celosia grows 3 to 10 in. (7.5 to 25 cm). The taller varieties grow up to 30 in. (75 cm), and add a striking accent into autumn.

When the soil is warm, cultivate thoroughly until it is fine, then add composted manure. Bedding plants are readily available. Choose young green seedlings and set them out 6 to 10 in. (15 to 25 cm) apart, in a sunny location. Alternatively, sow seeds directly in the garden, cover them with amended soil, and keep them moist until they sprout.

Water from beneath and feed once a month with plant food like 6-12-12.

Cleome

(Cleome spinosa)

Mark's rating: **7.8**

The tall elegant spires of Cleome are topped by lacy, 8-in. (20- cm) wide flower clusters with long needle-like stamens. New blossoms emerge as the flower ball extends upwards. Blossoms continue to appear until hard cold halts growth in autumn. Cleome, also known as Spider Plant, is available in shades of rose, white and rich purple. Seed pods are quite decorative.

Cleome grows 3 to 5 ft. (90 cm to 1.5 m) high and is usually placed at the back of a border. It is also effective massed together in an island bed, where individual flowers can lend one another support. It sways somewhat. Stake discreetly if you wish. Cleome grows well in hot, dry locations, and will also tolerate semi-shade locations.

Begin Cleome indoors as pot plants by mid-March for July blooms. Early May plantings outdoors will yield late summer blooms. Plant in full sun, spacing 15 in. (42.5 cm) apart. Do not overwater. To germinate seed, store in a refrigerator at 40°F. (4°C.) for 5 days.

Coleus

(Coleus blumei)

Mark's rating: **9.5**

Coleus' main attraction is its multi-coloured leaves, in variegated shades of purples, greens, and yellows. This plant is equally at home inside or outside. It can grow up to 3 ft. (90 cm) high in the garden.

Coleus prefers crumbly, well-cultivated soil mixed with lots of humus. Choose a spot in shade or filtered sunlight for best results. Set bedding plants 1 ft. (30 cm) apart.

Established plants can easily be propagated from cuttings. Just break off a side shoot, remove all but the top leaves, and place in rootings soil. When the roots are 1/2 in. (13 mm) long, put the shoot in potting soil and water regularly.

Coleus in the garden must be kept well watered to prevent drooping. Pinch back new shoot tips to encourage branching. Remove any little yellow flowers as soon as they appear. Feed Coleus every couple of weeks with a balanced high nitrogen fertilizer like 20-20-20. Watch for aphids and mealybugs.

In fall, dig up Coleus, pot, and bring it inside for the winter. It will thrive in bright, indirect light.

Cosmos

(Cosmos bipinnatus)

Mark's rating: **9.0**

Cosmos is Greek for "beautiful thing" and this plant certainly lives up to its name. I "discovered" Cosmos recently and save a special spot for it in my yard each season. It can grow to 3 ft. (90 cm) or higher, with delicate daisy-like flowers above long wiry stems and fine, feathery foliage. There are single and double forms in white, red, and shades of pink or gold, with tufted yellow centres.

Average soil, slightly on the alkaline side, is just fine. Sow directly into the garden about 2 ft. (60 cm) apart as soon as the earth is warm.

Cosmos does well so long as it gets plenty of sun. It does best at the back of the border, where it can be supported by sturdier annuals. Stake taller specimens at the base and shelter from strong winds.

Don't over-water, and don't fertilize or you'll get all leaves and no flowers.

Cosmos is a good flower for cutting. Immerse cut flowers in cool water immediately or they will wilt.

Try planting Cosmos in a border with Snapdragon, Baby's Breath, and Zinnia.

Dwarf Dahlia

(*Dahlia* hybrids)

Mark's rating: **8.9**

Dahlias were brought from Mexico to Europe in the late 1700s and named for the Swedish botanist Dr. Andreas Dahl. Today there are well over 14,000 varieties available.

Dwarf Dahlia is a bushy plant with at-

Coleus' main attraction is its multi-coloured leaves.

RULE OF THUMB

Every year new annual flower varieties are introduced. I was disappointed in annual Dianthus until I tried a new variety — Telstar. What a winner!

tractive shiny leaves and single or double flowers, which come in all colours except blue.

Dahlia generally grows from 1 to 2 ft. (30 to 60 cm) high with a similar spread. (Some decorative Dahlias will grow up to 5 ft. (1.5 m) high.) Their flowers are excellent for cutting. Many Dahlias are good middle-of-the-border plants. They bloom from early summer right through to the first frost. They are tender bulbs (tuberous roots), cultivated similar to Gladiolus.

The first year, set out seeds or bedding plants 10 to 24 in. (25 to 60 cm) apart in very warm earth. Choose a spot that gets full or lightly filtered sun. Before planting, cultivate the soil with plenty of peat moss and sterilized manure. To make plants bushier, keep pinching out the middle set of the 3-leaved shoots as the plants grow.

Although Dahlias like the sun, they also like cool roots, so keep a layer of peat moss or composted material around the base of each plant. Water well and feed regularly with phosphorus and potash (high second and third numbers in fertilizer formulae, if you are using packaged fertilizers such as 6-12-12). Don't add fertilizer with nitrogen, since this will weaken the stems and the tubers forming under the earth.

Remove dead flowers immediately to encourage growth, and pick flowers right down the stem as often as you can. Stake tall-growing Dahlias.

After the foliage has been frost-killed, dig up the tubers, put them in a paper bag (never plastic!) filled with damp peat moss, and store them over the winter in a cool dark place. Divide and set these out again in the spring. Propagate Dahlia from leaf-cuttings or grow from seed or use root divisions.

Dianthus or Pinks

(Dianthus chinensis)

Mark's rating: 7.5

Dianthus, the Gillyflower of Shakespeare, has been cultivated for thousands of years. It got the popular name Pinks not only from its colours, but also from the indented edges of the flowers, which look as though they have been cut with pinking shears.

Dianthus is a large family with includes

Carnation and Sweet William, a biennial. There are single and double forms in pink, white, red, or various combinations of these. Pinks form clumps of attractive grey-green foliage. They grow 1 to 2 ft. (30 to 60 cm) high, with flowers about 1 in. (2.5 cm) across, lightly to deeply serrated.

Sow directly into the garden, about 1 ft. (30 cm) apart. Pinks like neutral or slightly alkaline soil. Add lime if the soil is acid. Amend sparingly with enough peat moss to ensure good drainage. Pick a sunny spot, or a location with afternoon shade. You can also plant these flowers in rock gardens and patio containers. Sweet William self-sows profusely if it has the right conditions and is left undisturbed. Seedlings take two years to flower, as with other biennials.

Water moderately and snip faded blooms to promote further growth. Make sure you get the base of the blooms, cutting right down to the stem as often as possible to encourage growth.

Pinks, which have a slight spicy scent, love to be picked and make an excellent cut flower in arrangements.

Dusty Miller

(Senecio cineraria)

Mark's rating: **9.1**

Several plants are called Dusty Miller, including *Senecio cineraria* and the perennial Artemisia. *Senecio cineraria* is the most common Dusty Miller.

The silver-dusted leaves of Dusty Miller are a dramatic addition to a garden, alone or with brightly coloured annuals like Geranium and Lobelia. Dusty Miller looks lovely in the moonlight.

This plant is reliable until the first snow. Growth is usually 12 to 20 in. (30 to 50 cm).

Buy bedding plants. Dusty Miller isn't fussy about the soil, as long as it is well-draining. Add a bit of peat moss when planting, and plant in full sun.

Plants need little or no fertilizer and moderate amounts of water. From time to time, pinch out the little yellow flowers which form.

Dusty Miller is outstanding for cutting. The leaves continue to look fresh for weeks with a minimum of attention. Just change the water occasionally.

RULE OF THUMB

For drought tolerant annual flowers try Portulaca, Dusty Miller, and Verbena and Dwarf Zinnias.

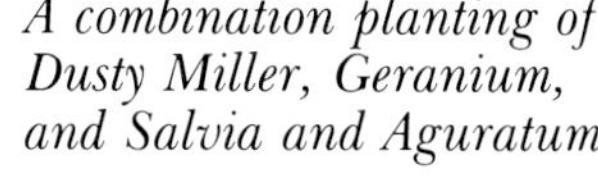

A combination planting of Dusty Miller, Geranium, and Salvia and Aguratum.

(Opposite) *Impatiens, Canada's most popular annual, flourishes in moist, shady conditions.*

Everlasting

Mark's rating: **8.0**

Several different species are often called Everlasting. They are everlasting in the sense that they retain little moisture, dry with ease and are very useful in artificial bouquets. They include: Strawflower (*Helichrysum*), Globe Amaranth (*Gomphrena*), *Rhodanthe* or *Acroclinium*, Common Immortelle (*Xeranthemum*), and Honesty or the Silver Dollar Plant (*Lunaria annua*).

All everlasting species originated in warm, dry regions like the Mediterranean or Australia. They prefer intense sun and are extremely heat-resistant. Plant in dry or average soil after all danger of frost is past. Most everlasting types do not transplant well.

Requirements differ for each species.

Gazania

(Gazania rigens)

Mark's rating: **8.0**

Gazania is very attractive and easy to grow. Long sturdy stems support pretty and multi-petalled flowers resembling Daisies, while fuzzy flat leaves hug the ground like a mat.

Gazania flowers love the sun so much they close up on cloudy days and at night. The colours are sunny too – cream, orange, yellow, bronze, pink and red. The flowers continue blooming well past the first frost of autumn.

Gazania likes sandy, well-draining soil. Avoid heavy clay or loamy earth. Set out bedding plants in a sunny location, or sow seeds directly into the garden. Gazania is delightful when massed or used as a ground cover, so plant a lot of them in one place.

Care is minimal. Don't fertilize, and add only a moderate amount of moisture, letting the earth dry out between waterings.

Gazania does well in containers and rock gardens, and thrives in all sorts of odd places so long as there's lots of sun. Try planting seeds between the dry-set stones in a walkway or patio. They'll grow well in the sandy soil beneath.

In autumn, pot your favourite Gazania plants and bring them indoors for winter.

Geranium

(Pelargonium hortorum)

Mark's rating: **9.2**

Geranium is a garden staple. Sturdy stalks hold up clusters of small-petalled flowers surrounded by large lily-pad leaves. Red, pink and salmon are the most popular colours, although orange and white are also available. Leaves are variegated with as many as four different colours.

You may grow Zonal Geranium from cuttings or seed. Begin seeds indoors in late December or early January. Take cuttings in late summer, before evening temperatures drop below 55°F. (13°C.)

Geranium will last more than one season if it is brought indoors. Dig up plants in the fall, pot them, and place them in a sunny window.

Buy your first Geraniums from a nursery. A first-year Geranium grows up to 2 ft. (60 cm) high with a similar spread, while 2- or 3-year-old plants are larger and correspondingly more expensive. Look for hybrids which are disease-resistant and heat-tolerant. Ivy Geranium (*P. peltatum*) is very popular, especially for hanging baskets and balcony plantings.

Set Geraniums out in soil well mixed with peat moss. Since this plant performs best when its roots are constricted, it does wonderfully in containers. Geranium loves acid soil, so add some apple cider vinegar to the water can occasionally. Fertilize every three weeks with 6-12-12.

When flowers fade, snip them right down to the stem to encourage new blooms.

Godetia

(Godetia amoena)

Mark's rating: **8.0**

Also known as Satinflower or Farewell-to-Spring, Godetia is a hardy annual that produces bi-coloured blooms in shades of pink, peach and burgundy. The four-petalled flowers are borne singly or in clusters on stalks that range between 1 to 3 ft. (30 to 90 cm). Poor soil in light shade is preferred.

Godetia is difficult to transplant. Sow seed in early spring for July blooms. Space seedlings 6 to 8 in. (15 to 20 cm) apart.

RULE OF THUMB

Don't be fooled by the appearance of bedding plants when you purchase them in the spring. Lavatera, for example, looks poor in a tray or pack in May but will impress anyone in the garden come midsummer. On the other hand, a full-flowering bedding plant may be past its prime planting stage.

Impatiens

(Impatiens Wallerana)

Mark's rating: **9.7**

Impatiens, often called Busy Lizzie, is the most popular annual flower in Canada, thanks to its profusion of red, white, and pink single-petalled flowers over waxy green leaves. It blooms through the summer until the first frost. Elfin varieties grow up to 1 ft. (30 cm) high, and Imp varieties grow up to 2 ft. (60 cm).

Superior bedding plants are available. Pick plants which are compact, not leggy. Select a spot in full or partial shade and cultivate the earth until it is light and crumbly. Add lots of peat moss or composted material. The distance between the plants should equal their anticipated height.

Impatiens requires very little care, but it has a succulent stem, and must never be over-watered. Keep soil moist at all times, but never soggy. If the ground dries out and the plants begin to wilt, a good drink will revive them. But don't do this too often or the plants will get spindly. Fertilize with 20-20-20.

Impatiens is wonderful for shade areas under trees or on the north side of a house. You can plant a twilight garden with white Impatiens and blue Lobelia or Browallia. It's also popular for use in hanging baskets, in shady places, out of the wind.

Lavatera

(Lavatera trimestris)

Mark's rating: **8.9**

Lavatera, commonly known as Rose Mallow, is one of the most underrated Boy Wonders. Once you have enjoyed its performance in your garden, I think you will be back for more.

Lavatera grows in one form as a wild flower throughout Canada. Its flowers resemble small Hollyhocks. Plants grow as small bushes, reaching 3 ft. (90 cm) in height, with almost equal spread. Available colours are limited to pink and white.

Lavatera can be transplanted, but only with care. Sow seed outdoors in mid to late May, when all danger of frost is past and the ground has warmed. Cover lightly and thin to 2 ft. (60 cm) spacing.

Livingston Daisy

(Mesembryanthemum criniflorum)

Mark's rating: **8.7**

The Livingston Daisy is a succulent that grows no higher than 3 in. (7.5 cm). Livingston Daisy forms a dense carpet of sprawling foliage, which in the warmest regions of British Columbia can winter over as a perennial ground cover. It produces wide daisy-type flowers in bright shades of pink creams or orange, often sporting a white centre. It blooms only in the sun, and makes a great colourful annual in "hot spots".

A close relative is Ice Plant (*M. crystallinum*), so called for its silver-white tinged leaves.

Seed can be sown directly, but in climates harsher than Zone 8 early blooms are more certain with potted seedlings. Ice plants require sustained warmth to reach maturity. Mesembryanthemum requires surface temperature of 70°F (22°C) for germination. Seed should be barely covered. Space plants 2 in. (5 cm) apart.

Lobelia

(Lobelia Erinus)

Mark's rating: **9.1**

Although Lobelia can sometimes be found in white, purple and even pink, deep blue is the most popular and striking colour. The small 5-petalled flowers with delicate green leaves grow profusely from a single plant.

Bush or upright Lobelia is for use in borders. The best upright variety, Crystal Palace, grows 6 in. (15 cm) high.

Trailing Lobelia are for use in containers. The best of these is Sapphire, which grows 1 ft. (30 cm) long.

Seeds take long to germinate, so buy bedding plants. Lobelia does well in all kinds of soil, but appreciates a bit of peat moss mixed into the earth in the planting hole. Full sun is fine if the summer isn't too hot and the plants get plenty of water, but Lobelia looks fresher and more intensely coloured in filtered sunlight or partial shade. The ideal location is sunny in the morning and shaded in the afternoon.

Keep the soil moist but not soggy, and try to soak it from underneath the plants so they don't get flattened. If they start to look scraggly in midsummer, cut them

back and fertilize with a solution of 20-20-20 for second growth.

Blue Lobelia is stunning at dusk, particularly when it's planted with white Lobelia, white Impatiens, or Dusty Miller. In a sunny location, try it massed with yellow or gold French Marigold.

Marigold

(Tagetes)

Mark's rating: **8.5**

Marigold, or Tagetes, was originally sent back from Mexico by the priests accompanying Cortez on his conquests in the 1500s. It travelled first to Spain, then to monastery gardens in France and Morocco. By the time it reached England, it was divided into French (*Tagetes patula*) and African (*Tagetes erecta*) species. The orange and yellow colours earned this plant the nickname Mary's Gold.

Both African and French Marigold like a sunny location with average soil mixed with a bit of peat moss. Buy bedding plants that are round and compact, not leggy. French Marigolds can also be sown as seeds directly into the ground. They will grow to 1 ft. (30 cm) and should be planted 10 in. (25 cm) apart. This is one of the easiest plants to grow from seed.

African Marigolds are tallest. The Climax and Jubilee series grow up to 3 ft. (90 cm). To help support them when they are large, set the young bedding plants about 3 or 4 in. (7.5 to 10 cm) into the earth. Break off the bottom foliage and pack the earth around the stem. Place them at least 2 ft. (60 cm) apart.

For bushiness on the taller plants, pinch out the axil growth between all the double leaves which form as the plants grow. Pinch off any faded blooms right down the stem. Give Marigolds plenty of water and fertilize with 20-20-20 every two weeks.

Mirabilis

(Mirabilis jalapa)

Mark's rating: **7.7**

The bright yellow, pink, red or white trumpet flowers of Mirabilis open in the late afternoon, hence their common name Four O'Clock. Mirabilis is a native of South America, also known as Marvel of Peru.

Mirabilis is an unusual plant, though easily grown. It somewhat resembles perennial Phlox in stature and flower-form. Frequently more than one colour of

Yellow marigolds add a mix of colour to a bed of annual flowers.

RULE OF THUMB

All annual bedding plants transplant best if the root mass is pre-moistened with a solution of water-soluble 20-20-20.

(Opposite) Nasturtium is valued equally for its blossoms, (which are edible!) and its distinctive round leaves.

bloom will appear on the same plant.

Mirabilis can be grown from seed or from small tubers which form at its roots. If harvested and stored over winter it can be planted again in May. Sow outdoors in late spring for August blooms. For earlier blooms, sow indoors.

Mirabilis reaches a height of 2 to 3 ft. (60 to 90 cm). Plant in sunny, well-drained locations, spacing seedlings 10 to 12 in. (25 to 30 cm) apart. This is an ideal annual for filling in large spaces.

Morning Glory

(Ipomoea)

Mark's rating: **8.3**

This lovely vine has heart-shaped leaves and fragile, trumpet blossoms that close in bright light. It's a fast-growing plant that captures the interest of children. Morning Glory comes in a wide variety of colours and bicolours, with a prominent distinctive star in the centre.

Morning Glory is useful as a vine, ground cover and container plant. New bush-type dwarfs are especially favoured for baskets and window boxes.

Plant in full sun, in poor soil, spacing 6 in. (15 cm) apart. Seeds require warmth for germination. Soak seeds overnight before sowing for quick germination.

Morning Glory takes a full two months after germination to begin flowering, and often doesn't bloom until late summer. Eager gardeners often want to give this plant a head start and put it out as potted seedlings. However, only the most carefully handled Morning Glories will survive transplanting.

Nasturtium

(Tropaeolum)

Mark's rating: **8.8**

Nasturtium's blossoms and its distinctive round leaves are equally attractive, and are both suitable for use in flower arrangements. This plant grows either as a vine or small bush. Its colour range is limited to creams, and shades of scarlet, orange, yellow and rose. Some bicoloured forms and varieties with variegated leaves are available. Double-flowering types possess a stronger tart fragrance than single-flowering cultivars.

Nasturtium can take as long as two months to bloom. Seedlings can be started indoors but they require extra care as transplant injury is common. Outdoors, plant Nasturtium after all danger of frost has passed, in sun or light shade, spacing 8 in. (20 cm) apart. Well-drained, warm soil is essential. Do not fertilize. Watch for aphids.

Nemophila

(Nemophila)

Mark's rating: **7.2**

The bright blue and white flowers of this sprawling, 1 ft. (30 cm) high plant make it an unusual eye-catcher at the front of a border. *Nemophila Menziesii,* commonly called Baby Blue Eyes, has fern-like leaves that tend to trail. Both it and *Nemophila maculata,* which has five blue-dotted white petals, are native to North America. Its bell-shaped flowers are 1 1/2 in. (3.8 cm) wide.

Nemophila prefers shade and somewhat moist soil, especially where summers are hot and humid. Sow indoors in April for June flowers, but transplant gently. Seeds sown outdoors will produce mid-summer blooms. Cover seed lightly and space 8 in. (20 cm) apart.

Nicotiana, or Oriental Tobacco

(Nicotiana species)

Mark's rating: **8.5**

Nicotiana, also known as Flowering Tobacco, has small trumpet-shaped flowers on long stems which bloom into the fall. The plants used to be famous for their sweet evening smell, although some of the newer varieties are less aromatic. The most fragrant varieties available are *N. alata grandiflora,* or *N. affinis.*

White is the most popular colour, but the flowers also come in red, crimson, lavender, and mauve. Nicotiana grows up to 2 ft. (60 cm) tall, and looks best massed or spaced between other annuals in a border as an accent.

Set out bedding plants 1 ft. (30 cm) apart as soon as the earth is warm. Choose a spot with partial shade or filtered sun, although some of the newer hybrids are now reliable bloomers in full sun. Cultivate the soil until crumbly and mix in plenty of peat moss.

Keep this plant away from Tomatoes. Nicotiana can contract tobacco mosaic virus. It won't hurt the flowers, but it will

RULE OF THUMB

Don't throw spent annual plants in the garbage, their soft stems, leaves and flowers produce great compost.

make the Tomatoes very sick indeed.

Nicotiana loves humidity, so keep soil moist. Fertilize every couple of weeks with a solution of 20-20-20, and keep weeds down by mulching with peat moss.

Nicotiana is good in large containers and planters around the patio where you can smell the flowers and watch the butterflies they attract.

Nierembergia

(Nierembergia)

Mark's rating: **7.6**

The intense, bright purple or white flowers of Nierembergia are chalice-shaped, hence its common name Cupflower. Its low, spreading habit makes Nierembergia an ideal choice for edging a border or for lending colour to a rock garden. Its thin, grassy foliage grows only 6 in. (15 cm) high.

Nierembergia likes a well-drained site in full or lightly filtered sun. It is a half-hardy annual which is best sown indoors. A January sowing will yield May blooms. Plant at intervals for steady bloom production. Space seedlings 6 in. (15 cm) apart.

Nigella

(Nigella)

Mark's rating: **8.0**

Nigella produces multi-petalled blossoms in gem-bright shades of blue, mauve, pink and white. Prominent stamens dominate Nigella's blooms. The blooms nestle amid fine, feathery foliage, almost as though trying to hide, hence the common names Persian Jewel, Devil-In-A-Bush, and Love-In-A-Mist.

Nigella is a hardy annual which deserves to be better known in Canada. Its seed will winter over in Zone 4 but colour selection is more certain if you purchase fresh stock and sow in very early spring. Successive sowings every two weeks will yield blooms all summer long. Nigella is not fussy about soil. Plant in full sun and space 6 to 89 in. (15 to 20 cm) apart.

Ornamental Kale and Cabbage

(Brassica)

Mark's rating: **8.3**

The popularity of flowering Kale and its close cousin the Cabbage seems to increase each year. Their brilliant, variegated leaves in rose, purple and white combine with a hardiness that places them among the sturdiest autumn plants. Cold weather actually deepens and improves their colour. Like other members of the Mustard family, Brassica tends to do poorly in summer heat.

Put out as seedlings either in early spring or late summer. Plant in a sunny site with well-drained soil. Thin to 15 in. (37.5 cm) apart. This plant will continue to flower weeks after other annuals have died – even up to Christmas in some areas.

Pansy, or Viola

(Viola species*)*

Mark's rating: **8.8**

Pansies and Violas are both members of the genus *Viola*, and come in both annual and perennial varieties. The Pansy, a very popular flower in the spring and early summer, is named for the French *pensée*, meaning thought. Large five-petalled blooms in velvety colours look out at the world from longish slender stems. The blooms are famous for their distinctive black markings or faces, and for their fragrance.

Violas don't have faces, but come in lovely muted shades of white, blue, mauve, purple and yellow.

Both are hardier than they appear, and are excellent for city gardens and containers. They grow successfully amid pollution and exhaust fumes. New varieties are being developed which can stand the heat of summer.

Pansy and Viola are best set out as bedding plants to exactly the same depth in the ground as they were in the flat. They should never be allowed to dry out. Before planting, amend the soil with peat moss or some other moisture-retaining material. Then put a good layer of mulch around the plants to keep the moisture level constant and the roots cool. To help the plants bloom as long as possible, choose a spot that gets the morning sun.

Plant out in your garden as soon as the

Pink Petunias amid a planting of bright red Geraniums.

ground can be worked. Don't worry when your neighbours laugh at you for it – you'll be rewarded with plenty of hardy, early-season bloom.

The flowers will start to bloom immediately. Pick them regularly right down the stem. Pinch back the plants constantly to prevent them from getting leggy, and to promote blooms. Keep watered. Fertilize with 20-20-20.

Petunia

(Petunia hybrida)

Mark's rating: **9.3**

Petunia, originally from Argentina, was the most popular annual in North America for a long time – Impatiens has since moved into the number one spot. It is famous for its dependability and variety of colour, including all shades of blue, red, and purple, as well as white and yellow and bicoloured. The flowers, trumpet-shaped and about 5 in. (12.5 cm) across, come in single or double blooms – fringed, bordered or streaked. Double-flowering types usually have fewer blooms, and need frequent deadheading.

Both compact and trailing varieties are available. Cascade is the best of the trailing varieties, and is excellent for use in containers. Double-bloom Petunias are also good in containers since they have a tendency to droop over in the garden, but these must be dead-headed frequently to encourage blossoming.

In the spring, as soon as the soil is warm to the touch, cultivate until crumbly and mix in some peat moss for good drainage. Buy bedding plants which are compact, not leggy, and plant them about 1 ft. (30 cm) apart. Pinch them back to 6 in. (15 cm). After the first bloom, cut them back again. This will delay early blooming, but it's worth it since it produces bushier growth and more flowers.

Water regularly and fertilize at least every three weeks with 20-20-20. Any faded blooms should be cut off right down the stem, not just pulled out of the bracket.

Petunia makes a very good and long-lasting cut flower with a spicy fragrance. Regular picking also encourages more blooms. If plants start to get leggy in midsummer, cut them back ruthlessly and give them a good feeding. In no time at all you'll have a spectacular second growth. With tender care, they'll bloom into autumn.

RULE OF THUMB

Are you a cottage gardener? Try Portulaca. It loves sand, sun and being ignored for days at a time.

Phlox

(Phlox Drummondii)

Mark's rating: **6.9**

A contrasting eye gives annual Phlox a "twinkle" effect. It grows in such a multitude of colour arrangements that they could never all be listed here. Blossoms are usually a solid colour with a highlighted or white eye.

Seed houses often advise gardeners that their weakest seedlings will provide the best colour blends and should be coddled. This species is native to prairie meadows and does not flag with intense heat. Dwarf strains are excellent at the front of a border. Taller forms grow as high as 15 in. (37.5 cm).

Plant in full sun or minimal shade. Cover seed lightly. Darkness and mild warmth is needed for germination. Seeds sown indoors in late winter should be ready to bloom by mid-May, at which time seeds can also be sown outdoors. Plant at intervals for successive blooms. Thin seedlings 5 to 8 in. (12.5 to 20 cm) apart. Shear back severely for rejuvenation.

Portulaca, or Rose Moss

(Portulaca grandiflora)

Mark's rating: **8.4**

Portulaca, often called Rose Moss, is a happy flower which will grow in even the poorest soil so long as it's sunny. This is a ground-hugging plant, which usually reaches a height of only 6 in. (15 cm). It features an abundance of single- or double-petalled flowers rising above a thick carpet of succulent foliage. The colours – red, yellow, orange, white and coral – are clear and brilliant. The flowers love the sun so much they close up when the sun goes down.

Portulaca loves sandy soil in sunny locations. For this reason, I often recommend it for cottage gardens. It is ideal around patios and between the stones of dry-laid walks. It is absolutely indispensable in trouble spots where other annuals die out.

When the earth is warm and all danger of frost is past, seed directly into the ground. Thin growing seedlings to 6 in. (15 cm) to promote bushy plants. You can also set out bedding plants 6 in. (15 cm) apart. Some varieties re-seed and come up the following year.

Portulaca is easy to maintain. It needs no fertilizer or grooming, and very little water. It deserves a place in beds, edgings and rock gardens, and troublesome areas like driveway strips. Try it with other ground covers like Alyssum and Vinca.

Evening Primrose

(Oenothera)

Mark's rating: **6.8**

This hardy annual is so prolific and successful at dispersing seeds that many gardeners argue it is perennial. Evening Primrose issues broad 4-petalled blossoms that open at dusk. They scent the evening air and remain throughout the following day. Many varieties change colour as they fade from white to pink, and from yellow to orange or red. Plants range from 6 in. to 6 ft. (15 cm to 1.8 m), depending on variety.

Evening Primrose is a wild meadow flower native to North America. It likes hot weather and is not fussy about soil. Plant indoors ten weeks before the last expected frost date or sow directly in late spring. Plant in a sunny or lightly shaded location in small clumps. It is a nice addition in the foreground of perennial gardens.

Salvia or Scarlet Sage

(Salvia splendens)

Mark's rating: **8.2**

Salvia is a dramatic tall-speared plant which can grow from 1 to 3 ft. (30 to 90 cm) tall. Famous for its red colour, it also comes in white, lavender, rose, salmon, and even a blue variety which looks great massed or combined with the red.

Salvia blooms all summer, thriving in the heat, but it seems to come into its own in early fall with the colours of autumn.

Salvia can be set out as bedding plants as soon as the soil is warm. Amend the earth with peat moss or other organic material, and cultivate until crumbly. Salvia prefers dry soil to wet. Plant about 1 ft. (30 cm) apart. This is a fiery, sun-loving plant, but it will also tolerate partial shade. It is a handy tall plant for tricky borders that don't get full sun.

Snapdragons are available in solid and bicolour shades of red, yellow, pink, wine and white.

Dwarf types are ideal for edging flower beds and planters.

Once a month, apply a half strength solution of 20-20-20 to keep the leaves green, but don't overfeed. Water frequently.

The sweet nectar in the flowers will sometimes attract bees, butterflies and hummingbirds. Try planting the shorter varieties in planters and containers with white Dahlia, and the tall red ones in a border with gold and yellow Marigold or silver-grey Dusty Miller.

Snapdragon

(Antirrhinum majus)

Mark's rating: **9.1**

Snapdragon florets, which line vertical stalks, sometimes snap open when squeezed, giving the flower its popular name.

Snapdragon comes in solid and bi-colour shades of red, yellow, pink, wine and white.

Snapdragon is my favourite cutting flower.

The plants grow from 6 in. to 3 ft. (15 to 90 cm) high and come in three varieties: dwarf, medium, and tall. The tall ones are good at the back of a border, the medium size in the middle to blend with similarly sized annuals, and the dwarf at the front, or massed in their own bed. The taller the plant, the better for cutting. But taller plants flower later in the season. They will continue to blossom until the snow flies.

Set bedding plants out as soon as the soil is warm to the touch in a location that gets lots of sun. Turn earth with a garden fork until crumbly, amending with lots of peat moss or compost, then plant seedling 6 to 12 in. (15 to 30 cm) apart, depending on the height of the variety. Pinch back as they grow to cause branching, and support the tall varieties with bamboo stakes.

You can fertilize in midsummer with 20-20-20, but don't overdo it. Water moderately from underneath so the leaves don't get wet, since Snaps are susceptible to rust. To be on the safe side, spray occasionally with garden sulphur.

If you want to keep your Snapdragons blooming all summer and into fall, keep them picked. Otherwise, they will go to seed and the flowers will stop developing. Besides, Snaps cry out to be picked for use in arrangements. They also go very well in a border with other cutting flowers like Aster, Zinnia, and Marigold.

(Opposite) Sweet Pea, a favourite annual for children, is ideal in summer bouquets.

Statice

(Limonium)

Mark's rating: **8.6**

A long-time favourite of florists, Statice, often called Sea Lavender, bears clustered paper-thin buds on long racemes that are perfect in fresh and dried arrangements. Blues, mauves, yellow and white are often combined in popular mixtures. Statice has a remarkable tolerance for salt and dryness, making it appropriate for maritime gardeners.

Plant seed outdoors in early spring. Thin seedlings 10 in. (25 cm) apart. Statice seed can be extracted from reasonably fresh bouquets and air-dried.

Virginia Stock

(Malcomia maritima)

Mark's rating: **7.2**

Stock is the name commonly given to two different but similar plants, which share a sweet scent and pastel colouring. Together with Cabbages, they are members of the Mustard family.

Virginia Stock *(Malcomia maritima)* is a hardy annual that grows only about 1 ft. (30 cm) tall. Its delicately shaded blossoms vary from soft rosy white to purple.

Common Stock

(Matthiola incana) and Evening Stock (Matthiola bicornis)

Mark's rating: **7.2**

Common Stock (*Matthiola incana*) is anything but common. Its pretty, flower-lined stalks are somewhat reminiscent of Brussels Sprouts. Two strains, Ten-Week and Trysomic, are available in a range of creams, blues and pinks. Both dwarf and tall forms are easily obtained. Over 80 per cent of most mixtures will have double flowers. Thin out singles by discarding seedlings that are less vigorous and that have lighter foliage.

A close cousin, Evening Stock (*M. bicornis*), has flowers resembling Virginia Stock. They open at night, lending a delightful fragrance to the evening air.

Both species of *Matthiola* prefer sun, average to alkaline soil, and cooler weather. They perform best in early or late summer, though heat-resistant varieties are frequently offered. Plant outdoors in very early spring, after hard freezing is over. Common Stock can be sown indoors in March. Thin 6 to 8 in. (15 to 20 cm) apart. Seed of Evening Stock should be broadcast in clusters.

Swan-River Daisy

(Brachycome)

Mark's rating: **6.8**

This demure little Daisy has a dark eye that beckons from nests of wispy, thin foliage. Flowers, which measure 1 1/2 in. (38 mm) are usually pastel shades of rose, white or blue. Brachycome is less than 1 ft. (30 cm) tall, and should be planted at the front of a border, in containers, or on small slopes as a ground cover.

Plant in a sunny, well-drained site. This plant can easily be transplanted or sown directly. Thin to 6 in. (15 cm) apart to allow for bushy, trailing growth.

Sweet Pea

(Lathyrus)

Mark's rating: **8.5**

With its ruffled blossoms, Sweet Pea has long been one of the most popular flowers of the early summer garden. It is another favourite annual for children. Sweet Pea almost always blooms in time to celebrate Canada Day. Originally it was a vine, with tendrils to cling, but hybridization has created strains that grow as mounding bushes which are ideal for borders, window boxes, planters, or cutting. Rainbow mixtures and solid colour seed collections are often sold. The colour range includes scarlet, maroon, salmon, pinks, blues and white.

Sweet Pea likes rich deep soil and cool temperatures. It will grow in full sun but usually withers once summer heat becomes intense. Cuthbertson strains tolerate higher temperatures. In order to get full enjoyment from Sweet Pea, plant indoors in late winter or outdoors in April. The hard seed can be pre-soaked for 24 hours before planting. Place in well-worked, mounded soil, spacing 8 in. (20 cm) apart. Prepare the soil in autumn so you can plant the seed early in spring.

To encourage maximum bloom from

RULE OF THUMB

Vertical colour is easy to grow and effective. Try these annual vines in the sun: Morning Glory, Sweet Pea, Thunbergia and Scarlet Runner Beans.

tall vines, pinch back seedlings to stimulate side shoot growth when they reach 5 in. (12.5 cm). To ensure repeat blooming, diligently cut back finished blossoms. Sweet Pea is a heavy feeder. Mulching with finely-ground bark helps to keep the soil cool.

Sweet William

(Dianthus barbatus)

Mark's rating: **6.1**

Sweet William is a member of the Dianthus family and a relative of Carnations and Pinks. It has thick stalks with green sword-like leaves beneath massed flower heads. The sweet spicy fragrance is delightful. The flowers come in wine and red. Some varieties are bi-coloured with white.

Sweet William ranges in height from 4 in. to 2 ft. (10 to 60 cm), so make sure you know what you've got before you decide where to put it in the garden.

Like its relatives, Sweet William prefers slightly alkaline soil. As soon as the soil is ready to be worked, fork it until it is crumbly, and add a generous amount of peat moss or compost. Dig in lime to bring up the pH at least to 7.0. Choose a spot that gets full sun or afternoon shade.

Set out bedding plants 8 in. to 1 ft. (20 to 30 cm) apart, depending on their mature height.

Sweet William is a hardy biennial which will sometimes last for a second season. However, it usually dies out by the second summer and should be replaced by new plants.

This plant requires only moderate watering and little fertilizing.

Plant Sweet William in a border with other alkaline-loving plants like Pinks, Carnations, and Cosmos, and with dramatically-coloured Salvia and Snapdragons.

Thunbergia, or Black-Eyed Susan Vine

(Thunbergia alata)

Mark's rating: **7.3**

Thunbergia is an excellent climbing vine which grows quickly to provide flowering cover. It is a tender perennial, grown like an annual in the moderate climates of the northern hemisphere. It has crisp leaves and bright flowers about 1 in. (2.5 cm) across. The flowers come in cream, orange, and yellow, with black centres or "eyes" and purple throats. Thunbergia cascades as nicely as it climbs. I like it in containers and hanging baskets.

Provide twining stems with a trellis or other support before you plant. Fork soil and amend with peat moss to ensure good drainage, then set out bedding plants 10 in. (25 cm) apart.

Thunbergia likes lots of water. But you don't have to fertilize them unless they are in containers, in which case you should give them a drink of diluted 20-20-20 every month.

Unlike the Sweet Pea, this vine doesn't have to be cut back or pruned. Just let it grow. If you have planted Thunbergia in containers, bring it indoors for the winter, container and all, cut it back, then set it outside again in the spring.

Vinca or Periwinkle

(Vinca rosea)

Mark's rating: **8.1**

Annual Vinca is a pretty plant which blooms continuously all summer with very little upkeep. Small five-petalled flowers, which are surrounded by shiny green leaves, come in white, rose-pink, and white with red centres, or pink with rose centres. Some cultivars have variegated leaves.

Vinca is adaptable for use in borders, as a ground cover, or in hanging baskets and containers. It stands up well to the stresses of city living, and thrives in hot humid summers. It is a spreading plant, rounded and bushy, which can grow over 1 ft. (30 cm) high.

Vinca does well in average soil, but a little peat moss added during planting helps with drainage. Choose a spot in full or lightly filtered sun. Seeds are slow to germinate, so buy bedding plants. Set them out 12 to 15 in. (30 to 37.5 cm) apart. Keep pinching out growing tips to encourage bushiness.

Water occasionally to keep the soil moist, but don't over-water or the plants will get spindly. Don't fertilize. Plant Vinca alone, or with Zinnia, Petunia, or Ageratum. It is ideal for containers, especially hanging baskets.

Zinnia

(Zinnia elegans)

Mark's rating: **8.9**

Zinnia has brilliant daisy-like flowers in single or double blooms. I love it as a cut flower and as a colourful attraction in my garden. It does particularly well in North America because of its fondness for long, hot summers. It is an all-purpose garden annual, which can be used any place.

Zinnia comes in a wide range of types and in all colours except blue, but it is famous for the sunny colours of red, yellow, gold and bronze. The flowers are held on stiff stems with undistinguished foliage, best hidden in a border with other plants. Multicoloured and striped cultivars are available.

Zinnia comes in dwarf, intermediate, and tall varieties, growing from 6 in. to 3 ft. (15 to 90 cm) high.

Zinnia is reliable and easy to grow. Turn the soil and add plenty of peat moss or other compost. Sow seeds 6 to 12 in. (15 to 30 cm) apart. If you buy bedding plants, be sure they haven't started to flower or set bud.

Choose a spot in full sun. Because Zinnia is subject to mildew, plant it where the air circulation is good and breezy. As the young plants grow, pinch them back to promote bushiness and blooms.

Water frequently but carefully. To reduce risk of mildew, water early in the day. Soak plants at ground level so the leaves don't get wet. One of the secrets of growing good Zinnias is to keep the leaves dry. Spray occasionally with garden sulphur and fertilize every couple of weeks with a solution of 20-20-20.

Pick often to encourage blooms. Pick early in the morning when the buds are just starting to open and the flowers will last a long time in arrangements, providing you change the water daily.

Zinnia comes in a wide range of colours, but is most famous for the sunny colours of red, yellow, gold and bronze.

POPPIES

The wide, bright blossoms of poppies bring irresistible cheer and colour to a summer garden. Most annual Poppies are very easy to raise. They are divided into five main categories with distinct flowering habits.

California Poppy

(Eschscholzia californica)

Mark's rating: **8.3**

California Poppy has a low, spreading form, and feathery, blue-green foliage. It grows to a height of 12 in. (30 cm) and issues blooms in various shades of orange, buff and rose. California Poppy is a sun-lover that closes whenever daylight fades. This makes it unsuitable for cutting. It is lovely combined with blue Pansy or Ageratum at the front of a border.

Mexican Tulip Poppy

(Hunnemannia fumariaefolia)

Mark's rating: **8.1**

Mexican Tulip Poppy closely resembles the California Poppy in foliage, flower form, and requirements but it is available only in yellow. Tulip Poppy grows 2 ft. (60 cm) or more and its flowers can be used in cut arrangements if the bottom of the flower stem is first singed with a match.

Iceland Poppy

(Papaver nudicaule)

Mark's rating: **9.0**

Iceland Poppy is the most easily transplanted variety. Its delicate pastel blossoms surround an attractive fringe of gold stamens. Salmon, gold, white and orange shades are most frequently available. Some have double blooms. A biennial, it is often treated as an annual. Seed takes ten months to reach maturity.

Flanders Poppy

(Papaver Rhoeas)

Mark's rating: **8.2**

This is the Corn or Flanders Poppy of poetic fame and of special significance to Canadians. The most popular form is the Shirley Poppy, often grown in single or double bi-coloured forms that lighten to white at their centre. The Shirley Poppy is available in every shade of red or pink imaginable and grows between 16 and 24 in. (40 to 60 cm). Its delicate, paper-thin petals last only a short while, but each plant can produce multiple buds over the course of a fortnight.

Opium Poppy

(Papaver somniferum)

Mark's rating: **7.8**

Somniferum is best known for its derivative opium. The wide open petals are often bi-coloured combinations of salmon and purple, pink and black, red and black or solid colour versions in an assortment of shades. Both single and double flower forms are available. Each flower lasts just one day.

RULE OF THUMB

Raising annual Poppies is truly foolproof. Since transplanting seedlings is seldom successful, sow *in situ*. Choose a sunny site with soil that is not too rich or damp. Broadcast seed at intervals beginning in early spring. Mid-April is not too soon. Poppy seed is quite tiny so a seed disperser is useful. Thin plants 8 to 10 in. (20 to 25 cm) apart.

(Opposite) California Poppies (Eschscholzia) make a bold contrast with deep blue Lupins.

CHAPTER 4

PERENNIALS

If your goal as a gardener is to produce as much colour as possible for as long as possible, perennials are not down your alley. Typically, perennials provide a burst of colour for a few days or weeks, then "foliate" for the rest of the season.

However, a limited experience with perennials may change your goals.

My dream of a perfect garden – one loaded with blossoms and fragrance, form and foliage – and my penchant for annual flowers and flowering shrubs, was shattered when I visited David Tomlinson and his wife Diedre at their home in Aurora, Ontario a few years ago. David and Diedre grow over 700 species of hardy, flowering perennials on a little more than an acre of land. For them, perennial gardening is more than a pastime, it's a passion.

My initial visit has since become an annual event for me and my whole family. Mid-July is generally considered peak time for perennials. But this lively couple has taught me to appreciate not just the glory of a perennial garden blooming in the July heat, but also the ever-changing personality of the garden throughout the growing season.

Perennials are generally reliable repeat performers. Like good friends, they come back year after year to spread their own particular charm – providing you do your part to keep the weeds down, keep competitive plants out of the way, and provide the desired nutrients. None of this should scare you off.

I am hooked. Perennials are a vital part of my garden these days. And if plants have personalities, I consider my perennials the most sociable, outgoing and interesting of my botanical buddies.

English style gardens rely heavily on the use of perennials for a prolonged season-long show of colour.

CARE AND MAINTAINANCE OF PERENNIALS

Characteristics of perennials

Perennials differ from annuals in several respects. They live year round and tend to be quite hardy, even where winters are severe. Many can tolerate climate conditions in Zone 3 or colder. They do not mature in a single season. Nor do they bloom for prolonged periods of time. They usually require a year to reach maturity when begun from seed and they tend to bloom for short, specific periods of time, once a year. Some will bloom a second time, e.g. Delphinium and Lupin.

There are very few perennials that cannot be propagated by division of established clumps. Since they also live more than one season, they are therefore one of the most economical forms of gardening. Once borders are established, costs are minimal.

Soil and site

Proper cultivation of the soil bed is an absolute prerequisite for perennial gardening. You achieve a thriving, mature border much more quickly if soil is well cultivated from the beginning.

Think of the soil as a home in which your plants will live the rest of their lives. It should have the tilth and friability to support large plants, yet be light enough that deep-rooting plants can extend downward with ease. It needs to retain moisture, but not too much. It also needs to be rich in elements. As I have previously discussed, the best way to achieve this apparently contradictory mixture of qualities is with organic amendments, preferably manufactured in your own compost pile. An application of ground limestone at 5 lb./100 sq. ft. (2.3 kg/9 m^2) at soil preparation time will help loosen the soil and raise the pH.

Choose a site free of tree roots, grass or weeds. All of these compete aggressively with your plants for space, moisture and nutrients. The site should also have adequate drainage. Perennial roots need moisture in summer, but any tendency for water to collect during winter months is lethal. Your site should also be able to accommodate any future expansion you may desire.

Border design

Since perennial borders tend to evolve over a number of years, they require careful attention to design. See Chapter 1 for more on this topic. Borders devoted entirely to perennials are traditionally large. This is primarily in order to accommodate the great number of permanent plantings required to produce variety in colour and successive blooms over an entire season.

A border should be wide enough to provide a rich, full effect and long enough to suggest a harmonious panorama. To accomplish this, they need to be at least three plant rows deep and about four times longer than wide. A background fence or hedge will cut the winds and help to show off your perennials and their ever-changing patterns.

Novices are advised to plant a perennial garden in stages. Build up your garden gradually, in keeping with your experience, budget, and plant stock.

Avoid overcrowding. Crowding results in leggy, unsatisfactory growth and creates extra thinning work in future. Plants need space to breathe and grow. Note the mature size of the plants and leave appropriate space in your design. Add a little extra to recommended spacing requirements both within and among plant groups. If your border abuts a wall or fence allow plants at the back of the border at least 6 in. (15 cm) for breathing space and air circulation.

Bare patches as a result of slow growth or generous spacing can be disguised with a little imagination. Mulches of organic material or decorative stone can be used to help separate or distinguish one group of plants from another. Annuals are also useful as a quick cover for any blank spaces in a youthful perennial bed.

Planting in groups

Perennial borders consist of patterned *groups* of plants rather than assortments of individual specimens. Each group should include at least three plants of the same variety and colour to create greater visual impact and avoid a scraggly or motley appearance.

Organize plant groups so that bloom schedule, colour and plant size effectively co-ordinate. This is certainly easier said than done – but if it was easy, perennial gardening wouldn't be recognized for the fine art that it is.

Select plants to ensure continuity of bloom throughout the growing season. Each row of your border could include plants that bloom in the early, middle and end of the summer. Plants should also vary in their colour and height to avoid the curse of uniformity. A border that features all June-flowering plants is tedious in August, and a border that features solid and unrelieved pink bloom becomes wearisome before summer's end. Borders of one colour *can* work, but they depend heavily on foliage, contrast and texture for their success.

Planting perennials

Prepare your perennial bed a season in advance if possible. The majority of perennials achieve their best growth if they are set out as nursery seedlings in late summer or early fall. Autumn weather conditions are less likely to induce dehydration or the other symptoms associated with root trauma. And perennials seek to maximize root growth even in cold weather. By the time spring arrives fall-planted seedlings have a considerable advantage over those placed in the spring.

All perennials benefit from a protective mulch during winter months. Plants that stay in the ground year round are particularly susceptible to heaving as the ground undergoes successive freezing and thawing.

Early autumn planting also makes sense if you opt to grow perennials from seed. Very few germinate and blossom in a single season. Some deep-rooted plants, like Peony, require several growing seasons to mature sufficiently from seed to produce flowers. Luckily, most will germinate one summer and flower

Perennial plants can often grow from seed, but if you want an early show of colour, box nursery plants are easier to use.

1. Dig hole larger than the rootball and sprinkle in a handful of 6-12-12 fertilizer.

2. Carefully place the rootball in the hole. Make sure not to let the rootball dry out before you plant.

3. Fill in with soil and gently tamp down.

4. Water frequently and generously until plant is established.

RULE OF THUMB

As a rule, plant the largest groups you can afford in order to obtain a lush, mature look earlier than you might otherwise. But numbers should also relate to habits of growth. Plants that proliferate slowly, like Balloonflower, can be planted in groups of eight with little likelihood of overcrowding, whereas fast multipliers, like Purple Coneflowers, would soon form a hedge if planted in those numbers.

the next.

For best results, plant perennial or biennial seeds in midsummer in a nursery bed, where seedlings can receive the coddling they require. Keep them well watered and mulched. They should be ready to be transferred to their permanent site in early September.

Staking

Perennials sometimes need help to maintain an orderly appearance. Heavy rains or winds can crush Peonies in full bloom, or make short work of low, densely grown perennials like Dianthus.

Bamboo or other long staking material should be used with tall-growing perennials like Peony or Delphinium. Insert stakes when plants are first set in the ground. As tall plants grow, they can be secured to the stake. Smaller species can be propped up with Tomato cages or short stakes, sometimes combined with string. Cages are ideal for Baby's Breath, but species like Flax, which seldom grow higher than 2 ft., can be prevented from flopping to the ground if staked corral-fashion with short sticks and twine.

General care

Every couple of days walk around your garden with a basket and knife in hand to collect faded blooms or discoloured foliage. This will encourage further blossoming. Pick up any debris that could camouflage or attract chewing insects.

Weeds should be mercifully rare if you maintain a good, thick mulch of ground-up pine bark or cocoa bean shells. Attack and remove weeds or grass on sight. Think of them as marauding thieves that will rob your cherished plants of nutrients.

Loosen the soil around perennials periodically to prevent soil compaction, using a cultivator or garden fork. Prod the earth gently to let in air and moisture, but not so vigorously that roots are damaged.

Perennials are happily healthy. If you practise good grooming, watering and mulching there is little chance of illness. Remove any diseased part immediately and put it in a plastic garbage bag – not your compost. Spores can survive for several seasons and infect otherwise healthy plants if they are disposed of carelessly.

Tackle persistent mildew problems by altering pH, adjusting watering procedures, or increasing plant spacing to improve air circulation. Garden sulphur applied to diseased plants should retard if not cure the problem. Contact a reliable nursery or government agriculture office for advice on any mildew problem specific to your area.

In the fall, cut dead or woody stalks and trim or shear back foliage. Dispose of healthy debris on the compost pile. Do a general clean-up before applying a winter mulch. Rake, and pull weeds and annuals. Otherwise, you'll encourage whole colonies of pests.

Thinning and dividing

Once perennials are established, periodically thin those which grow most rampantly. Keep aggressive growers in check or they soon overcrowd and kill their neighbours or themselves. Perennials die from their centre out when they become grossly overcrowded. If foliage clumps are wide and healthy in appearance, but blooms fail to appear, overcrowding may be the cause. Assume that most perennials need to be dug and divided every three or four years on average. Some require dividing more often, others less often. It will become obvious within a year or so which perennials in your border need more frequent reining-in.

Spring and summer flowering perennials are best divided in the late summer or fall. Autumn-flowering perennials should be divided in very early spring, as soon as the ground is easily worked. Follow these rules:

- Trim plants to 6 in. (15 cm) above ground and water them well the day before you intend to separate them.
- Use a garden fork to avoid unnecessary damage to roots.
- Dig out an entire clump, shake off excessive earth and place on a work table or plastic sheet.
- Trim and remove any unhealthy or dead portions. Cut the remaining healthy root portion into smaller clumps. If roots are very tangled they are best separated or cut by using two garden forks back to back.
- Add soil supplement in the form of mature compost or a low-nitrogen fertilizer to the site from which your plant was dug before replacing any portion of your trimmed root. Add coarse sand to help drainage and peat moss to suspend moisture.
- Replant the other clumps in new locations or distribute them to friends. Perennials make great gifts.

PERENNIALS

Descriptions and requirements

At the bottom of each description symbols have been used to indicate sun and shade tolerance, the minimum hardiness zone, moisture requirements, and soil pH requirements.

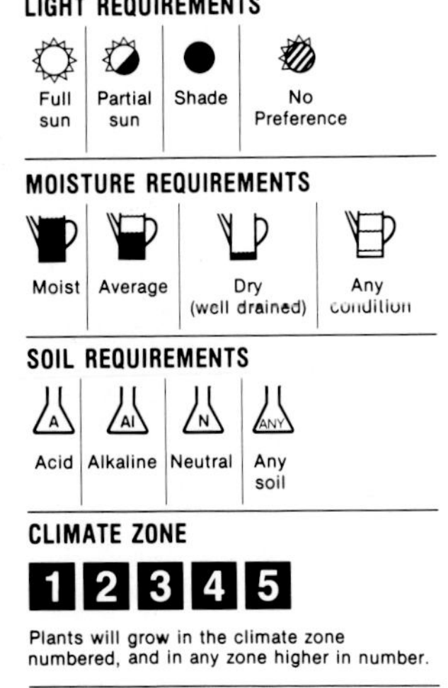

(Previous page) *Vibrant red Lupin, with its distinctive spikes.*

Achillea

(Achillea)

Achillea, also known as Yarrow or Milfoil, is a field flower deservedly promoted to the flower garden. Its grey-green, ferny foliage is topped by blossoming umbels of white, yellow or shades of pink, including carmine. Foliage usually has a rather pungent odour.

Achillea is extremely useful in the perennial border for filling in large gaps, forming a background and providing long-lasting displays of colour. Some varieties grow as high as 4 ft. (1.2 m) and blossom from summer through to fall. Dwarf varieties are also available. Choose and place carefully to avoid a weed-like effect. This plant needs frequent thinning to prevent overcrowding.

Achillea prefers sun, and soil that is well drained but not excessively rich. Cultivate by dividing clumps or sowing seeds directly. Achillea is an extremely hardy plant which easily withstands droughts and has few enemies. In windy locations, stake.

Arabis

(Arabis)

The ground-hugging succulent leaves of Arabis are smothered in clouds of pink or white blossoms for much of the spring. Flower clusters are produced atop stems ranging from 5 to 10 in. (12.5 to 25 cm) high. Plants can spread over wide areas, hence their common name Wall Cress.

Arabis prefers a sunny location and neutral soil. It is easily propagated by root division or started from seed. Space about 10 in. (25 cm) apart, or closer for a massed effect. Arabis becomes straggly and unkempt if it is not sheared back annually. Popular species are *A. albida* and *A. alpina*

Aubrieta

(A. deltoidei)

Sometimes called Purple Rock Cress, Aubrieta is ideal in rock gardens or at the front of a border. It produces profuse cascades of flowers with dark purple and rose tones over several weeks in the spring. Its slender trailing leaves become completely covered in blooms. Aubrieta can be invasive once it is established and may require periodic thinning.

Aubrieta prefers a sunny site, with soil that is slightly alkaline (high pH) and well drained. Aubrieta prefers dry rather than overly wet conditions. Where summer heat is severe it may prefer a partially shaded location. Divide established clumps or grow from seed.

Baby's Breath

(Gypsophila)

The perennial variety of Baby's Breath, also known as Gypsophila, is an airy, white spray popular in bridal bouquets and other arrangements. In borders it softens the shapes of other plants and adds interest. *G. paniculata* is the most popular species. Long stems branch out at the top carrying many small flowers, usually white but sometimes pink.

This plant loves well-drained, alkaline soil. Sow seeds directly in the ground in sun or partial shade or buy nursery plants. Store-bought plants may have been grafted, so plant the bud union just beneath the soil line. Train plants on Tomato cages or other supports.

Gypsophila blooms mainly in July. Shear back for renewed growth in late midsummer, following the first flowering. In fall, cut back. After the ground freezes, mulch with leaves.

Balloonflower

(Platycodon grandiflora)

Balloonflower is named for its buds, which swell and dilate just before opening. Large, star-shaped blossoms emerge on 2- to 3-foot (60- to 90-cm) high stems in midsummer. This plant, which is also known as Chinese Bellflower or Platycodon, is a favourite dried flower with many people. It needs a special spot in the garden where it won't be disturbed, and it requires several years growth before it begins to produce its blue or white blossoms.

It is easily killed by any disturbance of its roots. Balloonflower's habit of delaying new growth until late spring mistakenly leads many gardeners to believe it has died.

Provide with light shade and moist, well-drained soil. Plants are slow to spread so place them 1 ft. (30 cm) apart.

Bellflower

(Campanula)

Campanula is perhaps a perennial gardener's greatest blessing. It is available in a great variety of forms and colours, and it is both prolific and hardy.

Campanula produces tiny bell- or cup-shaped blooms in every conceivable shade of blue. White and pink are also available but less common. It comes in forms ranging from 4-in. (10-cm) ground-huggers to stately 4-ft. (1.2 m) bushes. *C. carpatic*, often called Harebell, is a favourite rock garden perennial.

Campanula generally prefers sun or light shade. It tolerates many soil types so long as drainage is good. Plants spread well. Set them about 1 ft. (30 cm) apart. Campanula can be propagated by root division or grown from seed but, since many varieties are biennial – e.g., the famous Canterbury Bells – the results are not reliable. Plant mature nursery stock in very early spring or grow from seed, starting a year in advance.

Bleeding Heart

(Dicentra)

Bleeding Heart is named for its heart-shaped flowers, usually red and pink, which hang singly from drooping branches. The airy, bush-like foliage remains attractive for many weeks. This plant brings to mind old-fashioned gardens, and lends elegance to awkward shady areas.

The familiar form *D. spectabalis* grows up to 3 ft. (90 cm) and blooms in May and June. *D. formosa*, or Western Bleeding Heart, is low-growing but blooms all summer. *D. culcullaria* is a dwarf novelty that bears white flowers.

Plant in partial to full shade, leaving room to spread. Soil should be rich and moist. Buy nursery plants, and divide grown plants in early spring to replant. Most varieties of Bleeding Heart self-sow as well. New foliage grows at the side of the plant. Be careful not to damage it in fall clean-ups.

Water frequently, but don't drown. Pinch spent blooms and cut plants back when blooms have faded.

Carnation

(Dianthus)

The Carnation variety available from florists, with its long stem and large fragrant flower, is difficult to grow and is best left to professionals. But a similar species, *D. plumarius*, also known as Cottage or Grass Pinks, is more co-operative. Its fringed petals look as if they have been cut with pinking shears.

Cottage Pinks are low-growing spraw-

Dicentra, or Bleeding Heart, likes rich, moist soil and partial to full shade.

RULE OF THUMB

Remove spent flowers of early season perennials to encourage late season flowering.

lers, perfect for use at the front of a border. Foliage grows to 6 in. (15 cm). Colourful, fragrant flowers rise another 6 in. (15 cm), blooming in June and possibly beyond. Single or bicolour combinations of pink, salmon, red, and white are common. Foliage is grey-green and inclined to mound or trail.

Set out nursery plants in well-drained alkaline soil. Plant 1 ft. (30 cm) apart in full sun, watering when dry. Remove spent flowers immediately to encourage progressive bud production. Shear back plants after initial bloom period for renewed flowering. Shear back again to 3 or 4 in. (7.5 to 10 cm) before winter.

These are hardy and long-lived perennials. Divide every 3 or 4 years in the early spring.

Centaurea

(Centaurea)

The lacy, fringed blossoms of this perennial closely resemble annual Cornflowers or Bachelor Button, but the flowers and leaves are larger and the leaves are dark green and somewhat hairy. Given the right conditions, Centaurea, sometimes known as perennial Cornflower, forms wide clumps that usually require annual division. Flowers are blue, pink, white, yellow or bicoloured depending on variety. Blossoms appear in early summer and occasionally continue until fall.

Varieties include *C. montana, C. hypoleuca,* and *C. macrocephala*.

Centaurea requires average to dry soil and full sun. It does best in Zone 4 or warmer. Sow seeds a year in advance or cultivate by dividing established plants. Thin 12 to 16 in. (30 to 40 cm) apart. Plants grow between 1 to 3 ft. (30 to 90 cm) and may require staking.

Chinese Lantern

(Physalis)

Chinese Lantern makes a colourful dried flower for winter arrangements and adds interest to the fall garden. It grows about 2 ft. (60 cm) high on woody stalks, and has a brilliant orange calyx which looks like a traditional Chinese red lantern. It blooms in October.

Chinese Lantern is easy to cultivate. It likes ordinary soil, and sun or light shade.

Sow seeds directly in spring, or plant cuttings from someone else's garden. Chinese Lantern spreads by rhizomes. To divide or control spreading, slide your spade down into the earth and lift out the cut-off part.

Chrysanthemum

(Chrysanthemum)

Chrysanthemum is a reliable staple of the perennial garden. It is also a favourite of the annual flower garden, as this plant looks best when many annual flow-

Chrysanthemum is a favourite in annual and perennial gardens alike.

ers begin to fade. There are about 100 species and thousands of hybrids and varieties to please (and confuse) everyone from the novice gardener to the advanced horticulturist.

Flowers are generally 2 to 4 in. (5 to 10 cm) across and are carried on many-branched stems. They are available in single, double, and semi-double varieties. Chrysanthemum comes in all colours, but is usually identified with sunny and autumnal colours like yellow, deep red, and bronze, or the white of Shasta Daisy (*C. x superbum*). There are also the brilliant pinks and burgundies of Pyrethrum, or Painted Daisy (*C. coccineum*), a popular summer-blooming species. Mums bloom in late summer and autumn.

Start seeds a year in advance for best results, or put out nursery pots in spring or summer in average well-drained soil. Large potted house mums can also be purchased and set out in late summer or early fall, often in full bloom. Plants do well in full sun or partial shade, but they must not be allowed to dry out. Depending on variety, intense prolonged heat can induce wilting.

Feed monthly during the growing season. Water regularly, reducing slightly once blooms appear. Encourage bushiness by pinching back growing tips continually until midsummer. Shear back after initial bloom period to encourage a second flowering.

Since Chrysanthemum roots grow close to the surface, you can dig and move these plants with minimal damage.

Mulch in the summer with ground-up bark mulch to prevent weeds. Cut plants to the ground and mulch heavily before freeze-up.

Columbine

(Aquilegia)

Columbine is a long-time favourite of many Canadian gardeners. Its delicate, long-spurred petals give it a fragile, fairy-like effect. Tubular sepals in white or yellow are embraced by a spur consisting of five outer petals coloured blue, burgundy or yellow, depending on the variety. Single-coloured varieties are also available.

Columbine flowers rise above mounds of lobed, pale green leaves reminiscent of Shamrock. Sizes range from rock garden dwarfs to the standard form, which is 2 to 3 ft. (60 to 90 cm) high and almost as wide. Foliage fades and declines once flowering is completed by early summer.

Columbine does best in moist, well-drained soil and light shade. But if the soil is well supplemented with organic material, the plant can withstand considerable heat. Columbine dislikes being transplanted. Buy or raise your plants in biodegradable pots and leave them in the pots when you plant to avoid transplant shock.

Plants which start from seed in midsummer flower the following spring. Thin 1 to 2 in. (2.5 to 5 cm) apart. Columbine plants tend to die out naturally around three or four years of age. Renew by seeding biennially.

Fertilize Columbine with mature compost, or a half-strength 20-20-20 formula. Keep well watered and mulched. Watch for signs of leaf miners and

Columbine is easily identified by its characteristic spurs, which extend back from five petals.

promptly remove leaves bearing discoloured circular trails. Miners hatch worms that will defoliate an entire patch of Columbine overnight. Columbine also attracts hummingbirds.

Coneflower
(Rudbeckia)

The most famous Coneflower is the Gloriosa Daisy (*R. gloriosa*), with its huge blooms of gold, bronze or mahogany combinations. There are also solid yellow forms. Coneflower is named for its prominent centre discs which are usually coloured dark brown. It ranges in height from 10-in. (25-cm) dwarfs to the standard 3 ft. (90 cm) of *R. gloriosa*, which makes a wonderful background in a bright, sunny perennial border.

Plant Rudbeckia in full sun or very light shade. Space plants about 1 ft. (30 cm) apart. Propagation by division of clumps is easiest. Start seeds a year in advance for best results. Seed-grown Gloriosa will usually bloom the first year.

Coral Bell
(Heuchera sanguinea)

Coral Bell is named for its tiny, bright flowers which come in many shades of pink and red. The flowers are borne on panicles attached to tall single stems towering above rounded clumps of foliage. Blooms are long-lasting. Coral Bell grows as high as 2 ft. (60 cm).

Plant Coral Bell in a sunny site with rich, moist soil. New plants can be started from seed but require a year to reach maturity. Established clumps are often the best source of new plants. A good cut flower.

Coreopsis
(Coreopsis)

The wide daisy-yellow blooms of Coreopsis bring cheer to any garden. Large-flowered forms grow as tall as 3 ft. (90 cm). Dwarf forms are also available. Some types are bicoloured. Most bloom for prolonged periods throughout the summer. Coreopsis is prolific.

Forms include *C. auriculata* and *C. grandiflora*.

Plant in full sun and well-drained soil that is not excessively rich. Plants are easily begun from seed or propagated from established clumps. Space Coreopsis about 1 ft. (30 cm) apart. Thin clumps every 2 years.

RULE OF THUMB

A very special gift idea is a perennial that flowers each year during a special occasion. For my mother, Delphiniums always remind her of her mid-July wedding.

Coreopsis has cheery yellow blooms.

Delphinium
(Delphinium)

Delphinium is not the easiest perennial to grow but its tall spikes of closely packed flowers bloom alluringly in summer. While Delphinium is famous for its beautiful blues, bicolours in purple, pink and white are also available. Plants reach 15 to 60 in. (42.5 cm to 1.5 m) or higher. Medium-sized Delphinium is most useful in flower designing and requires less care.

Delphinium is my mother's favourite flower. Her July wedding flowers featured Delphinium in a wide range of colours, picked that morning from her mother's garden. It's a story about perennials she likes to repeat annually.

Some excellent strains include the Pacific hybrids and the famous Blackmore and Langdon.

Set out nursery plants in well-cultivated alkaline soil. Plant in full sun, or in light shade where summers get very hot. Space about 2 ft. (60 cm) apart to ensure sufficient air circulation and prevent mildew. Staking is advised – Delphinium easily blows over in high winds. Shear back for a second bloom.

Delphinium clumps live about three years. Set out new plants every couple of years for continuous displays.

Top-dress with compost, or feed monthly during the growing season with a dry granular fertilizer like 6-12-12 or 8-10-12. Water from beneath, keeping soil moist but not soggy. Two in. (5 cm) of mulch helps to keep soil moisture constant and prevent black spot. Remove and discard any diseased leaves.

Euphorbia
(E. epithymoides)

There are many different types of Euphorbia but *E. epithymoides*, better known as Cushion Spurge, boasts large, distinctive flower heads atop naturally rounded clumps. Cushion Spurge is ideal for borders.

Spurge grows 1 ft. (30 cm) or more high and equally wide. Plants are easily grown from seed and tend to be long-lived. Plant 18 in. (45 cm) apart in full sun. Soil must be well drained.

False Spirea
(Astilbe)

Astilbe is one of my favourite shade-tolerant perennials. It forms small fern-like shrubs that thrive in moist, shaded conditions. In early summer, it sends forth feathery plumes in delicate shades of white through magenta pink, accompanied by deep red blooms. Given the right conditions Astilbe will bloom over a number of weeks. Varieties range in height from 10 in. to 4 ft. (25 cm to 1.2 m).

Astilbe will grow in full sun but is better off in partial shade. It is a heavy feeder. Amend soil frequently with peat moss, compost or fertilizer like 6-12-12 or 8-10-12. Space plants about 16 in. (40 cm) apart. Thin every couple of years for best results. Astilbe performs best in Zone 5 or warmer.

Perennial Flax
(Linum perenne)

Common Perennial Flax provides linseed, from which oil and Irish linens are made. Its flat brown seeds are also a useful source of fibre for breads and cereal. But flax is beautiful as well as useful. Grown in large clumps, *L. perenne* looks for all the world like a sparkling blue cloud. The perennial Flax family includes purely decorative yellow and white forms. There is also an annual red form.

Flax plants vary from 1 to 2 ft. (30 to 60 cm) high depending on variety. Support may be required. Flax prefers full sun and dry, well-drained soil. Sow seed a year in advance or by dividing established clumps to propagate new plants. Space plants 1 ft. (30 cm) apart. Flax is not likely to behave as a perennial in climates colder than Zone 5. Provide with ample winter protection.

Forget-Me-Not
(Myosotis)

The tiny azure blue blossoms of Forget-Me-Not are prettiest planted for mass effect. This plant makes an ideal ground cover for bulb beds or slopes. Myosotis plants grow thickly together, their long, somewhat furry leaves forming low but dense mounds. Flowers appear on stems 1 ft. (30 cm) or more in height.

RULE OF THUMB

Hummingbirds are frequently attracted to Lupins, Foxglove, Delphinium and Primrose.

Only one species, *M. scorpioides*, grows as a reliable perennial, setting seed that blooms annually. It will also flower periodically in the summer following its peak bloom period of May. Other forms should be treated as biennial. However, any Forget-Me-Not seed planted in midsummer will bloom the following year. Take care that you do not disturb foliage during fall clean-up.

Forget-Me-Not prefers sun or light shade and moist soil.

Considering that most forms are biennial, the only way to ensure bloom from year to year is to plant seed. If you buy nursery seedlings look for *M. scorpioides*. Biennial forms are usually in bloom by May and are unlikely to make any long-term impact on your garden.

Foxglove

(Digitalis purpurea)

According to one fanciful explanation, Foxglove got its name because the little flowers would make nice gloves for little foxes. Foxglove was used in folk medicine to treat heart disease.

The flowers are long spikes covered with small bell-shaped blooms, usually with speckled throats. Common Foxglove (*D. purpurea*) blooms in June to August in many colours, including pink, purple, white and red. It has leafy stems and dense foliage at the bottom. Some varieties grow to 4 ft. (1.2 m).

D. grandiflora is closely related to Common Foxglove but blooms a bit later, in July and August, and has densely packed blooms in a light creamy yellow. It will often bloom a second time if flower heads are removed shortly after the first blooming. But then it will not self-seed.

Choose a moist well-cultivated site that won't dry out in the summer sun. Shade is best. Set out nursery stock about 15 in. (37.5 cm) apart in early spring. Seed needs to be started a year in advance.

Although Foxglove is biennial, it self-seeds, so it tends to stay around longer than two years. Set out new plants regularly to ensure constant growth.

Care is easy. Mulch to keep roots cool and water occasionally. Stake plants. Old blooms left on plants will set out seeds for the following year. I don't recommend that you remove them unless space is a problem.

Foxglove features long spires covered with bell-shaped blooms.

Geranium

(Geranium)

True Geranium, often called Crane's Bill, is among the hardiest perennial plants. Clumps of foliage produce stems bearing solitary, long-lasting blooms in shades of blue through pink. True Geranium is quite unlike the clustered flower balls of the cultivated house Geranium *Pelargonium*. It is mostly winter-hardy to Zone 4 and spreads prolifically if provided with the right conditions and space.

Varieties include *G. dalmaticum, G. sanguineum*, and the cultivar 'Johnson's Blue'.

Many Geraniums grow naturally as wild forest plants. Sites with light shade and rich, moist soil give good results for most members of this genus. Mulches are necessary where summer heat is intense.

Seeds require a year to reach maturity. Potted nursery seedlings are likely to give the best results. Dividing established clumps can injure the plant unless it is very carefully done.

(Opposite) Forget-Me-Not, with its tiny azure-blue blossoms, should be mass planted for best effect.

Popular summer-blooming species of Chrysanthemums such as Pointed Daisy come in brilliant pink colours.

Globeflower
(Trollius)

The bright gold and orange colours of Globeflower are at home in any garden that boasts plentiful moisture. Its globe-shaped flowers will appear for many weeks in early summer if flowers are removed promptly as they fade. Most varieties grow to about 2 ft. (60 cm) or more.

Plant in full sun or partial shade. Wet, marshy ground ispreferred. Sow seeds in autumn or begin new plants by dividing established clumps. Space 1 ft. (30 cm) apart.

Hosta - see Ground Covers

Jacob's Ladder
(Polemonium)

The ferny leaves of Jacob's Ladder grow to 2 ft. (60 cm) or more, and are so prolific they almost obscure the demure, soft blue flowers that emerge in late spring. The leaves of Creeping Jacob's Ladder (*P. reptans*) grow only about 6 in. (15 cm), and the flowers, which appear in early spring, are somewhat more noticeable.

Jacob's Ladder withstands full sun if it receives ample moisture. Start plants by either root division or seed. Clumps often require thinning, or dividing every two years.

Lavender

(Lavandula angustifolia)

The intense fragrance of its sapphire-blue buds makes Lavender one of the most-loved aromatic perennials. It has been used by herbalists and soap-makers for centuries.

Lavender is an evergreen in climates kinder than Canada's. Here, wherever there is significant snow cover or intense cold, it tends to lose some of its silver-grey-green foliage. Most varieties survive with minimal winter protection in Zone 5 or warmer. Stems are wiry.

Lavender ranges in height from 1 to 3 ft. (30 to 90 cm). It prefers sunny locations and must have well-drained soil. It's ideal in rock gardens.

Propagate by stem cuttings or start new plants from seed.

Lavender plants will grow to the size of small shrubs in several years. Nursery seedlings are inexpensive and often have the advantage of several years' growth.

Lupin

(Lupinus)

Lupin flowers are tall spikes covered with pea-like blooms in vibrant colours, including red, purple, and salmon. After they bloom around June, remove stalks. Don't remove their attractive palm-like foliage, which adds interest to borders and strengthens roots.

Lupin dislikes being transplanted. Set out peat pots in groups of 3 to 5 in neutral or slightly acid soil well mixed with damp peat moss. Plant in sun. Russell Hybrid Lupin is most successful. It grows up to 3 ft. (90 cm) tall and should be planted about 18 in. (45 cm) apart. Dwarf varieties, half that height and spread, are also available.

Mulch to keep roots cool and water just enough to keep soil damp but not wet. Feed occasionally with a low nitrogen fertilizer like 6-12-12, or top dress with compost.

Successful Lupins will spread. Divide in the fall of the second season and replant.

Lychnis

(Lychnis)

One of the best-known members of the Lychnis family, Maltese Cross (*L. chalcedonica*), produces balls of multiple scarlet blossoms on stems higher than 2 ft. (60 cm). Another family member, Rose Campion (*L. coronaria*), has been a cottage garden favourite for hundreds of years. Its fluorescent pink single buds are borne on thick, woolly stems covered in fine white hairs.

There are white forms also. German Catchfly (*L. viscaria*) has double-pink flowers.

Lychnis does best in full sun. Soil should be moist but extremely well drained. Excessive winter moisture can inflict significant damage. Lychnis is easily grown from seed or propagated from mature clumps. Plants require a year or more to reach maturity and may need to be renewed by dividing roots after about four years. Space Lychnis plants at least 1 ft. (30 cm) apart.

Lythrum

(Lythrum salicaria)

Lythrum, or Purple Loosestrife, is a native wildflower which blazes to life in low-lying fields and marshes in early summer. Its colourful flower spires average about 3 ft. (90 cm) in height. This is a great perennial for naturalizing in wide open spaces. 'Morden Pink', from Morden, Manitoba, is a hardy deep-pink cultivar.

Plant in full sun and very moist soil. Otherwise you must be prepared to water frequently throughout the summer. Lythrum grows best by root division. Plants should be spaced 1 ft. (30 cm) or more apart. They naturalize along streams and ditches to provide a great midsummer show of colour.

Monarda

(M. didyma)

Sweet Monarda goes by many names, including Bee Balm, Bergamot, and Oswego Tea. It is a typical member of the Mint family – aromatic and shrubby in appearance. Bright-coloured flower bracts appear on stems ranging from 2 to 4 ft. (60 cm to 1.2 m). Flowers range in colour from pink to purple or red and attract butterflies, hummingbirds, and bees.

Monarda is often described as drought-resistant but it really appreciates full sun only if soil is moist. Otherwise growth is stunted and flowers are sparse. Under good conditions, it spreads rapidly and requires annual spring thinning or dividing.

Monkshood

(Aconitum)

The deep, sapphire blue of Monkshood has tempted many gardeners to overlook its extreme toxicity. Towering spikes grow as high as 8 ft. (2.4 m) and bear clusters of dark lapis and purple blossoms in late summer.

Never eat Monkshood, especially the roots. It contains dangerous alkaloids, including the cardiac and respiratory sedative aconite. One tbsp (15 mL) is a lethal dose. The yellow Wolfsbane type and bicoloured forms are equally dangerous.

Monkshood forms large, rambling clumps. Provide plants with ample room to spread and space at least 1 ft. (30 cm) apart. It can take several years to bear flowers. Avoid disturbing anestablished clump. Begin plants from seed or buy them from a nursery. Monkshood prefers partial shade and rich, moist soil. Although it is hardy to Zone 3, it benefits from winter protection.

Peony

(Paeonia)

Peony demands space, but it is worth it. In early summer, large, fragrant flowers rise out of thick stands of lush leaves. Double blooms with their frilly edges are especially beautiful. White, pink and red are the standard colours, but unusual cultivars in yellow and dark mauves are also available. This is a long-lived per-

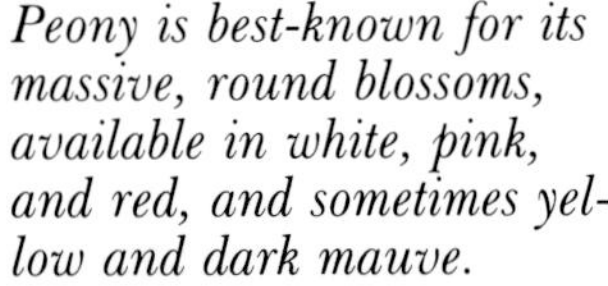

Peony is best-known for its massive, round blossoms, available in white, pink, and red, and sometimes yellow and dark mauve.

ennial, available with single and semi-double blooms. Stake the double-flowering types.

The most popular and easily grown variety is the herbaceous Peony *P. lactiflora*. Its flowers are wonderful and long-lasting for cutting, but remember to shake off any ants and earwigs before you bring them indoors. Ants are useful in the garden – they remove the protective honeydew from the blossom bud in order for it to open – but they are unpleasant in your house.

Peony lives 20 years or more and can easily take over a border. Restrain by dividing clumps for replanting.

Root cuttings with 5 eyes or stem buds are your best bet for propagating new plants. Get them from nurseries or established clumps. Set roots in deep holes in groups of 3 to 5, planting eyes about 1 in. (2.5 cm) below ground. I have found the greatest number of failures with Peonies are caused by planting the eyes too deep.

Peony stands grow 4 ft. (1.2 m) high and 4 ft. (1.2 m) wide, so choose a sunny spot with ample space. Cultivate with plenty of damp peat moss, and water occasionally with diluted apple cider vinegar to ensure acidity. Fertilize in May and June with 6-12-12 .

Phlox
(Phlox)

There is an incredible range of form among the brightly coloured members of the popular Phlox family. They include dwarf rock garden or ground-cover form (*P. subulata*), a creeping, woodland type (*P. stolonifera*), and a tall, garden variety (*P. paniculata*) which is excellent for cut arrangements.

All Phlox produce 5-petalled blossoms, commonly in shades of white, pink or blue. Bicoloured forms with contrasting eyes are also available. Many are sweet scented. Tall-growing types produce blossoms in umbels.

Most Phlox are spring-flowering, but Garden Phlox (*P. paniculata*) produces its peak flowers in late summer and then blossoms intermittently until fall. This species of Phlox puts on an excellent show when naturalized in low-lying, damp land near a pond or stream. Remove spent flowers to encourage new blossoms.

Perennial Phlox are most easily cultivated by dividing the roots of established clumps in very early spring or late fall. Seeds planted in late summer will flower in the next season. All forms will grow in partial shade. Garden and Moss Phlox (*P. paniculata* and *P. subulata*) tolerate full sun and drier soil. Other forms prefer moist but well-drained soils.

Oriental Poppy
(Papaver orientale)

Perennial Poppies produce single or double blooms above long, graceful stems. The flowers, which appear in early summer, are quite large – from 4 to 10 in. (10 to 25 cm) across – and they are dramatic and showy. Red, a popular colour, is usually set off with a black centre. There are also bicoloured varieties in white and purple, pink and red, and white and pink.

According to superstition, Poppies induce sleep. Some varieties provide opium, and Dorothy and her friends fall asleep running through a field of Poppies on their way to Oz. However, the vibrant colours of this plant are more likely to wake people up than put them to sleep.

Poppies need full sun. They like average, well-drained soil.

Set out nursery plants in early spring about 15 in. (37.5 cm) apart. Flowers grow up to 3 ft. (90 cm) high and may need support. Long tap roots are extremely sensitive and prone to transplant shock. If possible, purchase only stock growing in peat pots and plant well before or well after the peak bloom period or early to midsummer. Divide every five years, in late summer, exercising great care. Allow some spent flowers to mature and self-sow each season.

Potentilla
(Potentilla)

Potentilla, sometimes called Cinquefoil, is a relative of the Rose which includes many bright-flowering herbs and shrubs among its members. One of the best Potentillas for the flower border is *P. nepalensis*. Its large strawberry-like foliage sends forth 2-ft. (60-cm) high stalks bearing sprays of bicoloured peach and scarlet blossoms. Shrub varieties of Potentilla are described in the Shrubs and Vines

*Polyanthus Primrose (*Primula x polyantha*) is an alpine plant that blooms in early spring. But in most regions of Canada it survives only as a hardy annual grown in a cold frame.*

chapter.

Potentilla is an alpine which prefers sun and dry, well-drained soil. Soil should also be neutral or slightly acid. This plant does best in Zone 5 or warmer. Start new plants from seed, or divide established clumps. Take care in dividing roots – Potentilla dislikes being transplanted.

Primrose

(Primula)

English Primrose (*P. vulgaris*), sometimes called Polyanthus, is one of the most colourful harbingers of spring. Lovely clusters of flowers can grow up to 2 ft. (60 cm) high. Although Primrose is available in a wide assortment of colours, yellow is still the favourite.

Polyanthus (*P. polyantha*), the best-known variety, is available in all colours. Primrose likes cool, moist, acid soil. Plant in morning sun or shade. Set out bedding plants about 1 ft. (30 cm) apart and plant along with other spring-blooming perennials like Violet. Primrose usually blooms for several weeks.

Primrose blooms are good for cutting. Cutting also encourages new growth. Every couple of years, dig up plants and divide roots for replanting.

Pulmonaria

(Pulmonaria)

Bethlehem Sage (*P. saccharata*) is one of the prettiest forms of Pulmonaria. Bright rose and lavender blossoms emerge in spring above mounded clumps of white spotted foliage. Plants grow to about 1 ft. (30 cm) high and tend to spread or trail. This is an excellent ground cover, especially for use under mature trees.

Pulmonaria is a forest plant that requires shade and rich, moist soil. Plants sprawl limply and become dehydrated with the first blast of summer sun if given an unsatisfactory site. They also dislike being transplanted so it is wise to consider their placement carefully. They are well worth the extra effort they require. Sow seed or propagate by root division.

Purple Coneflower

(Echinacea purpurea)

Purple Coneflower, a member of the Daisy family, forms wide, tall clumps that begin to produce large flowers with a prominent centre disc in midsummer. The flowers are usually pink shaded and quite small to begin with. As they age, the ray petals enlarge and gradually extend downward, causing the centre cone bearing seeds to become distinct. Stands grow to 3 ft. (90 cm) or more in height, which makes this an excellent background plant in a perennial border.

Purple Coneflower prefers sun and likes most soils, with the exception of soggy, cold soil. It grows easily from seed but can also be propagated by root division. Thin clumps periodically to prevent overcrowding and to ensure vitality. Flowers can be dried for use in arrangements.

Ranunculus

(R. aconitifolius)

Some varieties of Ranunculus have butter-yellow flowers, as befits a relative of the Buttercup. Florepleno (*R. aconitifolius florepleno*) has double-flowered white flowers like pincushions. Both colours seem to catch the sun and shine, adding glisten to an early spring garden.

Ranunculus grows in clumps on arching slender stems and blooms in April. Florepleno blooms in May and June. The clumps grow 1 to 2 ft. (30 to 60 cm) in height and spread.

Ranunculus loves moist rich earth. It looks especially fine in the sun, but also grows in light shade. Set out nursery plants about 18 in. (45 cm) apart. Keep soil moist but never soggy. Propagate by division in autumn, every two or three years.

This plant is easily cared for. Pinch off dead flowers immediately to encourage new growth.

Red-Hot Poker

(Kniphofia uvaria)

Red Hot Poker, or Torch Lily, is aptly named for its brilliant velvety spikes of flowers. These are usually flaming red-orange, but they are also available in other colours, including white or yellow. These spikes or "pokers" grow 2 to 4 ft. (60 cm to 1.2 m) amid mounding grassy foliage.

Set out nursery plants in well-cultivated soil with lots of compost or leaf mould.

Plants are fully grown in four years, but last many years longer. Plant in maximum sunlight, leaving room to spread. Ask for varieties that bloom at both the beginning and the middle of the growing season.

Amend soil with manure every spring and water occasionally in hot spells. In fall, cut plants down. Mulch as soon as the ground freezes to prevent heaving.

Soapwort

(Saponaria)

Saponaria derives its name from the Latin word *sapo*, meaning soap, which can be made from this attractive perennial. The trailing green leaves of Soapwort become transformed by clouds of pink or white blossoms in mid-spring.

Saponaria prefers full sun and somewhat dry, near-neutral soil. Sow seeds or divide established clumps, spacing new plantings 1 ft. (30 cm) apart. Plants retain a neat appearance if they are sheared back yearly.

Veronica

(Veronica)

Veronica, sometimes called Speedwell, is a perennial member of the Snapdragon family which forms large rounded clumps of foliage and produces tall flowering spires. Height ranges from 1 to 6 ft. (30 cm to 1.8 m) depending on the variety, though rarely higher than 3 ft. (90 cm) in Ontario. Blossoms range in colour from bright blue to magenta pink, and last for several weeks.

Veronica appreciates full sun and ordinary, well-drained soil. New plants can be propagated from established clumps when flowering is completed. Dig and divide clumps every few years to ensure vigorous growth. Keep plants spaced at least 1 ft. (30 cm) apart as Veronica tends to fail if overcrowded.

Violet

(Viola)

There are over 300 species of *Viola*, including Sweet Violet (*V. odorata*), the purple Violet which blooms in the spring, smelling sweetly of romance.

V. odorata is a low-growing, spreading plant. It can be planted as a ground cover, in a spring garden, or in awkward spots at the bottom of a yard.

A hardy relative, *V. cornuta*, grows as high as 1 ft. (30 cm), has a good spread, and blooms from May to July.

Violet grows in ordinary soil, but does better if you add wet compost. Set out nursery plants about 1 ft. (30 cm) apart, in sun or partial shade. After plants are established, divide every fall and replant.

To extend bloom period, pick the flowers, or pinch out faded blooms.

Garden Pansy (*V. x wittrockiana*) is a member of the same genus. Pansy is a perennial, but it is not hardy in most of Canada.

CHAPTER 5

BULBS

Every Canadian gardener should try to visit Holland during the bulb blossom season (mid-April through the first week of May). I have been very fortunate to make the trip on two separate occasions. And in both instances, I was refreshed, inspired and rewarded by what I saw.

Imagine flying into Schiphol Airport on a clear day and taking in a patchwork landscape of solid colours – mostly red, purple, and yellow – from several thousand feet up. The colours cover acres at a time, as far as the eye can see.

If all this sounds a little overwhelming, take the trip anyway. And drive the residential areas of Holland. You'll be amazed how imaginatively and generously the Dutch have used spring-flowering bulbs around their own homes. Window boxes, patio planters, wooden shoes and postage stamp lots – all are packed with colour.

The Dutch purchase and plant over four times as many spring bulbs as Canadians per capita. The Germans and the British plant three times per capita what we do. But most Canadians enjoy a perfect climate for growing spring-flowering bulbs. Our cool autumn (however short in some regions) allows for strong root development. Our long, cold winter gives bulbs a generous rest – a needed time to stratify. And our cold spring encourages an unveiling of rich vibrant colours in succession over a period of weeks, sometimes months, that is akin to watching a great theatrical production taking place, scene-by-scene, in your own garden.

That said, spring-flowering bulbs are near foolproof. Good soil, drainage and fertility are musts, but bulbs are their own food factories. Inside many true bulbs is a miniature version of the mature thing. If you carefully dissect a Hyacinth bulb, you will see exactly what I mean.

Growing spring-flowering bulbs is a great way to get children into the garden. I would suggest you give your kids a patch of well-prepared soil and, with some direction, allow them to create their own splash of

(Opposite) Anemone (front left) are combined with Gladiolus (back left) and Lilium (right).

spring colour.

The fame of growing spring-flowering bulbs may rightfully belong to the Dutch, but there is no reason why the satisfaction of ringing in the new gardening season with a celebration of colour shouldn't also belong to you.

A patch of Anemone blanda *is pictured against a background of Trumpet Daffodils. For best effect, bulbs should be grown in groups rather than mixtures of individual plants.*

CARE AND MAINTENANCE OF BULBS

The miracle of bulbs

Bulbs are a unique life form. They are specially adapted storage organs, usually composed of stem tissue. In fact, they are modified stems. They function like chemical storehouses, supplying most of the nutritive enzymes required to bring individual plants into blossom. Some, like Crocus, Daffodil and Hyacinth, are so extraordinarily efficient at reserving food that they can be forced into bloom hydroponically using only water as their growing medium.

Complete, embryonic flowers are often enclosed within the fleshy, leaf scales of bulbs. In effect, bulbs are living plants and need to be treated with care. Even those that appear to be unpromising specimens – the pebble-like corms of Anemone, for instance – will deliver spectacular results if their needs are respected.

Bulbs have evolved a life cycle marked by four distinct phases: leaf growth, blossom development, decline and dormancy. Gardeners naturally attach the greatest significance to the flower stage, but the other stages are crucial to the plant's long-term health.

Foliage development is very important to food storage and reproduction. Even

in decline, leaves continue to process food. That is why it is important not to remove or greatly disturb the leaves of bulbs until they've withered naturally and the bulb is dormant.

Dormancy is a period of rest. Bulbs differ in their dormancy habits, apparently as an adaptation to climate. Spring bulbs like Tulip and Oxalis use dormancy to withstand severe cold and to gain advantage of the copious moisture associated with melting snow. Summer- and fall-flowering types like Dahlia and Gladiolus use dormancy to improve their resistance to prolonged heat and drought. Growth is triggered by seasonal rains late in the growing season.

Bulbs and garden design

Successful garden design with bulbs depends on an awareness of three main variables: colour, height and period of bloom.

Colour

Myriad colours are available, especially within the Tulip, Gladiolus, and Iris groups, and hybrid breeding by the bulb industry continues to expand the range. There are also new developments in blossom forms. Daffodils, for instance, are increasingly available in pink, double, cluster and reflexed forms.

Organizing an attractive bulb garden is a bit like dressing well. Contrast is the key. The best colour effects are achieved, not by mixing individual plants, but by planting a uniform group of bulbs next to another uniform group of bulbs in a complementary colour. Rather than mixing purple Parrots with double late white Tulips, you should plant stands of each side by side. There is an aesthetic as well as a practical consideration here. If you mix together individual bulbs of different varieties, it will be very difficult to sort them if you dig them up to redesign your garden.

If you decide you want to mix bulbs in rainbow combinations, soften the potentially chaotic effect by bordering with plants of solid colour.

Height

The original or species forms of most bulbs tend to be smaller than the hybrid forms. Among Tulips, wild species – e.g., *T. kaufmanniana*, *T. fosteriana*, and *T. greigii* – rarely grow above 1 ft. (30 cm) and are widely propagated for use in rock gardens, or as low-border plants. Hybridization, especially during the nineteenth century, created most of the cherished, long-stemmed Darwin and Cottage Tulips. Under optimal conditions, these varieties approach 3 ft. (90 cm), in contrast to many species types that measure under 6 in. (15 cm). Position bulbs according to their height, planting low-growing forms at the front of borders, and tall at the rear. Arranging darker colours in the background and lighter in the front gives the impression of greater depth.

Bloom schedule

Bulbs are usually separated into two broad categories, spring and summer, which in turn are separated into early, middle and late divisions. Galanthus blooms in Ontario before any other bulb and is classified as an early spring plant. Dahlia, which blooms in August, is a late summer plant.

Bloom schedule is affected by local weather conditions and varies tremendously across the country. In the mildest parts of British Columbia, spring can arrive as early as February, heralded by scads of Crocus. Most other provinces won't begin to enjoy the same display until April is well underway.

Local weather conditions also affect the progress of tender summer-flowering bulbs, many of which evolved in tropical climates. Acidanthera and *Anemone coronaria* progress so slowly from a spring planting that they don't come into bloom until fall in many temperate Canadian gardens.

Other design elements

Bulbs can be planted in formal beds dedicated solely to bulbs, or in groupings in a mixed border. They can also be naturalized in random clumps in a garden or lawn. Use them according to your design preferences. Planting techniques appropriate to each use are described below.

Combining bulbs with other plants, or overplanting, is an ideal way to obscure foliage as it begins to die back. Plant Tulip with complementary ground covers like Lamiastrum, Ferns, or Forget-Me-Not. In a combined bulb bed, Daylily interspersed with Tulip or Daffodil will begin to grow enthusiastically just as early-blooming spring bulbs start to decline. Many different combinations are possible. Experiment.

TYPES OF BULBS

Gladiolus: a corm. With the exception of Crocus and Dog-Tooth Violet, most corms need to be brought indoors over the winter. Each corm lasts just one season, and reproduces itself by growing a new corm on top of the old.

Daffodil (above) and **Tulip** (below): major or true bulbs. Note the onion-like appearance. True bulbs usually reproduce by growing juvenile bulbs clustered around a central parent.

Dahlia: a tuberous root.

Bearded Iris: a rhizome. Rhizomes send up new plants from root-like bud nodes which grow parallel to ground level.

Begonia: a tuber. Take care to plant tubers face up (concave side).

Grape Hyacynth: a minor true bulb, smaller but otherwise similar to major true bulbs like the Tulip and Daffodil.

Crocus: a winter-hardy corm.

Lilium: a true bulb, which can reproduce by seed, bulb division, and scale division, and from the miniature bulbs which form on its leaves and stems.

Anemone: a tuber. Anemone can be soaked overnight before planting to accentuate the leaf scars that distinguish top from bottom.

Hemerocallis (Daylily) root: a tuberous root.

RULE OF THUMB

The bigger the bulb the better the bloom.

Buying bulbs

Purchase the healthiest, best bulbs you can afford. Larger bulbs tend to produce bigger flowers. Avoid any that are desiccated and withered, or display symptoms of mould or rot. These are all signs of damage caused by improper storage. Discard any that have begun to sprout premature shoots. Bulbs overexposed to light or warmth in storage can begin leaf growth. Their immature root systems may ultimately result in weak, floppy stems.

Reputable nurseries and mail-order catalogues are the most reliable sources of bulbs that grow true to name. This is important if you're worried about colour co-ordination. It's frustrating when the statuesque white Darwin Tulips you planted emerge as orange Parrots, right beside your pink Darwins.

The Holland bulb trade is enormous and sometimes mix-ups in labelling occur during shipping and transportation. However, sources specializing in plants sell only premium bulbs and handle them carefully. Mislabelling occurs less often and, when it does, orders are normally guaranteed.

True bulbs

Hyacinth, Tulip and Daffodil are often classified as major or true bulbs. There are in fact many smaller, or minor, true bulbs as well. Scilla (Bluebells), Muscari (Grape Hyacinth), Allium, Chionadoxa and Snowdrop are some.

True bulbs are often described as a thick underground stem with a bud in which the embryo of the next year's plant is surrounded with plant tissue. Most true bulbs have the superficial appearance of onions – an oval or elliptical shape, a basal root plate, and an outer, papery sheath or tunic coat which protects their rigidly-compressed leaf scales from moisture loss.

The chief exception is Lilium, or Bulb Lily, which is easily recognized by loose, overlapping scales lacking a protective fibrous coat. An enlarged basal root system partially compensates Lily for its lack of protection, but it requires a continually moistened medium as it is never completely dormant.

Bulbs can reproduce by seeds, but they reproduce more efficiently by producing juvenile bulbs, sometimes called bulblets, usually clustered around a central parent. Some species will also produce tiny, miniature bulbs attached to the base of stems or leaves. Lilium is the most prolific in this regard. It can reproduce by seed, bulb division, and the miniature bulbs that form on its leaves and stems. It can also reproduce by scale division.

Every other season gardeners should dig and divide Tulip and Crocus to prevent overcrowding. Every three to four years they should dig up their Hyacinth and most other bulbs. Every seven or eight years they should dig up their Daffodil and Narcissus. Compact quarters result in smaller bulbs and a decline in the quantity and quality of flowers. Propagate by separating bulb offshoots, taking care to retain a portion of the parent basal plate, and plant them in a nursery bed if very small. Many offshoots will be large enough to plant directly in the garden.

Corms

The best-known garden corms are Crocus, Dog-Tooth Violet, Gladiolus, and Acidanthera. Only the first two are reliably hardy. The others are classified as tender and must be lifted, stored indoors over winter, and replanted in spring. Most corms originated in equatorial regions and continue to favour warm, tropical habitats. Delicate species like Freesia or Babiana may perform adequately when spring-planted in the warmest regions of British Columbia and southern Ontario, but most Canadian gardeners should be content to enjoy them as pot plants.

Flattened and laterally compressed, corms are composed entirely of stem tissue and do not contain dormant flowers. A central leaf bud or dried leaf base forms a tip at the corm's centre. Blossoms eventually grow from racemes or offshoots of the prominent sheathing leaves that emerge first.

Each mature corm lasts just one season. It expends all of its energy in producing a flower stalk and reproducing itself. Corms multiply by upward rejuvenation: a new corm grows on top of the old. Several juvenile cormlets may also be attached. They normally reach maturity and flower within two years given appropriate care and adequate space. Non-hardy species also require winter storage. Propagate by breaking off cormlets. Clean, dust with garden sulphur, and store in vermiculite in a dark, cool, porous container.

Rhizomes

Plants that spread horizontally by underground root stalks are known as rhizomes. The best-known and hardiest of these are Iris, Canna Lily, and Lily-of-the-Valley. Species appropriate to warmer climates include Brodiaea, a native to western North America, and Achimenes.

Rhizomes grow close to the earth's surface and bear lateral bud nodes that will produce upright leaf stalks and roots on their underside. Rhizomes often erupt from the earth to spread extensively. Hardy species can stand very cold surface temperatures.

Propagate by division. Simply lift and cut rhizomes into sections that bear at least two leaf stalks, trim and replant. Depending on growing conditions and plant vigour, divisions should be made every three to five years.

Tubers

Tubers are not easily recognized as a bulb. Some varieties look more like stones. Tubers lack most of the characteristics that would suggest their flower-producing potential, including basal root plates, exterior tunic cover, and discernible leaf scales. There is very little about the knobby, squat Anemone tuber that suggests it could produce blooms of enormous size and real beauty.

Even experienced gardeners can have difficulty distinguishing top from bottom. Some tubers, like most Begonia and Gloxinia, have visible leaf buds at the top. But in other cases, you have to look closely to discern the leaf scars or indentations from which new foliage will emerge. With very hardened tubers like Anemone, an overnight soak before planting can accentuate those indentations.

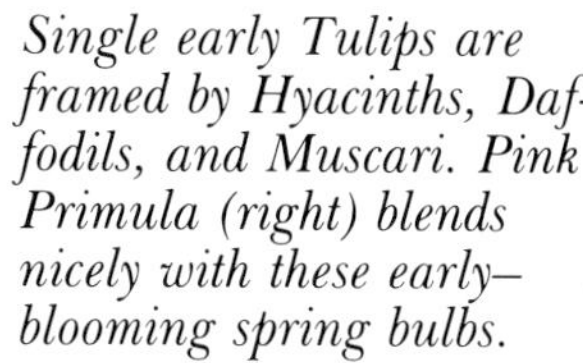

Single early Tulips are framed by Hyacinths, Daffodils, and Muscari. Pink Primula (right) blends nicely with these early–blooming spring bulbs.

RULE OF THUMB

There are many theories about how deeply bulbs should be planted. A standard rule is to plant the basal root plate at a depth 3 times the bulb's height. Thus, standard Daffodil, which is 3 in. (7.5 cm) from root plate to leaf crown, should be planted to a depth of 9 in. (22.5 cm) and covered with 6 in. (15 cm) of soil.

Fortunately, roots from improperly planted tubers will eventually find their way down into the soil. But whenever possible give tubers a head start by planting face up.

Tubers like Gloxinia and Begonia increase in size as they grow, and produce new buds as they process food. They can also be propagated by seed or leaf cuttings. With Caladium and Anemone tubers, propagation by division is most common. Horizontal offshoots produced by parent stock are simply split off. Tubers which retain three or more eyes are most productive. Store as for corms or tender bulbs.

Tuberous root

As the name suggests, tuberous roots are storage organisms composed of root tissue rather than stem tissue. Their ranks include Daylily, Dahlia, Ranunculus, Foxtail Lily and Winter Aconite. Tuberous roots reserve nutrients and moisture for flower production, just as the leaf scales of other bulbs do. However, they are incapable of growth unless their crowns bear stem leaf buds. Propagate by division. Separate roots so that each cutting includes at least one leaf bud. They are normally attached at the junction of existing stems.

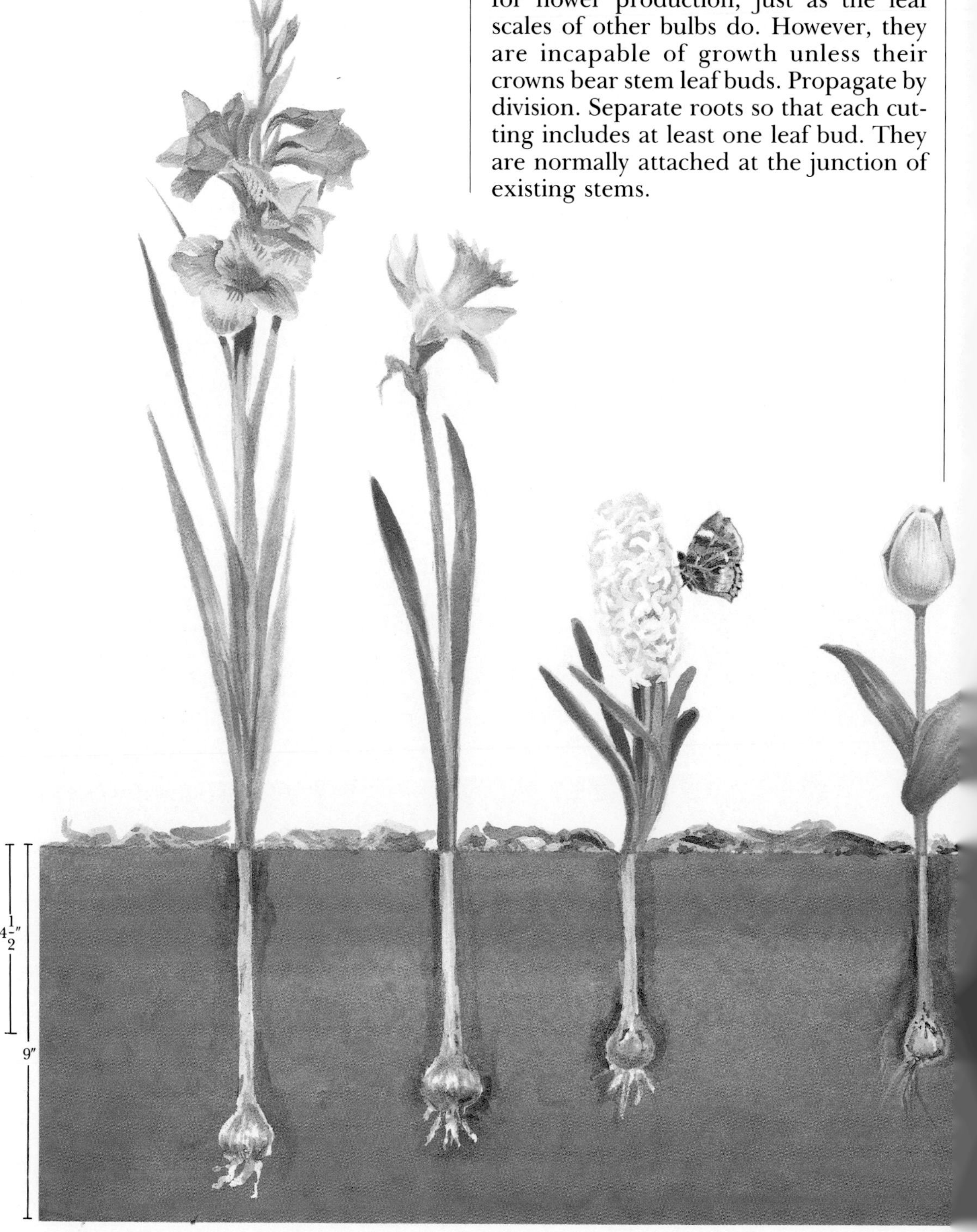

In general, the depth of planted bulbs should be three times the plant height. But, as always in gardening, there are exceptions.

Planting bulbs

Soil and water

Neutral to mildly acid soil (pH 6.5) is preferred by the vast majority of bulbs. The soil should be watered previous to planting, but not over-soaked. Bulbs are quite susceptible to fungus and mildew diseases that will spread in excessively wet conditions.

Planting depth

Of course, to every garden rule of thumb there are many exceptions. Shallow plantings are a must for rhizomes and a squat tuber like Begonia. Both should be placed so that their tops are level with the soil surface. Tuberous roots must be planted at sufficient depth for their fibrous roots but with stem buds near the surface.

Deep planting is recommended for many tall-growing varieties of different species. Daffodil, Tulip, Gladiolus, many Lilies and Hyacinths can all benefit from the additional support that extra-deep planting provides. Deep planting also protects the bulb from predators – squirrels love Tulips – and from moisture loss during intense heat. Soil that contains copious amounts of sand is helpful when planting tall bulbs, I have found. The added drainage helps prevent disease and assists with the "percolation" of oxygen and water down to the rhizome.

Size is another factor affecting planting depth. Small bulbs generally favour shallower planting, otherwise they exhaust their energy on root and foliage growth at the expense of blossoms.

On the other hand, tall varieties of hybrid Tulip and Daffodil may be overstimulated by sunlight and undergo rapid division of leaf scales. Mature bulbs will break up into many smaller ones, producing smaller and fewer flowers. Tall-growing Tulip and Daffodil varieties can withstand planting depths of 1 ft. (30 cm) in beds that have been well prepared and adequately dug.

Gardeners who take the extra time to carefully deep-plant will be amazed at their results. Deeply dug bulbs divide more slowly and have to be retrieved for division less frequently. Good drainage is vital for deep-planted bulbs. Make allowance for it when preparing the soil by adding sharp sand.

Soil and climate conditions should also determine bulb depth. Plant more shallowly in clay soils and increase your use of organic material. Plant more deeply in sandy soil or in windy locations. Plant more deeply in cold climate areas where intense freezing or repeated cold snaps could injure bulbs. To protect against cold, mulch with bark chips or fallen leaves.

Planting techniques

Planting techniques for bulbs differ depending on how you are using them, in formal bulb beds, in groupings in a mixed border, or naturalized in random clumps.

Bulbs in beds

A formal bed is usually grown intensively and should be well supplemented with organic matter deposited at root level. Using your garden plan, stake out and dig the area to the depth required. Work

Planting Bulbs

Bulbs can either be planted as single plants, or for a more intense display, in clusters as shown below.

2. Cover carefully with soil so as not to disturb the arrangement of the bulbs.

1. Arrange bulbs pointed tip upward on a layer of amended soil that allows for good drainage. Depth should be about three times the bulb's height.

3. Water thoroughly and deeply to settle the soil. Then water according to the particular requirements of the bulb type.

in a mixture of mature compost or composted manure with superphosphate and bone meal for best results. Other amendments like vermiculite and peat moss are also appropriate. Place the bulbs as recommended in the prepared bed and back-fill carefully. Protect your new bed with a covering of mulch. If you choose to fertilize the surface area, select a balanced mixture, or one that is low in nitrogen and recommended for bulb planting. I have had good luck with 6-12-12.

Bulbs in isolated groups

When planting in isolated groups it is usually not feasible to cultivate the entire bed. A good compromise is to dig a little deeper than necessary and insert a bit of prepared compost below root level before you place your bulbs. The extracted soil could also be combined with compost or other suitable amendments before being replaced. Fertilize as recommended for bulb beds.

A bulb-digger is more useful than a spade. A bulb-digger is a cone-shaped implement which narrows at the bottom, extracting a cylinder of soil where it is inserted. Properly used, it provides perfect bulb holes at the right depth.

Naturalizing bulbs

To achieve a casual, natural effect on a grassy area or beneath trees, take a handful of bulbs and scatter them. Plant them where they fall, using a bulb-digger. Choose hardy varieties that multiply vigorously for naturalizing. Otherwise, your plant is likely to be squeezed out by competition from existing vegetation. Minor bulbs like Crocus, Muscari, and Scilla are dependable spreaders. I like to drop them in holes punched in the lawn using a long metal crow bar. Hyacinth, Iris and Daffodil are also good naturalizers, but they're slower to spread, especially in dry or cold climates.

To achieve reliable results, you must resist the temptation to tidy declining foliage of bulbs, particularly bulbs planted in a lawn. Let bulb leaves mature over several weeks before mowing. If you remove foliage too early, next year's blooms will be reduced. If you disturb the foliage of true bulbs, you will affect not only reproduction, but also the development of latent flower embryos. Corm foliage can usually be safely cut or disturbed at an earlier date. For this reason, Crocus and Scilla are favoured surefire naturalizers.

BULBS

Descriptions and requirements

Symbols have been included at the end of each description to provide a quick reference regarding sun and shade tolerance, flowering season, and tenderness. Acidity (pH) has been noted where it differs from normal.

LIGHT REQUIREMENTS

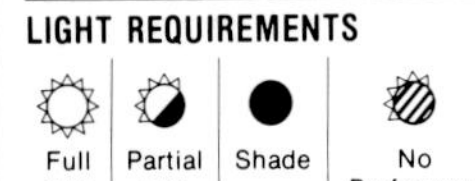

PLANT HARDINESS

Tender | Half hardy | Hardy

Tender: tropical origin killed by first frosts.
Half-Hardy: robust enough to withstand light frosts. Killed by heavy frosts.
Hardy: tolerant of successive frosts; seedlings may even overwinter. Poppies and Dianthus.

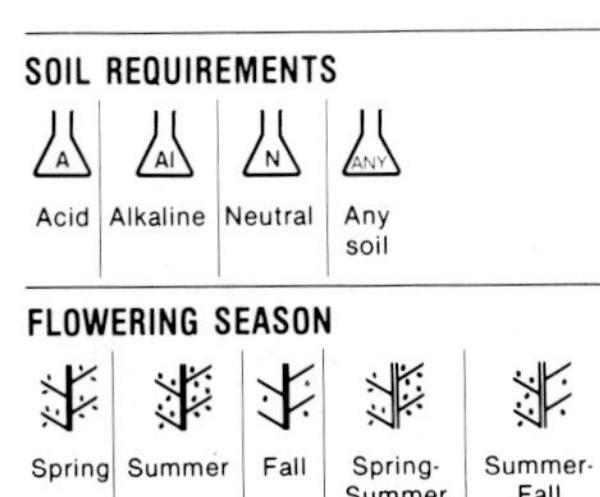

(Previous page) Crocus naturalized in a lawn brightens a spring landscape.

Achimenes

Achimenes is a continuous summer-bloomer. Hybrid varieties of this tender rhizome are available in shades of rose, purple and yellow. Its flowers have flat; outward-facing petals with bi-colour centres, resembling Browallia. Achimenes tends to trail and is ideal for hanging baskets. Culture as for other tropical species: warm temperature, light shade, and humidity.

Space 1 in. (2.5 cm) apart and cover lightly with soil that is rich in compost but also amended with sand to assist drainage. Remember to lift them and re-pot them before the cold weather arrives in autumn.

Acidanthera

A close relation of the Gladiolus, *A. bicolour* is a corm native to Ethiopia. Intensely fragrant, long-lasting, star-shaped flowers are produced on arching stems atop sword-like foliage. Acidanthera's lovely scent and delicate coloration have won it many fans among Canadian gardeners who grow it as a tender bulb in climates harsher than Zone 7.

Plant 4 in. (10 cm) deep and 5 in. (12.5 cm) apart, in full sun or filtered shade.

Agapanthus

(Agapanthus)

Africa Lily is a stately plant from South Africa that produces tall stalks topped by rounded umbels (bud clusters) in shades of white and blue. Many varieties are tall – some as high as 5 ft. (1.5 m). Massed together in a long border they are very striking.

Agapanthus is extremely susceptible to frost, and is grown as a tender plant throughout Canada. It is best suited to west coast gardens. Space 1 ft. (30 cm) apart, covering rhizomes lightly.

Allium

Allium is a large genus which claims several pungent members, including Garlic and Onions. Flowers are produced in bud clusters or umbels atop single stalks. Colours include rose shades, yellow, white and purple. Varieties range from diminutive rock garden plants to 6-foot (1.8 m) specimens. Dried flower heads are a favourite for designing.

Plant to a depth measuring three times the bulb's height in a sunny, well-drained location. Space according to bulb size, between 3 in. to 1 ft. (7.5 to 30 cm).

Anemone

Huge-blossomed varieties have been developed from the Greek wildflower Anemone. The best known of these, *A. coronaria*, is available in dark mauves through to red or white and features prominent stamens ringed by lustrous petals.

The smaller species types,*A. blanda* and *A. nemorosa*, sometimes called Windflowers, are delicate and best suited to rock garden settings or the foreground of perennial shrub borders. They only grow 2 to 6 in. (5 to 15 cm), compared to the larger hybrids which normally grow about 1 ft. (30 cm).

The tuberous rhizomes of Anemone often benefit from a pre-planting soak. Place them in water for several hours before planting.

Plant about 1 in. (2.5 cm) deep and space 5 in. (12.5 cm) apart in sun or light shade. Treat as a tender bulb in climates harsher than Zone 7. It is best to lift and store tubers over winter.

Begonia

Tuberous Begonia is demanding but its large pendulous blossoms give much beauty in return. Begonia colours are primarily pastels: yellow, pink, apricot, and white. Unless pampered, it does not thrive.

Like other tropical tubers it demands filtered light and gentle warmth. It prefers humidity. A tendency to stem rot can be moderated by providing good air circulation and by watering roots, not foliage. Begonia is frost-sensitive and should be spring-planted after the risk of frost has passed.

Plant tubers in a rich, sandy loam, barely covering them.

Remember to plant the hollow side of tubers up and the rounded side down. Space mature tubers 1 ft. (30 cm) apart, or start them in pots indoors in mid-March in a mixture containing at least 1/3 peat moss.

Brodiaea

'Queen Fabiola' is the best known variety of Brodiaea grown in Canada. It bears narrow, grassy foliage and clusters of violet, tubular-shaped flowers held on spreading umbels that grow 1 ft. to 18 in. (30 to 45 cm).

Plant corms 3 in. (7.5 cm) deep and 3 in. (7.5 cm) apart in full sun.

Caladium

(C. x hortanum)

Caladium is grown for the decorative, bi-coloured leaves it sends forth. A tradi-

(Left) Tuberous Begonia needs to be pampered, but this plant is worth the effort.

(Below) Anemone, available in dark mauves through to red or white, is a marvellous cut flower.

tional jungle species, Caladium requires warmth and can be grown only as a tender bulb. Its tubers require bright but indirect light for maximum growth. Caladium is frost-sensitive and is best suited to pot culture in climates harsher than Zone 8.

Spring plant 6 in. to 10 in. (15 to 25 cm) apart in good soil. Cover with 1 in. (2.5 cm) of earth.

Canna Lily

(Canna)

This is a stunning tropical and subtropical plant which adapts well to life in temperate climes, so long as the soil is right. The leaves range in colour from green to bronze, and resemble Banana leaves. The flowers, which resemble Lilies, are held on long stalks and come in a variety of colours, including whites, pinks, oranges and reds.

Canna Lily (*C. generalis*) can grow to a height of 6 ft. (1.8 m). A dwarf variety, Phitzer Dwarf, reaches only 3 ft. (90 cm), and is good for containers.

Soil should be rich and well drained. Amend it with finely composted humus from your own compost bin or a nursery. Plant the tuberous rootstalks 5 in. (12.5 cm) deep and 10 in. (25 cm) apart as soon as the earth is warm in the spring. Choose an area where the plants will get maximum sunlight.

Canna is spectacular in borders, and wonderful around a pool so long as the ground isn't too soggy. The flowers are best left on the plant until they fade, then carefully pruned to make way for another bloom. The colourful leaves can be cut and used in arrangements.

When the foliage begins to fade, dig up the rootstalks and store them for the winter in a cool dry place. Plant again the following year.

Chionodoxa

There isn't a prettier blue in early spring than Chionodoxa (*C. luciliae*), also known as Glory-of-the-Snow. Its reflexed petals surround a white eye formed by cup-shaped stamens. Buds are borne in clusters on leafless, 6-inch (15-cm) racemes. White and pink cultivars of rare species types are increasingly available.

Plant close together in a sunny spot in September or October and cover with 2 in. (5 cm) of soil. Chionodoxa spreads well and is most effective in a massed group.

Clivia

Sometimes called the Kaffir Lily, Clivia (*C. miniata*) produces huge orange-shaded trumpet flowers with long gold stamens. It is borne on 2-ft. (60-cm) umbels in groups of 6 or more. Planted in a mass, which is its preference, Clivia produces wide, dark evergreen foliage, providing a beautiful, carpeted background.

Grow as a tender bulb in Canada or for pot culture. Clivia is an excellent potted house plant. Spring plant rhizomes 6 in. (15 cm) apart in a shaded, warm location.

Pretty blue Chionodoxa planted amid yellow Daffodils produces a perfect colour contrast.

Colchicum

Colchicum, also known as Autumn Crocus (*C. autumnale minor*) is not a Crocus but actually a member of the Lily family. It has the same flower form and small stature as the spring-blooming type, but usually flowers in September in Canadian gardens. It produces foliage several weeks after it flowers.

Colchicum is also surprisingly self-sufficient, and is capable of blooming without the aid of soil or water. Shades of pink, white and yellow are available.

Plant in fall, spacing 6 in. (15 cm) and covering with 3 in. (7.5 cm) of soil. Sunny locations are best in climates harsher than Zone 6. Maintain soil moisture year-round.

(Opposite) The flamboyant Canna, is a native of tropical and sub-tropical climes and likes Canadian summers.

Convallaria

Better known as Lily-of-the-Valley (*C. majalis*), this intensely fragrant little bell-flower grows from rhizomes that are hardy to Zone 3. Convallaria grows rampantly and can even be used as a ground cover. Flowers are produced on racemes and surrounded by wide green leaves that thrive all summer long.

This is one of my favourite permanent ground covers in shaded areas.

Convallaria prefers slightly acid, rich soil. When planting, space 5 in. (12.5 cm) apart and cover with 1 in. (2.5 cm) of soil. Provide light shade for best results. Keep well watered until established.

Crocus

The cup-shaped blooms of Crocus open wide only when the sun shines bright. Otherwise they close up to protect their lovely gold stamens, the source of saffron. Available colours include rose, blue, white, yellow and even striped variations. The familiar large Crocus are Dutch hybrids developed from small species types, which are also widely available.

Plant corms in full sun, spacing 4 in. (20 cm) apart. Depending on bulb size, cover with 2 to 4 in. (5 to 10 cm) of soil.

Cyclamen

The hardy species Cyclamen, a member of the Primrose family, is a dwarf compared to those sold in flower shops, but lovely just the same. Some flower in early spring while others produce their exotic miniature blooms in fall.

Plant tubers in fall, spacing 2 in. (5 cm) apart and covering lightly. A shady location is best. Cyclamen is hardy to Zone 4 but needs ample winter protection.

Dahlia

The towering star of the late summer garden, Dahlia produces multi-petalled flowers in a spectacular range of colours and forms. Their numerous cultivars are sorted into groups, including bicoloured, single, pompon, cactus, peony, and others. Dahlia normally grows to heights of 1 to 5 ft. (30 cm to 1.5 m), though tree forms exist.

Plant tuberous roots in spring, about 3 in. (7.5 cm) deep. Space at least 1 ft. (30 cm) apart, more for large, spreading varieties. Dahlias are extremely frost-sensitive, and must be dug and stored over winter.

Species Cyclamen features exotic miniature blooms.

Dwarf Dahlias can now be grown from seed, sown indoors in late winter and set out in late May after frost is finished. They are treated like annuals.

Endymion

Commonly called Bluebell or Scilla, Endymion commonly takes the form of a hardy, blue, Campanula-type bellflower appearing in low-growing masses in spring. Taller species, such as Spanish Bluebell (E. hispanicus), grow to about 18 in. (45 cm) high and are most frequently offered in shades of white and pink.

This plant is a favourite of mine naturalized in the lawn or under deciduous trees.

Lightly-shaded, moist sites give best results. Space 6 in. apart and cover with at least 1 in. (2.5 cm) of soil depending on bulb height.

Eranthis

Eranthis, commonly called the Winter Aconite, closely resembles its cousin the Wild Marsh Marigold. It bears open,

(Opposite) Colchicum, which usually blooms in September in Canadian gardens, is also known as Autumn Crocus.

RULE OF THUMB

To determine the viability and health of a true flower bulb (for example, a tulip or a daffodil bulb), look for the texture and firmness of an onion.

bright yellow blossoms in early spring for several weeks.

Plant in sun or shade, spaced 3 in. (7.5 cm) apart and covered with 2 in. (5 cm) of soil. Eranthis is hardy to Zone 4 and prefers a very moist environment and wind protection.

Eremurus

Foxtail Lily (*E. robustus*), a native of the Himalayas, produces tall flowering spears in many shades, 3 to 8 ft. (90 cm to 2.4 m) high. Modern cultivars include gold and pink forms, but white is most common.

Eremurus is hardy to Zone 5. Plant tuberous roots 6 in. (15 cm) deep and 1 ft. (30 cm) apart. Handle gently and spread roots carefully. Eremurus resents being moved so provide it with a sunny location where it has room to spread. Winter protection is essential.

Erythronium

It's easy to recognize this native woodland plant by its brown-spotted leaves and extremely recurved petals. Erythronium, also known as Dog-Toothed Violet (*E. dens-canis*), has yellow, pink, or white blooms carried on flower stalks as high as 14 in. (35 cm). This plant is hardy to Zone 3, and needs shade and rich organic soil. Plant corms 3 in. (7.5 cm) deep and 6 in. (15 cm) apart.

Freesia

The intoxicating scent of Freesia inspires even some gardeners who should know better than to try planting them outdoors. But after all, gardening is a challenge. Tubular blossoms in yellow, white, pinks and lavender are borne on wiry racemes atop 1 ft. (30 cm) high foliage resembling Gladiolus.

In Zone 8, plant in fall. Elsewhere in Canada, treat as a pot plant or try sowing corms in spring for summer blooms. Space 2 in. (5 cm) apart and 4 in. (10 cm) deep in a sunny warm location that is well drained. Freesia is extremely tender and should not be exposed to prolonged freezing. However, like most spring bulbs, it withstands moderate cold and light frost.

Fritillaria

Even the appearance of Fritillaria bulbs, with their large stem hole, indicates the unusual nature of this plant. It produces down-facing blossoms on single stalks. In the case of the exotic Crown Imperial variety, *F. imperialis*, the clustered blooms form an umbrella over Lily-type foliage. The checkered *F. meleagris*, with its purple and white squares, is borne singly on thin reed-like stems.

Hardy to Zone 3 with winter protection, Fritillaria bulbs prefer rich, well-drained soil. Plant bulbs on their sides to prevent them from becoming waterlogged. Plant the large form 10 in. (25 cm) apart and cover with 6 in. (15 cm) of soil. Small varieties can be planted closer together and 3 in. (7.5 cm) deep.

Fritillaria looks better than it smells. While in Holland I learned that Fritil-

laria bulbs help to repel garden moles and chipmunks. Plant 1 large bulb/5 sq. ft. (0.46 sq. m).

Galanthus

The Common Snowdrop, *G. novalis*, enjoys widespread popularity simply because it appears at winter's end. Galanthus is impervious to snow and produces pendulous, tiny white blooms that droop from a prominent green ovary. Some variation in leaf form is found among different species. A double-blossom form is available.

Prepare the soil well, and Snowdrops will thrive undisturbed for years. Plant in sun or filtered shade, spacing 2 in. (5 cm) apart and 2 in. (5 cm) deep. Spreads best in shady, moist ground. If you must move them (after flowering), dig in large groups. Otherwise they are easily set back.

Gladiolus

Gladiolus, the Queen of the August garden, is so easily hybridized that it is available in a wider range of colours and hues than perhaps any other flower.

Gladiolus produces multiple florets on tall stalks borne by sword-like foliage. Its large, outward-facing blossoms are ideal, long-lasting cut flowers. Many gardeners think Gladiolus looks better in a vase than a garden.

This flower's rigid, straight form sometimes reaches 5 ft. (1.5 m) and is difficult to combine with other plants in a mixed border. Many gardeners plant Gladiolus in its own bed. Others create harmonious arrangements by selecting low-growing and miniature forms for the front of borders, using tall Glads where hedges or shrubs form backdrops.

Plant ordinary garden Gladiolus in early spring in full sun, in well-drained soil. Space corms 6 in. (15 cm) apart and 6 in. (15 cm) deep. To prevent tall Glads from blowing over in a stiff wind, plant bulbs in a 1 ft. (30 cm) deep trench and back-fill as the stem of each bulb matures.

In climates harsher than Zone 7, treat as tender and store over winter. Hardy Gladiolus, which tends to be short and to bear fewer flowers, is planted in fall for early summer bloom. *G. Byzantinus* and *G. Carneus* are hardy to Zone 5. Winter protection is advised.

Hemerocallis

A favourite, low-maintenance perennial, the Hemerocallis is better known as Daylily. It produces long flower stalks that can bear numerous buds, each of which bloom for just one day.

Hybridization has encouraged the development of many blossom colours, including cream, purple, pink and shades of peach. Tall, reed-like foliage spreads vigorously. Daylily is extremely adaptable, and can thrive in a wide variety of growing conditions. Its standard height is 3 ft. (90 cm), although miniatures and enlarged forms can be found.

A tuberous root that is very cold-hardy, Daylily is best planted in either spring or fall. Plant so that the crown of each root

(Left) Erythronium, the Dog-Toothed Violet, is easily identified by its extremely recurved petals.

This summer garden features tall stalks of yellow Gladiolus in the rear, orange and red Dahlia in the left foreground, and orange Lilium in the right foreground.

is just lightly covered. Space at least 1 ft. (30 cm) apart. Plant it in the spring and it will bloom the same summer.

Hyacinth

(Hyacinthus)

The reflexed bell flowers of Hyacinth, borne on tall, blunt stalks, are a familiar sight of spring. Their scent is memorable and can haunt a room for days. Dutch hybrids are available in varied hues of white, blue, and pink. Yellow, orange and crimson blossoms have also made recent appearances, as have miniature forms. Some varieties bear multiple spikes.

Plant in sun or shade, spacing 6 in. (15 cm) apart, and cover with 6 in. (15 cm) of soil. It will grow in almost pure sand. The largest Hyacinth bulbs are normally sold for indoor culture as they produce such full, heavy flower stalks that they can be easily damaged by wind. Protective mulches are often needed, even for those sold as winter-hardy.

Lilium

Lilies are everything a flower should be – beautiful, fragrant, prolific and adaptable. Hybridized versions of wild species have produced wide variations in height, blossom colour, blossom form, and growing requirements. Lilium is said to be the oldest-known cultivated flower. Many Lilies are native to this country.

There is a Lily for every garden. With careful selection, many Canadian gardeners could plant for continuous summer bloom. Horticulturists have separated Lilium species into nine categories characterized by bloom type, size, schedule, and plant height. The categories are Asiatic, Martagon, Candidum, Longiflorum, Aurelian (trumpet), Oriental, unclassified hybrids, and Species types.

Asiatic and Martagon Lilies bloom in early summer. The rest bloom intermittently between July and August, excepting Oriental Lily, which blooms only in August. Heights within each category range considerably, from as little as 2 ft. (60 cm) to as much as 8 ft. (2.4 m). Flowers may face down, up or out. Some are described as trumpet- or funnel-shaped. Others bear petals that recurve, some extremely so.

Plant in the fall or spring according to the variety. Many Lilies thrive in shade but a few require sun. Lilies generally need to be spaced 1 ft. (30 cm) apart and to be planted twice the depth of their bulbs. Unlike other tall bulbs, they don't necessarily benefit from deep planting. Most Lilies (e.g. Madonna) form roots from the base of the bulb, but some (e.g. Regal) form roots on the stem between the bulb and the soil surface. The latter should be planted deeper.

Muscari

Grape Hyacinth (*M. armeniacum*) is the most common member of the Muscari genus. One sniff will tell you how it gained its nickname. Tightly clustered purple flowers ring 8-in. (20-cm) high stalks and smell just like grape juice. White and even feathered forms of Muscari are available. Bulbs of this species are so prolific, hardy and inexpensive that every garden should have some.

Plant in any soil, 3 in. (7.5 cm) apart and 3 in. (7.5 cm) deep. Hardy to Zone 2. Muscari is ideal in groups in rock gardens, and foreground areas of borders.

Narcissus

The golden-trumpeted flower known widely to gardeners as Daffodil is actually a hybridized member of a very large flower genus, *Narcissus*. The lesser group of sweetly scented types known as Jonquil is a species of Narcissus. Many other forms of Narcissus are also available to home gardeners, including the popular Hoop Petticoat (N. bulbocodium) and Poeticus Daffodil (*N. poeticus*).

I admit a weakness for most Daffodils. They are early, hardy, often fragrant. They make great flowers and the squirrels don't like them.

Like other large bulb groups, the Daffodil family boasts thousands of cultivars that cover a wide range of flower types and height. They are classified according to such characteristics as flower length, schedule of bloom and place of origin.

Cultivation techniques vary little among the various Daffodils. Most are hardy to Zone 4. Plant them three times the depth of their bulb and space 6 in. (15 cm) apart. Daffodil bulbs can have several noses, indicating their potential for multiple stems.

Wherever a naturalized effect is not desired, dig and divide every few years to ease overcrowding. Dig in summer when the bulbs are dormant. Ensure that each separation retains a portion of the parent basal plate for reliable development of root structure. Narcissus begin new growth of both crown leaves and roots in the late fall.

Ornithogalum

Star of Bethlehem (*Ornithogalum*) is a charming species which produces 1-ft. (30-cm) umbels of clustered, star-shaped flowers. The variety *O. umbellatum* is prolific and hardy in Zone 5. In springtime, flowers open in the morning and close in late afternoon.

This plant is not fussy about soil requirements. Plant in sun or shade. Cover bulbs with 2 in. (5 cm) of soil and space 4 in. (10 cm) apart.

Oxalis

Bushy, low mats of clover-type leaves precede the appearance of large, lilac-

IRIS

According to Greek mythology, Iris, the Goddess of Rainbows, was a messenger of the gods. It seems only appropriate that one of the loveliest early spring flowers should bear her name.

Hybridization has created multitudinous forms and colours, as well as some confusion. Iris, sometimes called Flag, grows by bulbs or rhizomes. Both types produce elegant, reed-like foliage which varies in width and height according to type. There are variegated foliage varieties also. Iris blossoms have strictly organized their petals into upward standards and down-facing falls, with prominent styles and, sometimes, beards.

Bulb Iris

The popular Dutch hybrids are the best known forms of bulb Iris, and are also the easiest to culture outside of the west coast of Canada. But even the Dutch hybrids are persistently hardy in Canadian gardens only when given ample winter protection.

Conservative gardeners living in climates harsher than Zone 6 treat them as tender. Dutch Iris grow to 2 ft. (60 cm) and are so sylph-thin that they can be closely planted for a good mass effect. Space them 4 in. (10 cm) apart and cover them with 5 in. (12.5 cm) of soil.

August is the ideal time to transplant Iris, but new plants can also be started in spring. Shallow cultivate, otherwise roots near the surface will be cut.

I. reticulata is a low-growing miniature which is the earliest-blooming Iris. Its richly veined flowers, in purple, yellow and blue shades, bear lovely contrasting crests in yellow, orange and white.

I. reticulata is perfect in rock gardens or massed together at the front of borders. It effectively completes the spring garden when combined with Crocus, miniature Tulips or Arabis in complementary colours. Tall, sword-like foliage spears the air for several weeks following flowering. Plant in full sun, 3 in. (7.5 cm) apart and 3 in. (7.5 cm) deep. Protect well, outside of Zone 5. Hardy.

Rhizomatic Iris

Rhizomatic Iris comprises the vast majority of known Iris species. The largest sub-group of these is the bearded Iris, *I. x germanica*. Hybrid beardless forms include Japanese and Siberian Iris.

Bearded *I. x germanica* is the standard Iris found in most gardens. It increases to form massive clumps and is extremely hardy. There are six recognized categories of Bearded Iris, varied in their height, and the size, number and period of bloom of their flowers. They are available in all colours of the rainbow and then some. Hardy.

The Japanese Iris (*I. kaempferi*), with its flat, beardless blooms, can be grown only by gardeners with rich, moist (even wet), acidic soil. If you have the right environment, give it a try. The richly veined blooms in shades ranging from white to blue, pink or purple can spread 10 in. (25 cm) wide and are quite spectacular additions to the summer garden. Hardy to Zone 5. The Japanese Iris should be planted at least 1 ft. (30 cm) apart, and lightly covered. Mulch heavily in winter. Half-hardy.

I. sibirica has the reed-thin quality of Dutch Iris but is hardy to Zone 3. Like other beardless types, it prefers rich, moist soil. It achieves heights of 3 ft. (90 cm) and ranges in colour from white, blue to shades of purple. Cover rhizomes lightly and plant 15 in. (37.5 cm) apart as they can form thick clumps. Hardy. Clean up the Iris bed in fall to discourage the Iris borer from overwintering.

pink flowers. *O. adenophylla*, ideal for rock gardens, is the most common species offered in Canada. A native of the Andes, it is also the hardiest. Oxalis can be grown in pots and hanging baskets.

Oxalis can be grown in regions colder than Zone 6 if well protected. Plant in full sun, spacing 2 in. (5 cm) apart and 2 in. (5 cm) deep.

Puschkinia

The blue veined white flowers of Puschkinia (*P. scilloides*), often compared to Scilla, in fact closely resemble a miniature Hyacinth. Puschkinia is a good multiplier and soon forms thick mats. It is native to dry regions such as Afghanistan, and adapts to dry soils. It is much favoured for naturalizing in grass or planting in rock gardens.

Plant in full sun, spaced 3 in. (7.5 cm) apart and 3 in. (7.5 cm) deep.

Ranunculus

One of the most exotic members of the Buttercup family, *R. asiaticus* bears multi-petalled blossoms on 18-in. (45 cm) stalks. Their colour range and blossom form, available in shades of rose, yellow, orange and white, closely resembles Begonia. Ranunculus is a tuberous root that is treated as non-hardy in climates harsher than Zone 8.

Plant in full sun, spacing 6 in. (15 cm) apart and 2 in. (5 cm) deep. Tubers look like large dried-up raisins. Soak them before planting. Grown plants like their crowns dry and their roots slightly damp.

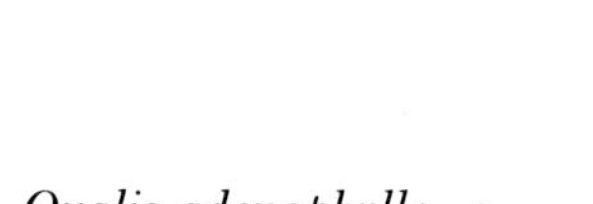

Oxalis adenophylla, a native of the Andes, blooms in early spring.

TULIPS

Since the days of Tulipmania in the seventeenth century, when Tulips were given the status of money, this versatile bulb has been a recognized treasure. Its contribution to the spring garden is invaluable.

Hundreds of named varieties of Tulips are available commercially. Horticulturists group them into classes according to shared bloom characteristics in an effort to maintain order. Only about 15 divisions have importance to most gardeners.

Tulip breeding has developed tall, late bloomers able to withstand the hot temperature of late spring. You should custom order bulbs adapted to the Canadian climate.

Species Tulips comprise the little-known group of original Tulips from which many popular hybrids were developed. Many are native to mountainous regions of eastern Europe and are extremely robust. They can be counted on to provide the first blooms of early spring. Some of the better known species Tulips are *Tulipa greigii* (variegated foliage), *T. kaufmanniana* (large blossoms, useful to hybridizers), *T. fosteriana* (extremely large) , *T. tarda* (multi-stemmed), *T. praestans* (multi-flowered), *T. eichleri* (coloured centres), *T. clusiana* (striped petals), and *T. saxatilis* (wide yellow centres).

Single Early and Double Early Tulips bloom next in early spring. They are followed by **Mendel Tulips** which are good examples of the earliest Dutch hybridizing efforts.

More vigorous stems resulted with the development of **Triumph Tulips**, a cross of Single Early Tulips and Darwin hybrids.

The Darwin Hybrid Tulip was obtained by crossing Darwins with the species *T. fosteriana*. The resulting large-cupped flowers grow to a height of about 30 in. (75 cm) and are extremely vigorous. They bloom in late spring.

Darwin Tulip is the classic Tulip. It is a separate category of late-blooming flowers, with solid colour blossoms that may be slightly fringed. It includes the tallest, strongest-stemmed Tulips, which are unfailingly popular.

Lily-flowered Tulips bloom in late spring with the single late Tulips. Their reflexed petals, which curve outward, distinguish them among other Tulips. They may have been derived by combining the sharply pointed species forms *T. clusiana* and *T. acuminata* with other more robust forms.

Parrot Tulips are fringed solid-colour or streaked Darwin blossoms that mutated naturally. All Parrots are late spring bloomers, usually accompanying Darwins and Lily-flowered strains.

Double Late or Peony Tulips bloom in late spring and are substantially taller than Double Early cultivars. They are considered a type of double triumphs and bloom one week later.

Large, egg-shaped blossoms borne on stems as tall as 3 ft. (90 cm) are the earmark of cottage and Darwin Tulips which were recently jointly reclassified as Single Late Tulips. They provide some of the healthiest, most vigorous tulips, in the best colour range.

Multicoloured Tulips are classified according to flower shape and derivation as either Breeder, Rembrandt, Bizarre or Bybloemen. Although multiple crosses brought them into being, these types share broken or variegated markings that make them quite distinct among Tulips. The "breaking" of colour in these groups is associated with the mosaic virus which affects colour genes and is assumed to be inherited, or transmissible from one generation to another.

Despite the vast array of forms, Tulips have fairly standardized cultural preferences. Plant according to bulb size, at least three times the bulb's depth in well-drained soil. Tulips can be planted extra-deep – 10 in. (25 cm) or more – thus saving the bother of digging them up to make room for annuals. Simply tie the foliage together after flowering in mid-May and plant your favourite annuals between them.

Space 3 to 8 in. (7.5 to 20 cm) apart, depending on size, and plant in full sun or moderate shade, such as that provided by deciduous trees. They are very cold hardy and have a preference for climates with markedly frigid winters. What better terms could Canadian gardeners have?

Zantedeschia

In most of Canada, spring-planted Calla Lily (*Zantedeschia*) rhizomes will produce blooms of yellow, white or soft pink in mid to late summer. Most varieties of this large funnel-shaped flower are not hardy beyond Zone 8. The common white form *Z. aethiopica*, or Crowborough Lily, is an exception. With protection it can overwinter in Zone 5. Cultivars of various heights ranging from 6 in. to 4 ft. (15 cm to 1.2 m) are available.

Plant in well-drained, rich soil, spacing 1 ft. (30 cm) apart and 2 in. (5 cm) deep.

Zephyranthes

The bright rose-pink blossoms of the Zephyranthes or Fairy Lily bring to mind a tiny Daylily. They form mounding clusters about 8 in. (20 cm) high which are entirely appropriate to rock garden settings. This is an unusual and interesting small bulb. White and autumn flowering forms are available.

Plant in full sun, spacing 2 in. (5 cm) apart and 2 in. (5 cm) deep. Hardy to Zone 7, they are grown as tender bulbs elsewhere in Canada.

Golden Apeldoorn Tulips have fine red markings on their petals.

CHAPTER 6
HERBS

Herbs are among the oldest cultivated plants. Their aromatic flavours and medicinal qualities inspired their early domestication and continue to inspire many modern gardeners.

Herbs are attractive garden plants, often bearing lovely flowers or exhaling wonderful scents. They are also indispensable in the kitchen. A kitchen garden of frequently used herbs and flowers will provide efficient garden-to-stove-top results. It's a lot easier (and tastier!) to use Shallots and Parsley on the spur of the moment if you are able to cut them outside your back door instead of travelling to buy them from a market or specialty food shop.

CARE AND MAINTENANCE OF HERBS

The best gourmet restaurants often grow their own herbs and vegetables, or contract with a local gardener to obtain produce that is not reliably available from local markets, or to ensure absolute freshness. You can achieve the same gourmet quality in your own back yard.

Well-tended perennial herbs can usually be harvested over most of the summer. Start annuals inside and set them out as seedlings when spring arrives. They need to be planted in a well-prepared bed, liberally amended with mature compost and other organic material. Mulches are ideal for keeping in moisture and preventing weeds.

Fertilizer is seldom necessary. Many herbs do better without chemical fertilizers, which can encourage legginess.

Plan your herb garden to be readily accessible and easily cultivated. You should be able to harvest without straining to reach. If beds are too wide they are difficult to use, especially by hurried cooks. Paths or stepping stones can be incorporated to solve that problem. Many gardeners follow ancient traditions and plant herbs in formal patterns that include walking strips.

Combining herbs with low-growing ornamental flowers is also a nice touch. Urban gardeners pressed for space often incorporate herbs such as Lavender, Chives, and Thyme, in their regular flower borders.

Enthusiastic herbalists often pot their garden herbs and bring them inside to winter over. This helps to reduce replacement costs for tender perennial herbs. And it turns your kitchen window into a mini-herb garden, which keeps winter meals savoury. When bringing plants indoors, use appropriate potting material and sterile containers, and trim back specimens as needed.

Descriptions and Requirements

Basil

(Ocimum)

Basil is arguably the most versatile of common garden herbs. Its pleasant, pungent flavour is an ideal accompaniment to dishes which feature eggs, cheese, Tomatoes, Garlic or meat. It is great used fresh on salads, dressings and in Italian dishes.

Leaf size varies with variety. The most popular forms on the market are standard Sweet Basil (*O. basilicum*); Bush or Globe Basil (*O. basilicum minimum*), which are both small-leaved; and Ornamental Basil (*O. basilicum* 'Dark Opal'), which is a red, large-leafed form. This red-leafed Basil always generates many questions when we plant it at Cullen Gardens. Height ranges from 10 in. to 2 ft. (25 to 60 cm).

Sow seed directly in average soil when the earth is warm, or set out seedlings. Basil is quite tender and dies with the first frosts of autumn. It prefers sun. Pinch back to remove flowers and to promote bushiness.

Caraway

(Carum carvi)

Like Dill, Caraway is a Carrot relative that produces seed on 2 ft. (60 cm) high umbels. This seed is used as a seasoning in casseroles and breads.

Caraway is a biennial which should be sown from seed in spring or fall and harvested in its second summer. It will not survive harsh Canadian winters without being well mulched. Plant in full sun and provide average, well-drained soil for best results.

Chives

(Allium)

Chives, a member of the Onion (*Allium*) genus, forms rounded clumps of hollow, grass-like reeds that taste distinctly of Onion (*A. schoenoprasum*) or Garlic (*A. tuberosum*). Onion-flavoured Chives produce pretty purple-flowered heads, while the Garlic type produces white flowers. Chives are perennial bulbs.

Chives grow to approximately 1 ft. (30 cm) high and are ideal at the front of a border. They are often finely chopped and used as a garnish. I like chives mixed generously in sour cream, which I apply even more generously to my baked potatoes.

Chives will grow from seed but root division is the chief method of propagation. They like full sun or light shade, and average soil. Provide protection in winter, especially for Garlic Chives.

At the bottom of each description symbols have been used to indicate sun and shade tolerance, the minimum hardiness zone, moisture requirements, and soil pH requirements.

LIGHT REQUIREMENTS

Full sun | Partial sun | Shade | No Preference

PLANT HARDINESS

Tender | Half hardy | Hardy

Tender: tropical origin killed by first frosts.
Half-Hardy: robust enough to withstand light frosts. Killed by heavy frosts.
Hardy: tolerant of successive frosts; seedlings may even overwinter. Poppies and Dianthus.

MOISTURE REQUIREMENTS

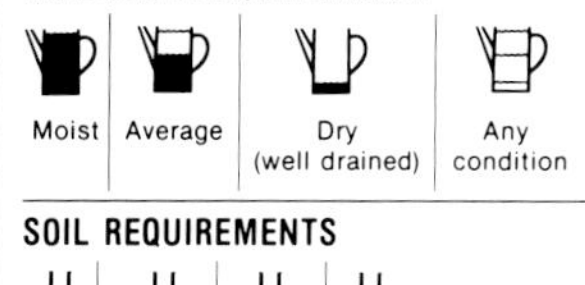

Moist | Average | Dry (well drained) | Any condition

SOIL REQUIREMENTS

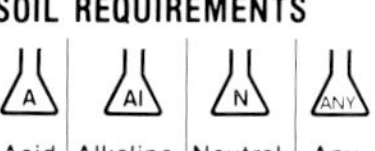

Acid | Alkaline | Neutral | Any soil

Dill

(Anethum graveolens)

Dill is a hardy annual grown for the sharp, tangy flavour its stem and seeds impart to preserves, bread, salads and many other foods. Seeds are borne on tall umbels that grow 3 ft. (90 cm) high, surrounded by feathery green foliage. Harvest flower heads before they open fully. Cut long stems and hang to dry.

Dill is easy to grow if provided with full sun and average, well-drained soil. Potted seedlings do not transplant easily. Sow Dill directly in the garden in very early spring. Give Dill lots of space.

Garlic

(Allium sativum)

The rich, odoriferous flavour of Garlic is considered invaluable by cooks around the world. Garlic is a perennial. Whole white or pink bulbs can be obtained by setting out individual cloves in early spring or preferably in autumn.

Like its cousin the Onion, Garlic produces tall, pungent stalks that produce white flower buds. But its foliage is narrow and flat rather than hollow. Garlic will grow over 2 ft. (60 cm).

Plant cloves or "sets" 2 in. (5 cm) deep and 5 in. (12.5 cm) apart. Garlic prefers a rich, well-drained site with full sun. Plants that winter over need a protective mulch in climates harsher than Zone 5. Bulbs are ready to be harvested when leaves begin to droop. Pull bulbs and allow them to dry a few days before removing foliage and roots.

Marjoram

(Marjorana hortensis)

Fragrant, sweet Marjoram is a white-flowering annual that grows a little over 1 ft. (30 cm) high. Its woody, upright stems are clothed in clusters of small, oval green leaves.

Marjoram can be easily grown from seed planted in early spring. Plant it in full sun. Soil should be alkaline but not too dry. Keep flowers pruned to encourage tender stem and leaf growth. Use Marjoram with salad, jellies, teas, or to flavour meats and vinegars.

There is nothing like fresh herbs such as Oregano to make your cooking come alive.

Mint

(Mentha species)

There is probably no more varied perennial herb group than the Mint family. Some, like Peppermint (*M. piperita*) and Spearmint (*M. spicata*), are tall, upright plants. Others, like Pennyroyal (*M. pulegium*), are low-growing carpet ground covers. Nearly all are prolific, rampant growers when provided with ideal growing conditions. Mints provide pretty flower stalks of blue or mauve as well as great flavour for beverages, jellies, meats and salads.

Get your kids involved in growing Mint. It is fool-proof, propagates easily, and has a taste they can relate to.

Propagate by dividing mature plants. Mint grows best in light shade and slightly moist soil. To keep your Mint under control, plant in a large juice tin with the bottom removed and the top rim of the tin extending 2 in. (5 cm) above the soil surface.

Oregano

(Origanum)

Greek Oregano (*O. heracleoticum*) is the tastiest, hardiest Oregano. This perennial produces pretty violet flowers atop

sprawling, spreading foliage that grows 2 ft. (60 cm) high and equally wide, if allowed. Oregano is used in many sauces, soups and dressings. It is a popular ingredient in several Italian dishes.

Plant seedlings in full sun. They're quite drought-resistant. Oregano is a rampant grower that may need to be trimmed occasionally. Can be used as a ground cover on dry embankments.

Parsley

(Petroselinum)

Parsley is universally popular as a garnish or flavour enhancer. It is also a remarkable source of iron and vitamins, and it is said to diminish breath odour caused by Garlic or alcohol. Parsley is available in curled (*P. crispum*) and plain leaf (*P. filicinum*) forms, as well as dwarf varieties.

Leaves and roots will hold their flavour if dried or frozen.

Parsley sometimes takes several weeks to germinate. The process can be speeded by soaking seeds overnight in warm water before sowing. Potted seedlings are difficult to transplant so use extra care. A tender biennial, Parsley is usually grown as an annual in Canada. It prefers average to rich soil that is moist or lightly shaded. Thin Parsley seedlings approximately 10 in. (25 cm) apart. Parsley will sometimes self-sow.

Rosemary

(Rosmarinus officinalis)

This tender perennial produces intensely aromatic and spicy, needle-like leaves that are favoured in a variety of meat dishes. In its natural habitat, Rosemary produces lovely blue flowers in spring. Both upright or trailing forms are available. Rosemary stalks can reach heights of 4 ft. (1.2 m) or more.

Plant seedlings in early spring. Rosemary requires full sun and prefers poor but well-drained soil. It can withstand frosts and cold but is unlikely to survive winters in climates harsher than Zone 8.

Sage

(Salvia species)

The leaves and scent of Sage are among the prettiest in an herb garden. Ordinary green Sage (*S. officinalis*) has long been popular in meat dressings. There are also Sages with variegated purple, red and yellow leaves ('Tricolour'), and one form that borrows its aroma from the pineapple (*S. gracilistyla*). Sage has long, thick leaves.

Plant Sage from seed, stem cuttings, or root division. It requires somewhat dry soil and full sun. Plants require generous room. They can grow to a height of 2 ft. (60 cm) or more and achieve equal spread. Cut leaves and stalks just as flowering begins.

Tarragon

(Artemisia)

The pointed, thin leaves of fresh Tarragon have a slight licorice flavour. Dry, they are sweet and mild. Plant only French Tarragon, (*A. dracunculus*) which has superior flavour. It produces sprawling, perennial clumps that die back in severe cold unless protected by a thick mulch.

Unlike its inferior relation, Russian Tarragon (*A. dracunculoides*), French Tarragon is infertile and spreads only by rhizomatic roots or stem propagation. Plant in sun or light shade in well-drained soil.

Thyme

(Thymus species)

There are more kinds of Thyme than any one gardener could grow, including Lemon Thyme (*T. citriodorus*) and Caraway-Scented Thyme (*T. herba-barona*). Thyme is also frequently grown for the flowering, dense carpet-like mats it produces. Blossoms range from white to bright burgundy. Vita Sackville-West, the famous English gardener, grew several Thyme varieties in different colours in adjoining patches to obtain a marbleized Thyme lawn. Depending on type, leaves are variegated grey, plain green, or yellow.

Sow seeds directly or plant seedlings in sun or light shade. Thyme sends out wiry strands that form small rambling clumps about 6 in. (15 cm) tall.

HERBS

Herbs are very easy to grow indoors. Plant a variety of herbs in small pots which you can keep on a kitchen window sill. This way you'll always have fresh herbs available for cooking.

Oregano

Sage

Mint

Thyme

Chives

Basil

Tarragon

Italian Parsley

Dill

CHAPTER 7

ROSES

Some say Roses are the oldest garden plants in cultivation. Maybe so, but hybrids are relatively recent. The first hybrid tree was produced in our Year of Confederation, 1867.

In 1982 I visited an acquaintance in British Columbia, Brian Minter, who had recently opened a show garden to the public. Brian impressed me as a truly inspired gardener with a talent for promoting two key ideas: that gardening improves the quality of Canadian life, and that it is easy to succeed at it.

Brian led me through his garden, waving his hands enthusiastically from planting to planting, barely taking a breath while explaining how his paradise garden had come about, nestled between two gorgeous snow-capped mountains.

When we arrived at the Rose garden, he stopped. No explanation was necessary. Brian had designed his huge Rose garden for mass appeal. The garden could be seen in plain view from the Trans-Canada Highway, and in the background he had boldly planted Begonias in the form of an enormous Canadian flag.

As Brian's garden confirmed, Roses are for sharing. I like to plant Roses in a highly visible spot in my own garden, where neighbours and passers-by can enjoy their ever-changing personalities and colour.

I like to cut Roses and bring them in to my wife Mary. I take them to neighbours and my secretary at the office.

Is it any wonder that Roses occupy a place of pride in most of the great Canadian gardens, including the Montreal Botanical Gardens, the Royal Botanical Gardens in Burlington, Cullen Gardens and Miniature Village in Whitby, Queen Elizabeth Gardens in Vancouver, and the most famous of all, Butchart Gardens in Victoria.

Roses are in a class by themselves. They deserve special attention regardless of where you live.

CARE AND MAINTENANCE OF ROSES

Preparing the soil

Adequate soil preparation guarantees years of success. It also makes planting easier.

Availability dictates that most Roses are planted in spring. However, Rose experts suggest planting Roses in fall for early spring growth. Where the winters are very severe – Zone 3 or colder – it may be safer to plant in early spring.

In spring, as soon as the ground can be worked, turn over the soil to the depth of a spade. To this loosened soil, add 1/3 to 1/2 as much again of composted humus like leaf mould, peat moss, or composted manure, together with coarse sand. Work the soil at least one month before planting to allow time for the soil to warm up, air to circulate, and compost to break down.

Roses like a fairly neutral soil (about 7.0 pH) but they are fairly adaptable to a variety of soil conditions.

Planting Roses

For years experts have disagreed about how deeply to plant Roses. Ideally, the bud union (the large bulbous part between the canes and roots) should be above ground to encourage new cane growth. But if the bud union gets damaged by cold, that's the end of the Rose. Therefore, many people plant the bud union under the ground. As a practical compromise, you can plant the bud union just above the soil line, then cover it with earth just before the cold weather arrives.

There are two ways of buying Roses for planting, bare-root and potted:

Planting Roses

1. Work soil at least a month before planting, adding composted organic material and coarse sand.

2. If you plant potted Roses in a peat or paper pot, make two slits down the sides of the container before putting it in the ground.

3. Adjust planting depth so that the bud union is visible just above the soil line.

4. Tamp and water heavily as you fill the hole with soil.

Bare-root

Some Roses come with bare roots and a short amount of cane above. To the uninitiated, they often look dead, but a good soaking will prove otherwise. As soon as you get them, remove the plastic casing and cut off any broken or extra-long roots. If roots are mushy-soft, discoloured or broken, prune them back until the pith is firm and cream-coloured.

If you can't plant them right away, put them back into the plastic wrap along with dampened moss or peat moss, and store them in a cool dry place or place them in a pail of water mixed with half rate 20-20-20 for up to a week. Or heel them in a corner of the garden, making sure over one half of the stem area is covered with soil.

When you're ready to plant, soak the roots in lukewarm water for an hour until they have plumped up. If they don't plump up, they won't grow, and you should take them back to the nursery.

To plant bare-root Roses, dig a hole deep enough so the bud union will be in the right place. Dig the hole to fit the direction of the roots, either spread out in a circle, or bent over to one side. Loosen the earth at the bottom of the hole and mix it with a spadeful of peat moss and a handful of bonemeal. If the roots are fanned out, you can make a mound at the bottom of the hole for the roots to spread over.

Put the dampened plants into the hole and spread the roots out with your fingers so they won't tangle or wind around the stem. Lean the plant slightly to face prevailing winds from the northwest, which helps to protect plants with weak bud unions. Then carefully back-fill to halfway up the hole with the earth you previously removed. Tamp this down gently with your foot, then fill with water and leave for an hour. Tamp down again. This will get rid of any air pockets

which would harm the growing Rose. (Instead of tamping, you can gently jiggle or shake the Rose in order to settle the soil around the roots. This helps to prevent excessive soil compaction.)

Fill up to the soil line, tamp and water again, and then mound any remaining earth up around the canes. This will keep roots moist and protected until after the plant has started to grow.

After a month, level the earth down to the soil line again. Leave a slight depression in a circle around the stem to catch water, which will permeate down to the roots.

Potted

Roses which have been started in containers by a nursery have several advantages. They have a head start on growth, sometimes displaying the colour and shape of the blooms before you buy them. And they can show immediate progress.

Potted Roses need little preparation. Water well an hour or two before planting. Dig a hole twice as big as the earth ball. Prepare the bottom of the hole as described above without any mounding. Make sure the bud union will be just above the soil line when the Rose is planted.

If the container is a peat or papier maché material that will break down on contact with wet soil, make two complete slits down the sides of the container before putting it in the ground.

Plastic pots must be completely removed. To remove the container, tap it on the bottom with a trowel and loosen by running a knife around the inside perimeter between the earth and the container. Ease out the Rose and immediately place it in the hole. Continue with the planting method described for bare-root.

Watering

Roses don't like to get their leaves wet. Drops of water on the leaves can cause burning, and lead to black spot disease. Always water from underneath, soaking the earth until it is damp but not soggy.

It's better to water thoroughly once a week than lightly several times in the same period. If you give Roses too much water, they'll drown. Water in the morning or at least four or five hours before dusk so that any excess moisture can be absorbed by the heat of the day.

Mulching

Roses like consistent moisture – not too much or too little. Keep the soil around roots cool and damp by mulching. Use good organic material like home-made humus, leaf mould, or peat moss, or longer-lasting materials like ground up pine bark chips. When you've decided which type of mulch to use, use it consistently. A layer of mulch 1 1/2 to 2 in. (3 to 5 cm) deep must be applied to really do the job right.

Mulch can also discourage black spot disease by reducing splashing. When drops of water hit bare earth, they can send up the spores of the black spot fungus, which then settle on the underside of leaves. Spores develop into little black spots which eventually turn the leaves yellow.

Feeding

Top dressing with organic compost or manure tea produces good results. If you use a dry granular fertilizer, feed your Roses about three times during the growing season – at the end of May, June and July. Feeding in August encourages growth which will likely be winter-killed. Feed with a solution of 6-12-12 at the rate of 1 cup (250 mL) per plant.

To get the darkest, greenest glossy leaves, professional growers apply 1 cup (250 mL) of epsom salts around the base of the plant at the beginning of the growing season and water it in.

Pruning

Shrub Roses, most Climbers and Miniatures should never be severely pruned. But grafted types like Hybrid Teas, Floribundas, and Grandifloras should be pruned annually, and drastically. If you remove up to 90 per cent of the top growth from these types of Roses each spring, they will produce vigorous new growth bearing beautiful flowers. Pruning helps to produce larger flowers and more of them. It also helps them to resist disease and stand up to insects.

The rules for pruning vary somewhat with the type of Rose. However, certain rules apply to all Roses:

- Always prune 1/4 in. (6 mm) above an outward-facing bud. This rule applies when you are pruning, cleaning away dead blooms, or cutting flowers at their peak. (Buds are nodes which eventually develop into Roses. They form at the

RULE OF THUMB

Plant sugars are highest in the mid-afternoon. This is the best time of day to cut rose flowers.

juncture of a cane and a leaf formed of five or seven leaflets. Often the bud will be visible in the leaf axil between the leaf stem and the cane.)

* Use a sharp knife or hand pruners (secateurs) to minimize damage, and cut at a 45 degree angle so the water will run off the cane.
* Never prune in fall. Just remove dead foliage, mound new garden soil around the plant, and wait until spring. Do not use soil from around the root zone of your Rose bushes to winterize.
* Hybrid Tea Roses need major surgery every spring. After the danger of hard frost is passed, remove all but four strong, evenly-spaced canes. For Hybrid Teas and Grandifloras, cut back each of the remaining four canes to an outward-facing bud 4 in. (10 cm) from the base of the plant.
* See below for special advice on pruning Climbers. Species, Shrub, and Old Garden Roses generally require only light pruning.
* Take as little stem as possible when cutting blooms from recently planted bushes. This allows the leaves which are left to work at full capacity for new growth.
* The best time to cut blooms for arrangements is in the afternoon. Plant sugars are at their peak during this time of day.
* Remove flowers as their petals begin to fall, cutting them back to the first bud.
* To encourage larger flowers, remove any secondary buds that form in the axils between the top leaves and the stem. This reserves all the nutrients for one Rose bloom at the end of the cane, resulting in a larger Rose.
* Suckers are shoots growing from the roots below the bud union, as distinct from new canes coming from the bud union. Follow them down with your finger to where they begin and carefully remove them. Cutting them off merely encourages regrowth. Be especially vigilant in spring and summer in removing any new green growth from *below* the graft. Otherwise, the vigorous root stock will grow its own plant and withdraw support for the Rose grafted onto it. The grafted Rose will die and be replaced by a thorny briar with smaller and fewer flowers which are unlike those you anticipated.

Pest and disease control

The most common diseases of Roses are black spot, a black bull's eye in a yellow target on the green leaves, and mildew, a white powder usually found on new stems and leaves. Affected canes should be removed. To prevent the spread of disease, clean your clippers with a solution of about 1/2 cup (125 mL) bleach to 1 quart (1 L) water. In late fall, rake and dispose of all Rose foliage to prevent black spot from overwintering and annoying your Roses the next year.

If you find any yellow leaves on your Roses, pick them off and burn them right away, or put them in a plastic garbage bag away from other plants. Then lay down fresh mulch and dust the leaves with garden sulphur.

Pruned Roses should be well sprayed with dormant oil in combination with lime and sulphur to kill insect eggs and fungus spores. Spray before the buds have burst in the spring.

Keep your Rose bed tidy, and prune Roses to ensure good air circulation, which helps to prevent disease.

Pruning Roses

1. Remove Rose blossoms which have begun to fade, cutting back to the first bud.

2. Always prune 1/4 in. (5 mm) above an outward-facing bud.

3. Prune to an outward facing bud. This will encourage a full rounded flower.

ROSES

Descriptions and requirements

Roses are classified into types according to ancestry, bush shape, and flower form and size. Some are repeat bloomers, some have multi-petalled buds, and some have single blooms. Some are scented while some have negligible perfume. Ask for help at the nursery to make sure you get what you want.

Hybrid Teas

Many people think these are the loveliest of all the Roses, and almost half of all Roses sold in Canada fall into this category. Long slender buds turn into luxuriant double blooms with outstanding colour and a beautiful scent. Hybrid Teas also make excellent cut Roses.

Most varieties of Hybrid Teas grow from 3 to 4 ft. (90 cm to 1.2 m) high. The top is grafted onto the roots, so be sure to get plants which have been developed for Canadian winters. These have hardy rootstalks, unlike some of the varieties available from enormous growing centres in other climatic areas.

New Hybrid Teas are being developed all the time. Here are some of my favourite proven varieties:

Crimson Glory - *Dark velvety red with a deep memorable fragrance.*

Chrysler Imperial - *Deep red with a heavy fragrance.*

Tropicana - *Orange-red with a heavy fragrance.*

Peace - *Yellow blend with a heavy fragrance.*

Tiffany - *Pink blend with a heavy fragrance.*

Floribundas

Floribundas feature clusters of flowers in a wide variety of colours. They create a wonderful display, whether grown as a single plant, massed together to form an edging or hedge, or incorporated into the foreground of an established Rose garden. They are usually hardy and bloom throughout the growing season.

Like Hybrid Teas, Floribundas are grafted, so be sure you buy Roses suited to your climate. They usually grow up to 3 ft. (90 cm). Popular varieties include:

Fashion - *Pink blend with a light fragrance.*

Carousel - *Deep red with a good fragrance.*

Circus - *Yellow-red and pink with a good fragrance.*

Cathedral - *Exotic fusion of salmon and apricot. Reliable ever-bloomer.*

Grandifloras

This class of Rose combines the attributes of the Hybrid Teas and the Floribundas. The flowers form clusters, but with Hybrid Tea-like blooms. Like Hybrid Teas, they are available in a wide assortment of colours. Grandifloras are excellent for beginners. They bloom in profusion and are easy to grow, usually reaching heights of 3 or 4 ft. (90 cm or 1.2 m).

Ask for new varieties as well as these old favourites:

Queen Elizabeth - *Medium pink with a good fragrance. Grows to over 4 ft. (1.2 m). Considered the world's most popular Rose.*

Golden Girl - *Medium yellow with a nice fragrance.*

Camelot - *Salmon-coral with a pleasant fragrance.*

John Armstrong - *Dark red with a mild, agreeable fragrance.*

Climbers

This class of Roses is an assortment of various types which share a tendency to produce long, flexible, flowering canes. Unlike true vines, Climbing Roses do not produce hooks or tendrils. They often grow in rambling fashion, over low walls or fences, but they must be manually fastened to a vertical support, like a trellis, if upward growth is desired.

The best-known Climbers are cultivars of Hybrid Teas, Kordesii Roses, Hybrid Wichuraiana, and Hybrid Multiflora. Climbers developed from the latter two groups are not repeat bloomers.

Climbers may be Hybrid Teas, Floribundas, or sometimes other types. Make sure you know what you are getting. Popular varieties include:

Blaze Improved - *Outstanding crimson colour with a good fragrance.*

White Dawn - *White with a good fragrance.*

Golden Showers - *Double yellow with a good fragrance.*

America - *Large and abundant double coral pink flowers with a spicy fragrance.*

Climbing Roses have some special pruning requirements. Rather than cutting them right back to several inches (centimetres) every year as recommended above for Bush Roses, remove one old cane for every strong new one produced, cutting it off at the base or at the strongest side branch near the base. Remove canes which are diseased, dead, or in decline. However, if your Climber fails to bloom it needs more extensive pruning than you have provided.

Cut back lateral canes, leaving four to eight buds. Where laterals are overcrowded, remove some completely to give the others room. Remove all suckers, pulling them off at the base while still young.

Ever-blooming Climbers should be pruned when they are dormant, between late fall and early spring. Remove the flowers of ever-blooming Roses as they fade, taking the flowers only, no leaves.

Climbing Roses which produce flowers only once a season should be pruned when their blossoms fade in midsummer.

As Climbers grow, tie new canes to a support as soon as they are long enough. As the season progresses, the bark toughens and it becomes much more difficult to position canes where you want them. Cut long growth back to the support.

Species Roses

Species Roses is the botanists' name for wild Roses. These are the original plants from which all other members of the family *Rosaceae* have derived. They tend to flower in late spring, producing blossoms which are always single, self-pollinating, and five-petalled. Blooms rarely repeat. Plants form sprawling or rambling type bushes which can often be trained to climb.

Juvenile plants resemble the parent in every detail.

There are several hundred types of Species Rose. As a group, they tend to be easily hybridized and cultivated. Specific members of the group – *Rosa wichuraiana*, *R. multiflora*, *R. rugosa* and *R. spinosissima* – have given rise to many valuable cultivars in the Climber, Polyantha and Shrub categories.

Like Climbers, Species Roses which bloom once during the season should be pruned after their flowers have faded. Those which bloom all season long should be pruned during the dormant season. Species Roses don't require major surgery. Just clean them up.

Shrub Roses

Pillar-type Roses which stand independently are often referred to as Shrubs. They are a modern invention, mostly developed by hybridizers over the last 100 years. Their multi-branching growth is shrub- or tree-like, and they have a tendency for repeat blossoms.

Modern Shrub Roses owe much to the Species form *R. rugosa*, which has produced many of the best and hardiest cultivars. Unlike the true Species Roses, some shrubs have double or semi-double flowers. They need light pruning after early-summer blossoms. Remove spent blossoms.

Quite happily, many of the Shrub Roses currently growing in popularity were developed by Canada's Federal Department of Agriculture. Look for ***Champlain*** (red), ***Martin Frobisher*** (pink), and ***John Franklin*** (red).

Old Garden Roses

Antique or old Garden Roses are mainly double, multi-petalled forms primarily raised in Europe before the mid-1800s. They boast ancient ancestry and are assumed to have been the first cultivated flower. Their intense fragrance has made them essential to the perfume industry for centuries.

Antique roses include ***China, Bourbon, Moss, Noisette, Gallica, Damask, Centifolia, and Alba types***.

Alba is white or pink, and often so thickly petalled that flowers don't open completely. It is thorny, tall, and large-leaved. ***Great Maiden's Blush*** is a famous variety.

China Rose is a continuous-blooming dwarf. It bears the standard cup-shape of commercial cut Roses. Blooms are yellow. Tea-scented types were used in development of Hybrid Teas. ***Archduke Charles*** is well known. Many modern miniatures are derived from China roses.

Damask is hardy, with greyish foliage, thorny, arching canes, and flowers in groups of three or more. Semi-double blossoms sport pretty gold centres. It often requires support to prevent sprawling. ***True Red Tuscany Rose*** is famous.

Bourbon is a natural hybrid of China and Damask Roses, growing as large shrubs, often with a fruity scent. It prefers mild climate regions. ***Souvenir De La Malmaison*** is popular.

Centifolia is also called a Cabbage Rose because of its tightly-packed, overlapping blossoms. Foliage is slightly reduced, but very hardy. ***Petite de Hollande*** is a popular, small form.

Gallica is best known for bicoloured pink and white types or dark purples such as ***Cardinal De Richelieu***. Both single- and double-blossoming types are available. It has reduced thorns, dark green colouring and upright growth habit.

Noisette has smaller blossoms, produced in clusters. It is upright, with reduced thorns, and it is not hardy. ***Champney's Pink Cluster*** is the forerunner.

ROSE TYPES

Polyantha "The Fairy"
Grandiflora "Gold Medal"
Meidiland "White"
Miniature "Debut"

Shrub Rose "Champlain"
Floribunda "Cathedral"
Climbing Rose "Improved Blaze"
Hybrid Tea "Pristine"

SECTION III

Ornamental Gardens

ORNAMENTAL GARDENS, INCLUDING lawns, trees, shrubs and vines, are generally permanent and hardy. They improve from year to year until they reach a natural state of maturity. This can take 10 to 15 years in the case of fast-growing flowering shrubs, or up to 50 years in the case of a well-maintained evergreen garden. Shade trees are in a class all by themselves: they often last many generations before they need replacing.

Not to be discounted is the lawn. The lawn is the wrapping of the landscape package or, as I like to describe the front yard, the welcoming mat that creates a lasting first impression.

The "ornamentals" discussed in this book add up to what most of us think of as a "home landscape". This section is a thorough compilation of the many hardy, woody (and non-woody) plants a Canadian gardener should consider before making the very important decision about what permanent plants to place in her yard.

Make special note of the hardiness, soil, and light requirements, as indicated by the symbols included, then cross-reference with the Climate Zone Map.

Then, go to it! And may the permanent plants in your landscape truly improve each successive year – which they will, given proper selection, planting, and year-to-year maintenance.

CHAPTER 8

LAWNS

Recently, I learned that golf course greenkeepers are among the highest-paid professionals in the horticultural industry. Like a good chef at a high-class restaurant, the greenkeeper can make or break the reputation of a course among finicky golfers.

It's small wonder. The turf must withstand very heavy foot traffic. The putting greens must be smooth and flat, almost like a billiard table, so as not to deflect the path of a small, dimpled white ball as it rolls toward the hole.

Some homeowners seem to emulate golf course greenkeepers. They strive for a lawn that looks as good all season as it did after the first cut in spring.

I admire these dedicated souls, but I don't exemplify them. You see, my lawn is the gift-wrapping to my garden, not the present inside. My lawn has to look good enough to complement the rest of the landscape – and it has to be tough enough to withstand all the play, work, and other activity which takes place on it – but it doesn't have to be perfect.

Therefore, this chapter won't tell you how to produce a golf green, but it will tell you how to enjoy a good-looking lawn that meets your needs without breaking your back, or your bank account. It includes some valuable shortcuts to lawn care which will free you to spend more time getting your hands dirty in the rest of your garden.

The chapter also includes a review of alternative ground covers. Although no ground cover can meet the rigorous demands you impose on your lawn, they have their place, in dense shade, where a tough, green lawn is virtually impossible to maintain.

Your lawn: A gentle green welcome mat that sets the stage for house and garden, and provides a rugged surface for family activities.

RULE OF THUMB

Avoid highly soluble fertilizers, which are available in liquid or granular form. They are like fast food. Just as a sugar doughnut gives you a burst of energy, fast-release heavy-weight fertilizers green up your lawn very quickly. But the effect is short-lived. And your grass develops a shallow, lazy root system. It becomes dependent on more and more fertilizers "fixes". Look instead for slow-release fertilizers with natural source nitrogen or sulphur-coated urea.

THE SECRET TO HEALTHY GRASS

Healthy grass out-competes most weeds, and resists pests and diseases. If you adopt good turf maintenance practices, your lawn can kick its dependence on manufactured chemical pesticides and fertilizers. You'll have a great lawn, and you'll feel happier watching your children and pets play on grass grown without harmful toxins. It may take two or three seasons to make the transition from chemical dependence to organic resilience, and you may have to put up with some pests in the interim, but it will be worthwhile.

Soil

Good soil, rich in nutrients and beneficial organisms, produces strong, healthy, pest-resistant grass. See Chapter 2 for more information on soil preparation.

If you are creating (or re-creating) a lawn from scratch, you can get top quality soil by amending it as required. Good sandy loam topsoil should be free of stones and other debris, and it should crumble easily when it's moist. If your soil is more like pudding than chocolate cake, it needs more organic material. Peat moss is considered best, but peat moss mixed with composted manure or leaf mould will do the job for soil with adequate sand content.

Spread 2 in. (5 cm) of organic material on top, and work it into the top 6 in. (15 cm) of the soil. You can do the job by hand with a garden fork and rake, but it's hard work. A rotary tiller with the tines in the back and powered wheels in the front is easiest to operate.

If your yard is slippery when wet and dries hard as rock, you probably don't have *any* topsoil. Don't even try to fix what's there. Buy 4 to 6 in. (10 to 15 cm) of good, weed-free sandy topsoil and spread it on top. Pay special attention to the drainage, making sure that water drains *away* from your home.

If necessary, use ground limestone to lower the soil pH to 6.5. If you are adding synthetic chemical fertilizers, use a high phosphorus starter formula such as superphosphate 0-20-0.

For large lawns, a fertilizer spreader ensures an even layer of fertilizer with a minimum of water.

WHEN TO APPLY FERTILIZER

April-May

Get your lawn off to a strong start with a formula like 21-7-7 (slow-release) at 5 lbs./1000 sq. ft. (2 kg/100 sq. m) and make two applications six to eight weeks apart to reduce the danger of burning.

July-August

Your lawn has a reduced appetite for nitrogen through the summer months. Apply a formula like 10-6-4 (slow-release) at 5 lbs./1000 sq. ft. (2 kg/100 sq. m). Apply only when your lawn is "active" – not during a drought. Water in thoroughly, or apply before a good rain.

September-November

I have always contended that this is the most important time to apply fertilizer. Just as a bear eats most heavily when it is preparing to hibernate, your lawn needs a good feeding before it takes a four-month rest. Apply 10-5-20 (*extra* slow-release) in October through mid-November.

Hand mower (left) and power mower: The scissor blades of the hand mower are gentler, and the quiet is welcome. But the power rotary mower does a better job of levelling tall weeds and over-long grass.

Fertilizing

Grass needs a great deal of the three main nutrient elements – nitrogen, phosphorus, and potassium. Nitrogen makes your lawn green, phosphorus produces healthy roots, and potassium builds hardiness. Grass also needs calcium, magnesium, and the other elements, but it can usually gather them unassisted from the soil, air and water.

On the other hand, composted organic material or premium quality, slow-release fertilizers act like a complete balanced meal – including the dessert. These amendments may cost more than the heavyweight fertilizers (unless you make the compost yourself), but they last so much longer they are actually a better buy. They won't burn your lawn if you apply a little too much. If applied in late autumn (October or November) they will hold back some nutrients to release in early spring, when the lawn is too wet for a new feeding. Look for a slow-release lawn fertilizer that contains sulphur-coated urea.

Mowing

Never cut grass by more than one third its length. The lower blades of grass, which have been shaded, might get burned by the sun. The only time you should cut your grass shorter (but not too short!) is the last time you mow in the fall. This helps to prevent snow mould by eliminating tops that might fall under the weight of snow and moulder. Rake all the clippings before the snow flies.

Always mow when it's dry. Wet grass sticks together then lies down when the mower wheels roll over it, resulting in an uneven cut.

Newly planted lawns should be allowed to grow to 2 in. (5 cm) or more before they are mowed. Test the earth for softness and wait until it is firm enough to support the mower.

Keep the blades of your mower sharp. A hand reel-type mower is best. It's light and its scissor blades are gentler than the blades of a rotary mower.

Mowing slopes can be tricky. Mow across the slope, starting at the bottom until it gets too steep to hold a straight line. Then mow down from the top. That way, if you stumble and let go of the mower, it's not going to run over you. A friend used to get his brother to stand at the top of the hill holding the other end of a rope tied to the mower. With that extra support, he could mow across the slope right to the top.

If clippings are over 1 in. (2.5 cm) long, they should be raked and thrown on the compost. Otherwise, they should be left as a nutrient-rich mulch. If you remove clippings regularly, you will have to fertilize to compensate for the loss of nutrients. Some power mowers can chop grass clippings into small "digestible" pieces for use as mulch.

RULE OF THUMB

Here's some good news for people who hate to cut the lawn: grass should be left relatively long – at least 2 1/2 in. (6 cm). If you keep grass long, especially when it's hot and sunny, you promote stronger roots and spreading.

Watering

If your lawn turns brown, this is a pretty good sign that it has become "dormant" due to lack of water. After a rain, you can sometimes see the colour coming back as if someone were turning up a light. But you can also tell your lawn is thirsty if the grass loses some of its strength and doesn't spring back after you walk on it, or if the colour turns from bright green to a dull blue-green.

Short, frequent watering encourages shallow roots, which die as soon as the weather turns really hot. Keep your lawn lush all summer by watering deeply and less frequently. Apply at least 1 in. (2.5 cm) of water every week. The water should soak to a depth of 1 ft. (30 cm) in good topsoil – deeper in sand and shallower in clay, but in any case deep enough to promote deep root development where the ground stays cool.

To avoid evaporation, water in the evening, or in the morning before the sun gets hot.

But don't expect your lawn to grow fast all season long. Lawns are like people – they need a rest now and then, especially in late June. This is the natural time for grass to go to seed, followed by a period of dormancy.

RULE OF THUMB

To figure out how long you need to leave your sprinkler in one spot, set a couple of pans on the lawn, and time how long it takes them to fill with 1 in. (2.5 cm) of water. As a rule of thumb, leave an oscillating sprinkler on for an average of 2 to 2 1/2 hours at a time on average soil. Impulse sprinklers may take a half hour more to cover a larger area as thoroughly as an oscillating sprinkler.

Aerating

With the passage of time, heavy foot traffic, and hundreds of rainfalls, the soil under your lawn becomes compressed, crowding the roots and attracting weeds. Use an aerator to open up the soil. Aerators have sharpened tubes that lift up plugs of earth, leaving hundreds of little holes about 3/8 in. (1 cm) in diameter and 2 to 3 in. (5 to 7.5 cm) deep. These holes, which are familiar to golfers, cave in and loosen the soil under the grass. Aerate once a year, in fall or spring. Apply compost and new seed as needed. I normally don't recommend aerating until a lawn is five years old, unless it is a heavy traffic area.

You can also reduce soil compaction by top-dressing with sand and sieved compost.

Dethatching

Grass spreads by rhizomes – thick rootlike stems that grow out from each plant to start new plants every inch (2.5 cm) or so. A healthy lawn grows such a mat of these rhizomes that air, water, and fertilizers can have difficulty reaching the roots. Thatch also encourages diseases and insects.

Thatch becomes a problems when it gets thicker than 1/2 to 3/4 in. (13 to 21 mm).

This problem can be remedied by raking, or by using a dethatcher. A dethatcher is a machine with vertical knives to cut through the thick thatch of grass and lift bits of it to the surface. Dethatchers are available from most rental stores.

If you have been caring for a lawn for three or more years and you have never dethatched it, do it this year. Once very three to five years should be plenty.

Dethatch in fall or spring. Unfortunately, dethatching is often followed by a

Dethatching with a rake cuts through lawn thatch, improving access to roots for air, water and nutrients. But be careful not to overdo it.

With work, a lawn suffering from weeds and bare patches can usually be refurbished.

flush of weeds, because it gives weed seeds a place to call home. Top dress with 1/4 in. (6 mm) of topsoil or soilless mix, and overseed your lawn with fresh grass seed. Keep well watered until germinated.

Weeds, pests and diseases

A weed-free lawn is an unrealistic goal, and is often unnecessary. Clover, for example, is actually beneficial because it fixes nitrogen in the soil. Establish your tolerance levels for weeds, then monitor your lawn regularly – at least once a week – to ensure weeds don't exceed acceptable levels.

Common lawn weeds include Dandelion, Crabgrass, and Wild Morning Glory. Most can be controlled through careful mowing, digging, pulling and aeration. A forked knife on a long handle is useful for digging out the roots after a rainfall or heavy watering.

Also watch for pest infestations during regular monitoring. Insect pests affecting lawns include aphids, ants, caterpillars, chinch bugs, cutworms, and white grubs. Lawns may also be afflicted by diseases such as slime mould, snow mould, rust fungi, dollar spot, and mildew. For information on these weeds, pests, and diseases see the appendix to this book.

Refurbishing a lawn

If you lawn has been taken over by weeds (more than 50 per cent of the vegetation), it may need major repair. Some gardening books recommend that you blanket your yard with a broadleaf chemical herbicide, like 2-4-D, combined with other chemical herbicides, to get rid of all the weeds so you can start fresh. As a non-chemical alternative, dig out the weeds manually. In areas of concentrated weed growth, dig up the lawn and start from scratch, carefully removing all weeds. Alternatively, cover the patch with black plastic for a week or ten days. That should be long enough to kill the vegetation.

Rake any leaves, sticks, dog bones, and so on. Level the site, filling the valleys with topsoil and leaving the hills alone. High spots in your lawn dry out quickly and are scalped by the lawn mower. Valleys are flooded, drowning grass roots or placing them under stress.

Spread 1/4 to 1/2 in. (6 to 12 mm) of fresh topsoil or a soilless mix over the entire lawn. Sow with a suitable grass seed mixture, and keep the area well watered. Sow heavily on the prepared barren areas, cover them lightly with peat moss, then roll them and keep them evenly moist until the seeds germinate. If you have children or cats, cover the seeded areas with dead branches to prevent foot traffic.

If you're filling in bare patches with sod, cut well into the surrounding grass so you don't have a thin spot around the sod. Cut the sod to fit the hole, set it down, and press it in place by standing on it with flat-soled shoes.

Water is essential to the growth of new grass. Grass seed must be kept cool and moist in order to germinate, then maintained at a constant level of moisture once it has started growing until the roots get well down into the earth.

Sod, too, needs to establish roots well into the earth before it can take a little parching. You've got to soak right down into the topsoil beneath.

SEED AND SOD

Your lawn should be seeded or sodded with competitive grass species. If one species is damaged, the other will usually continue to grow.

For a lawn in the sun, use a seed mixture of Canada #1 Kentucky Bluegrass (at least 50 per cent), Creeping Red Fescue (about 25 per cent), and Perennial Ryegrass (about 25 per cent).

For a lawn in the shade, use a mixture of Creeping Red Fescue (40 to 60 per cent), Kentucky Bluegrass (30 to 35 per cent), and Perennial Ryegrass (15 to 25 per cent).

Laying a Sod Lawn

1. Rake out the surface to ensure that it is level, smooth and free of rocks and debris.

2. As you roll out the sod, use a plank to kneel on already sodded areas if the sod is wet or soft. Make sure to lap the edges of sod layers together tightly.

3. When laying joints together, overlap one surface, and then cut with a knife so that the edges butt together tightly.

4. Roll over the sod surface with a heavy water-filled roller to ensure firm soil-root contact, then water heavily and frequently.

Starting a new lawn

Before you set out to create a whole new lawn, make sure it's necessary. If half your yard is grassy, you're better off to refurbish than start over. It's less work, less expensive, and faster. But if the soil under your lawn is so heavy with clay it strangles all your new grass, or so light with sand that the grass just dries up and blows away as soon as the sun hits it, then dig up your lawn and replace it from scratch.

It's important to clean up all the weeds. Even 1 in. (2.5 cm) of Quack or Twitch grass rhizome can reproduce, creating headaches later.

Prepare and amend the soil as described in the soil section above. Dig and level. Attach a rope to both ends of a plank and drag it across the area in order to find the high and low spots that need further levelling with the rake.

Planting a Lawn from Seed

1. Rake out the area to remove stones and level the surface. Spread lawn seed evenly over the surface.

2. Lightly rake over the surface to ensure that the seed is covered and just below the surface.

3. Cover with a thin layer of peat moss. The peat moss keeps the seed from blowing away, and also helps retain moisture .

4. Compact and smooth the surface with a heavy water-filled roller.

Roll it and rake it again. Don't use a heavy roller to do this – you want just enough weight to compress the soil you have levelled. Be careful not to overly compact your soil, pushing out all useful pores in the soil in which oxygen is exchanged for moisture. If there are any high and low spots left, rake and roll again, since even a small depression can cause uneven distribution of grass seeds.

You have two choices: seed or sod. Sod is faster to put down and looks like a lawn right away, but it is more expensive. Seed is more economical. And there is an added advantage – you have more control over the mix of varieties, and you know what variety of grass to sow if you ever have to repair your lawn.

Pick any nice weekend from mid-August through mid-September. Cooler weather is best. Seed as described in the seed section above, or lay down sod, taking special care to water generously and protect the new lawn from foot traffic.

CHAPTER 9

GROUND COVERS

Awkward spaces or gaps are a scourge to gardeners. Ground covers are an ideal solution for those blank or troublesome spaces in a landscape which are weedy or otherwise difficult to maintain.

Gardeners who dislike mowing lawns may find a ground cover more to their liking. Ground covers are commonly used to control erosion on inclines, provide colour beneath trees or shrubs, hide the foliage of bulbs in decline, and generally serve as a filler for empty spaces.

Ground covers are distinguished by their ability to naturalize and form colonies. Some species are particularly rampant growers. They suppress weeds and require little maintenance. But, given the right conditions, many plants can be encouraged to spread and form dense clumps. Perennial Geranium, Campanula, and various herbs can form immense borders and provide lovely colour, texture and scent, even though they are seldom sold as ground covers or listed in the literature as such.

Ground covers provide a colourful and multi-textured alternative to lawns.

Frustrated with the demands of lawn care and limited space, big city gardeners have set the standard for imaginative use of ground covers. But they can be equally useful in a small urban rectangle and a generous country lot.

Ground covers should create a rug-like effect. To encourage rapid growth you need to be very careful to select site-appropriate plants and to prepare the bed thoroughly. Weeds, unsuitable light conditions, inadequate moisture, and poor soil conditions will all impede rapid establishment. Gardeners dealing with a steep slope face potential erosion problems if their ground cover fails.

Mulch newly planted ground covers, especially those on inclines. Cold areas and low-lying regions may need winter protection as well. Use an organic mulch such as well-shredded tree bark, Cocoa Bean shells, or mulched leaves.

GROUND COVERS

Descriptions and requirements

English Ivy is excellent for carpeting the ground in dense shade.

Bearberry Cotoneaster

(Arctostaphylos)

An excellent low-growing evergreen, Bearberry Cotoneaster grows in spreading mounds that are not partial to pruning, so allow them adequate space. This plant issues small flowers, followed by bright red berries. These contrast well with its glossy, dark green foliage. It grows in full sun and is ideal for use on slopes, though it is somewhat slow growing. Cotoneaster is unique among evergreens in that it prefers neutral or alkaline soil. Hardy to Zone 5.

Bugleflower

(Ajuga reptans)

A low-growing runner, *Ajuga* produces clusters of blue, white, or pink flowers atop short stalks in spring. Varieties with variegated leaves provide colour all summer long. They will grow in sun but absolutely require moist soil, which is more likely to be found in partial shade.

Ajuga is a member of the Mint family which boasts many genera ideal for use as ground covers. These include Lamiastrum, Lamium, Nepata, Lavender and Salvia. Hardy to Zone 4.

(Previous page) Japanese Spurge (Pachysandra) is a large-leaved evergreen which requires moist, acid soil and partial shade.

Goutweed

(Aegopodium podograria)

There is probably no better known ground cover than this very successful relative of the Carrot, also known as Bishop's Weed. Its 1 ft. (30 cm) variegated leaves adapt to both sun and shade. There is not a more accommodating and easily grown ground cover.

Its umbel, or spike, of clustered white flowers identifies Goutweed as a relative of the wild Queen Anne's Lace and the blue annual Didiscus. Hardy to Zone 4.

Ivy

(Hedera)

Ivy is generally an excellent plant for carpeting ground in dense shade. It also clambers up rocks and walls. Two evergreen varieties – English Ivy (*H. helix*) and Baltic Ivy (*H.h. baltica*) are hardy throughout much of Canada but may require winter protection. They thrive only in rich, moist soils, preferring shade to strong sun. They are slow to establish, but strong growers after the third year. They are self-clinging, with semi-evergreen foliage. Hardy to Zone 5.

Japanese Spurge

(Pachysandra terminalis)

A large-leafed evergreen, Pachysandra is an exceedingly attractive and neat border plant, ideal for filling in gaps beneath trees or shrubs. It requires moist, acid soil and partial shade. Pachysandra attains a mature height of just 8 in. (20 cm) and spreads very gradually. A variegated form is available, but it is less vigorous.

Don't confuse Pachysandra with Euphorbia, also referred to as Flowering or Cushion Spurge. Its growing requirements are quite different. Euphorbia is partial to full sun and drier soil. Hardy to Zone 5.

Periwinkle

(Vinca minor)

Periwinkle is a mounding vine with glossy, dark green leaves and a distinctive bright blue flower that appears in May. Depending on the weather, Periwinkle may flower intermittently again in late summer. It loves shade and can form a 6-in. (15-cm) deep layer of trailing vines that spread continuously outward if provided with the right conditions.

Periwinkle grows best in rich, moist soil that is protected from direct sun. Encourage it to spread by eliminating competing vegetation. Provide a well raked weed-free bed, unencumbered by grass, and mulch well. Set new plants 1 ft. (30 cm) apart.

Like other perennial vines, Periwinkle benefits from a protective winter mulch in cold areas that may have inadequate snow cover. Hardy to Zone 4.

Plantain-Lily

(Hosta)

This mounding, graceful plant is appreciated more for its decorative foliage than its inconspicuous, stalked flowers. It grows outward in clumps and come in many variegated forms. Provide Hosta with rich, moist soil and partial shade for the best results. Propagate by dividing clumps in early spring and fall. The Hosta family includes hundreds of varieties, so take your time shopping for one best suited to your garden.

Hosta is Lily, a family which includes another robust grower often used as a ground cover, Daylily. Hardy to Zone 4.

Snow-in-summer

(Cerastium tomentosum)

This popular rock garden plant produces cascades of small white flowers on spreading stems. Its silvery foliage often needs cutting back. *Cerastium* spreads best in full sun and requires good drainage.

It is a member of the Pink family, which includes other fast-growing ground cover plants: Saponaria, Gypsophila, and many varieties of Dianthus. Hardy to Zone 2.

Stonecrop

(Sedum)

Sedum is a prolific succulent that comes in many forms and colour combinations. It trails low to the ground over slopes and rocks. It appreciates poor soil and sunny, dry locations. Its fleshy leaves often take on a red glow as cold weather approaches. Propagate by division year round. Hardy to Zone 3.

Crown Vetch

(Coronilla varia)

Vetch is a high-growing member of the Bean family that trails and flowers abundantly. Its mauve-pink blossoms resemble Clover and are ideal for attracting bees. Vetch is often perfect to control erosion on steep hillsides. It is invasive and spreads both by seed and roots. It's quite adaptable and tolerates most conditions.

Crown Vetch is a legume – it attracts bacteria which collect and store nitrogen nodules in the roots. If the plant is used as a green manure and ploughed under, the nodules decay and add nitrogen to the soil. Hardy to Zone 3.

Wormwood

(Artemisia)

The silver-grey and fringed foliage of this herb is ideal for hot, dry sites. Many varieties emit a spicy, pungent odour. They vary in mature height from 4 in. to 5 ft. (10 cm to 1.5 m).

Artemisia shares membership in the Daisy family with several other ground covers: Achillea or Yarrow, Chamomile, Ligularia, Santolina, and Centaurea, including Dusty Miller. Hardy to Zone 4.

RULE OF THUMB

Estimating coverage with ground covers is sometimes a mug's game. Before embarking on a massive planting programme create a test bed of the specimen you've selected. Then you'll have a better idea of how it will respond to the conditions in your garden, and you will be able to assess how much is needed.

RULE OF THUMB

There can be too much of a good thing when it comes to ground cover. Plants that spread don't know when to stop. Restrain growth by installing a barrier, like plastic lawn edging, at root level. Trim periodically. Remove flowerheads to limit self-sowing.

Versatile Boston Ivy, primarily used as a climbing vine or ground cover, once established provides a thick green cover that requires little maintenance.

CHAPTER 10

TREES

Trees provide many benefits – shade, colour, flowers, wind protection, fragrance, privacy screening, fruit, and a haven for birds or children. They come in an extraordinary range of shapes and sizes.

Trees cleanse and purify the air. They contribute oxygen to the atmosphere and consume carbon dioxide. They provide protection from the heat of summer and they'll help you save on winter heating costs by providing wind protection.

Trees define landscapes. They establish boundaries, frame the horizon, and lend *permanent* character to a garden. Their integral importance to landscaping demands that they be carefully selected.

Like a stock portfolio, trees are an investment in the future. When your investment matures, you'll have something beautiful to lean on while you watch the grass grow.

Don't forget to consider their unattractive features as well as their attractive ones. Weeping Willows may lend grace and grandeur to parks and golf greens, but they can quickly outgrow an ordinary suburban lot. Their invasive roots, plentiful leaves and allure for insects are apt to induce weeping in novice gardeners who plant them without thinking about these unwanted consequences.

A Weeping Willow looks gorgeous at the side of my in-laws' country pond; it would look ridiculous at the front of our suburban home.

Visit a garden centre to view stock, study shapes, and investigate what's new. It seems that a couple of new varieties become available every year,thanks to modern grafting and hybridization techniques. The great bulk of these are ornamentals, created by grafting traditional shrubs to treestock. Many are very new or rare, and you won't find them listed in books or catalogues. If you want to know what's new in trees, go exploring.

Touring well-stocked nurseries will give you an appreciation of the colour variation from tree to tree. Bark colour and texture often vary within the same family. Foliage colour may change markedly from the fresh colours of juvenile growth in spring to the mature leaf or needle colour in autumn. Tree blossoms can range from yellow, white, red, pink to purple or blue. Blossom colour can vary

greatly within species. The Malus and Prunus families, which comprise the Crabapples and Cherries, are perhaps the best examples.

If you are serious about making the right selection of shade tree (remember their permanence!) then pick up a couple of nursery catalogues from your local garden centres. And when buying, don't start too big. As a rule of thumb I like to plant shade trees that are no taller than 8 to 10 ft. (2.4 to 3 m); any bigger and you will pay more money to wait much longer for substantial new growth to develop. Young trees put down roots quickly. They also produce green top growth quickly.

Trees can provide a wealth of benefits, including colour and fragrance as well as shade, privacy, and dramatic effect, as in this street scene in Vancouver, B.C.

RULE OF THUMB

If you want a tall, straight tree, choose tall, straight nursery stock. The leader, or top growth, should not be forked, bent or broken. Damaged or badly pruned leaders will limit height and growth rate. As the tree matures forked joints can become so strained that they eventually split.

CARE AND MAINTENANCE OF TREES

Hardiness

Select trees that are designated hardy for the climate zone in which you live, as indicated for each of the trees listed below. Don't gamble with zone hardiness unless you have good reason to believe that your local microclimate is more moderate than the climate in your general area. A tree may survive an inhospitable habitat until a particularly severe winter comes along, or it may linger for years, terminally ill. Trees planted outside of their recommended zones can fall prey to insects and disease which would normally not afflict them.

Purchase only from a respected garden centre. Most reputable nurseries in Canada guarantee their treestock for one year following purchase. They take great care in selecting specimens known to transplant and winter well. Nursery staff can also be relied upon for advice about winter protection and other requirements. Nurseries often invest up 10 years or more raising tree saplings. With a commitment like that, you can be confident that everything possible will be done to deliver stock to you in prime condition.

The shape of things to come

Think ahead. Trees have a habit of growing up to obscure windows and shade gardens. If that's what you want, fine. Otherwise, choose trees that won't get in the way as they mature, or be prepared to follow an annual pruning and maintenance programme.

Trees grow in characteristic forms: pyramidal, rounded, pendulous, columnar, upright and spreading, or low-growing and spreading. Natural shape can be adjusted with pruning, but it's easier to choose a tree that is the right shape to begin with.

Upright, columnar trees are ideal for creating hedges and windbreaks, or for lining a driveway, but they can look oddly out of place towering above a ranch-style bungalow. Instead, choose low- or slow-growing forms, like Paper-birch, Dogwood, Hawthorn, Amur Maple, or Japanese Cherry.

Your choice of permanent shade tree will be your most important landscape decision.

Selecting a tree

"As the twig is bent, so grows the tree."

Trees are more apt to spread nicely if their branches are spaced evenly up and down and around the trunk. Unless you

Trees come in a variety of characteristic shapes, including pyramidal, rounded, pendulous, columnar, upright, and spreading, or low-growing spreading.

A Climbing Rose (right) intertwined through a Fir tree makes an unusual and striking combination in this Quebec garden.

RULE OF THUMB

Tree roots may be damaged during harvest or transport. If your nursery stores bare-rooted trees in a moistened top-dressing like sawdust, withdraw the tree and examine the roots yourself to determine their state of health. Otherwise, check the container for evidence of mistreatment. Avoid trees in broken or dented containers, or trees with burlap-wrapped rootballs that are split or lopsided. There may not be severe damage, but it is safer to choose containers in perfect condition. Why take unnecessary chances?

intend to plant along a fence or a wall, avoid lopsided nursery stock.

Examine young trees for nicks, cuts or bruises that may indicate rough handling. Small broken branches can be pruned but large damaged branches may cause long-term problems. Also avoid specimens with split or cracked trunks, if a significant amount of bark has worn or chipped off.

Transplanting

A young tree deserves the best possible care if it is to reach its potential.

When transporting nursery stock, lift young trees by their containers, not their trunks. Tender roots can be badly damaged if they are strained against the weight of moistened earth. Have a wheelbarrow handy to receive your new purchase when it's unloaded. You'll also need a shovel, a large square of canvas or polyethylene, pruning shears, guy rope or wire, stakes, a short piece of old water hose, compost or other organic soil amendment, planting fertilizer and water.

Your landscape plan tells you where your new tree will go, but there are some fine details that can only be settled when the tree is on-site. Strong, lower branches should be pointed away from paths. Branches don't move up as trees grow, so a limb 3 ft. (90 cm) up the trunk of a sapling will still be 3 ft. (90 cm) off the ground when your sapling has matured. Similarly, upper branches should be a minimum of 7 ft. (2.1 m) from the ground if you expect them to overhang a walkway.

Think twice about mature size and spread, listed below in each tree description. Don't plant too close to walls or other permanent structures. You may have to chop down a tree at its prime because it no longer fits the space you left for it. Double-check the planting chart and the tag that accompanies your purchase.

Plant an adequate distance from eaves and house walls to ensure that your tree will receive ample sun and water. Plant an adequate distance from other trees to avoid competition for available nutrients. When planting a grove or orchard, consider the full size your trees are likely to attain. Trees may look sparse when they are planted, but in time they will fill in. Be patient. It will pay off in the long run.

When to plant

The ideal time for tree planting is autumn, when young trees are dormant. Deciduous trees have then lost their leaves and evergreens have hardened their new growth in preparation for winter. Fall planting provides trees and

Planting a Tree

1. Before planting a tree in a fibre pot, cut slits in the side with a spade.

2. Remove the rim to avoid drawing moisture to the surface.

3. Amend the soil in the hole with moistened peat moss and composted organic matter.

many shrubs, including Roses, with an invaluable head start. It allows tree roots time to become established before freezing and it encourages new growth immediately when spring arrives.

Spring plantings are risky. Most plants are dormant only until very early spring. If your planting is delayed by frozen or wet ground you may lose a season's growth. Certain flowering trees, like Magnolias, can be so traumatized by late plantings that they will fail to bloom for a year or more. If you have no choice in the matter, spring plant only those plants grown in fibre containers. They can be put directly in the ground, which reduces the chance of transplant shock considerably by minimizing the disturbance to fine roots.

Digging

There's an old adage that a $5 plant needs a $50 hole. That's certainly true of trees. Holes should be twice as wide and half again as deep as the rootball. Put the soil from the hole into your wheelbarrow, or onto a canvas or heavy plastic sheet.

Next, fill the hole with water and let it drain. If water lingers after two hours you've got a drainage problem. You can either plant a tree that likes wet conditions, or you can improve the drainage. Sometimes you can do this simply by digging a bigger hole and amending soil to improve water absorption. If the problem is more extreme, consult Chapter 2 for a description of the available remedies.

Unless you're very lucky, the soil you have removed will require amending. Mix in moistened peat moss, composted manure, or composted vegetable matter (2 parts topsoil to 1 part peat and/or compost). Work together until the mixture is of a moist crumbly tilth and then begin back-filling around the rootball.

When planting in exposed locations, lean the tree about 5 degrees toward the northwest. As it grows it will eventually straighten out. Otherwise, it may appear to be blowing over backward in the wind.

Bare roots may need to be gently spread apart to encourage straight, even development. Roots that grow in a gnarled, twisted clump, without room to spread outward, can become so choked they strangle. Trim long roots to fit the hole. Clip any which are broken or discoloured.

Burlap-wrapped rootballs should be back-filled the same way. But untie and roll back the burlap so that it is well covered by amended soil. This will allow for more rapid growth and prevent the burlap from stealing moisture from the tree.

Plastic or metal containers are non-biodegradable and should be carefully removed and then discarded. If the plant

RULE OF THUMB

Position the tree so that the soil line of the trunk is 3 in. (7.5 cm) above the ground. The soil line is a mark where bark texture indicates what portion of the trunk was previously submerged in soil. Pack the back-fill with the ball of your foot, using the full weight of your body. If your soil is very heavy, you will have to remove it and replace it with fresh sandy loam or top soil. Again, add 1 part peat or compost to 2 parts soil. As a rule of thumb, if you need a pick axe, or if your shovel bounces off the "soil" surface when dry, you should replace it altogether.

4. Position the tree in the hole, creating a well in a circle around the trunk.

5. Fill the well with water, repeating as required over the next few days until the ground has hardened.

6. Stake new trees over 2 feet (60 cm) for at least the first year.

doesn't slip out easily, cut the container away. It is extremely important to minimize transplant shock, particularly for trees in leaf, by keeping roots and the soil that protects them undisturbed.

Fibre containers made of recycled newspapers decompose after their rims have been removed. They can be put directly in the ground. Cut slits down the sides to allow easier root extension. Position and backfill in the same manner as with bare root plantings.

Watering

For fall-planted trees, build a small wall of earth in a circle around your newly positioned tree, about the same radius as the roots. Fill the circle with water. In a few days, water again. If the surface soil dries out, repeat the process until the ground has hardened.

Saplings planted in spring need one soak with water alone, followed by an application of water combined with composted manure or 20-20-20 fertilizer. For the rest of the season, apply water regularly and ensure that the surface soil never dries out. Summer plantings need frequent watering to prevent severe leaf wilt. In the case of specimens planted in fibre pots, watering is a priority to speed the breakdown of the container. Mulch with a layer of straw compost, dry grass clippings or finely-ground bark to aid moisture-retention.

But don't overwater. You can drown your young trees. Enable them to make efficient use of the moisture they receive by shading them from intense heat, misting leaves with water, and applying thick mulches composed of leaves, Pine bark, Cocoa hulls or similar organic material.

Staking

New trees higher than 2 ft. (60 cm) should receive support for a minimum of one year to encourage straight, appropriate growth. Don't rely on a single stake pounded in next to the trunk to do the job. You could injure your tree rather than encouraging good growth. Instead, use three stakes and a guy rope. Place the stakes at a distance equal to half the height of your tree. Space them evenly around the tree and insert to a depth of 10 in. (25 cm) at a 45° angle. Be sure to tie a bright ribbon around the stakes about halfway down to avoid tripping over them.

Wrapping young trees and shrubs provides some protection against pests, diseases and the elements.

1. Secure the wrap at soil level with wire or rope and wrap upward in a diagonal fashion.

2. Wrap to desired height and secure with tie.

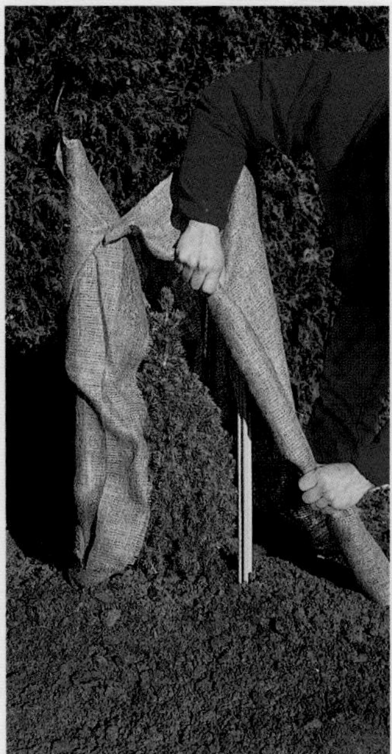

1. To protect shrubs against winter damage, install posts that are taller than the bush you want to protect.

2. Cover by wrapping mummy-fashion and folding over the tops so the top of the bush is completely covered.

DECIDUOUS TREES

Descriptions and requirements

For each variety I have indicated the harshest climate zone, the range of mature size in ft. and metres, and the shape of the foliage.

Alder

(Alnus)

Quick-growing, and native to moist habitats, Alder is a useful screen plant. Black Alder is the hardiest and best-known variety in Canada. Bright green leaves are preceded in early spring by catkins. This is a good bush or small tree for locations too wet for more desirable types.

Black Alder; *Zone 3; 40 to 50 ft. (12 to 15 m); upright*

Red Alder (A. oregona); *Zone 8; 30 to 50 ft. (9 to 15 m); conical*

White Alder (A. rhombifolia); *Zone 5; 40 to 65 ft. (12 to 19.5 m); pyramidal*

Ash

(Fraxinus)

Ash is a gardener's delight. It can withstand winds and pests, and it is able to tolerate a range of soil types, including fairly heavy clay. It is not difficult to establish, and it grows quickly. It provides yellow through to deep purple fall foliage.

It is one of the last trees in spring to leaf out and the first in autumn to drop its leaves. Fallen leaves may mat together and smother grass in autumn.

Green Ash (F. pennsylvanica lanceolata); *Zone 2; 40 to 50 ft. (12 to 15 m); spreading*

White Ash (F. americana); *Zone 3; 50 to 70 ft. (15 to 21 m); rounded*

European Weeping Ash (F. excelsior pendula); *Zone 5; 40 to 65 ft. (12 to 19.5 m); pendulous*

Flowering Ash (F. ornus); *Zone 7; 30 to 45 ft. (9 to 13.5 m); rounded*

Moraine Ash (F. holotricha 'Moraine'); *Zone 7: 30 to 45 ft. (9 to 13.5 m); rounded*

Beech

(Fagus)

Beech, a native of Canada, is among the most stately and impressive of shade and lawn trees. It is a shallow-rooted plant that needs room to spread without interference – even a nearby hard-surfaced path can obstruct healthy growth. Derivatives of the European Beech are more popular because they transplant with greater ease. Nurserymen have produced forms which are purple, fern-leafed, pendulous and copper coloured. Check tags carefully to be sure you get the variety you want and hardiness appropriate to your area.

American Beech (F. grandifolia); *Zone 4; 60 to 100 ft. (18 to 30 m); pyramidal*

European Beech (F. sylvatica); *Zone 5: 40 to 70 ft. (12 to 21 m); multi-shaped*

Birch

(Betula)

Birch symbolizes the forest for many Canadians. It is among the cold-hardiest of all species. Birch has a short life – it tends not to live beyond age 25 – and it is prone to borer and minor infestations. But thanks to its great beauty, small size and bright yellow fall foliage, many gardeners grow it anyway, most with good results. Its white bark provides an ideal contrast to evergreens. Birch also performs well fairly close to a house.

Paper Birch (B. papyrifera); *Zone 2: 30 to 50 ft. (9 to 15 m); upright*

Gray Birch (B. populifolia); Zone 3; 15 to 25 ft. (4.5 to 7.5 m); conical

Cherry Birch (B. lenta); *Zone 4: 35 to 45 ft. (10.5 to 13.5 m); upright*

European White Birch (B. pendula); *Zone 2: 20 to 40 ft. (6 to 12 m); upright*

European (Cutleaf) Weeping Birch (B. pendula gracilis); *Zone 2: 20 to 40 ft. (6 to 12 m); pendulous.*

Youngi Ornamental Weeping Birch (B. verrucosa pendula 'Youngii'); *Zone 4; 12 to 14 ft. (3.6 to 5.2 m); pendulous*

White Birch is popular for its distinctive bark and bright yellow fall foliage, and it grows well in most parts of Canada.

*(Previous page) The notched blossoms of a Red Dogwood (*Cornus florida rubia*).*

Umbrella Catalpa forms a naturally rounded head with pruning.

Catalpa

(Catalpa)

Catalpa is often called the Bean Tree because of the 1 ft. (30 cm) seed pods which follow immense white blooms in early summer. Leaves are an attractive heart shape. The Common variety is frequently used for ornament because it can be pruned to maintain a neat rounded or umbrella shape. Northern Catalpa grows rapidly to attain mature height and spread, easily withstanding pests, drought and clay soils. Look at the blossoms carefully and you'll notice the florets resemble tiny Orchids. Not coincidentally, Catalpa is a remote member of the Orchid family.

Common or Umbrella Catalpa (C. bignonioides); *Zone 5; 15 to 30 ft. (4.5 to 9 m); rounded*

Northern Catalpa (C. speciosa); *Zone 5; 40 to 70 ft. (12 to 21 m); rounded*

Cherry

(Prunus)

Prunus is a broad genus belonging to the Rose family, which boasts many of the finest flowering ornamentals, including Apricot, Almond, Peach and Plum. All have been developed for their beautiful blossoms at the expense of fruit. Some members of Prunus grow large enough to furnish shade, especially on the Pacific coast, but generally Prunus varieties are among the smallest ornamentals. Transplant shock can delay blossoms in the year following planting. To promote the next year's bloom, prune radically. Plant in full sun.

Flowering Almond (P. triloba); *Zone 3: 5 to 15 ft. (1.5 to 4.5 m); spreading*

Higan Cherry (P. subhirtella); *Zone 6; 20 to 35 ft. (6 to 10.5 m); weeping*

Purpleleaf Sand Cherry (P. cistena); *Zone 3; 5 to 25 ft. (1.5 to 7.5 m); rounded*

Sargent Cherry (P. sargentii); *Zone 5; 20 to 40 ft. (6 to 12 m); rounded*

Japanese Cherry (P. serrulata 'Kwanzan'); *Zone 6-9; 20 to 30 ft. (6 to 9 m); vase-shaped*

Purple Leaf Plum (P. cerasifera pissardi); *15 to 25 ft. (4.5 to 7.5 m); rounded*

Chestnut

(Aesculus)

Chestnut is prized for its nuts, for its shade, (cast by its palm-like leaves), and for its large flowerheads of white, light yellow, and red, which grow upwards. Varieties differ in the colour and form of their flowers. Only the Ohio Buckeye colours in fall. Chestnut is a good city tree, particularly the sterile Baumann's variety, which produces lovely double-blooms but not nuts. Once it becomes established, Chestnut resists pollution. It can adapt to various soil types so long as it receives sufficient water. Most parts of this tree are poisonous, including the raw fruit. Buds are large and very sticky. Chestnut does not transplant easily, so plant only specimens under 8 ft. (2.4 m) tall. You will find it grows rapidly once

Chestnut is prized for its flowers and its palm-like leaves.

established.

Common Horse Chestnut (A. hippocastanum); *Zone 5; 40 to 70 ft. (12 to 21 m); rounded*

Baumann Horse Chestnut (A. h. baumannii); *Zone 5; 40 to 70 ft. (12 to 21 m); rounded*

Ruby Horse Chestnut (A. carnea briotti); *Zone 5; 30 to 45 ft. (9 to 13.5 m); rounded*

Ohio Buckeye (A. glabra); *Zone 2; 20 to 30 ft. (6 to 9 m); rounded*

Crabapple

(Malus)

There are too many varieties of Crab to list them all here. This immensely colourful and varied species includes trees that are miniature, conical, and pendulous. Blossoms may be single or double, and are found in every gradation of hue from white to red. Leaf colours vary from green to purple to bronze. Even the fruit, produced in alternate years in some varieties, boasts a range of colours. Look for specimens that are scab- and disease-resistant. All do well given a sunny location and moderately acidic soil. Some of the most prolific Crabs are prairie-bred and extremely hardy. Check carefully to be sure you get a variety that suits your climate and landscaping intentions. Some Canadian introductions have large edible fruits. Dolgo produces good canning fruit.

Dolgo Crabapple (M. 'Dolgo'; *Zone 2; 35 to 40 ft. (10.5 to 12 m); spreading*

Japanese (Showy) Crabapple (M. floribunda); *Zone 5; 25 to 30 ft. (7.5 to 9 m); rounded*

Profusion Crabapple (M. 'Profusion'); *Zone 2; l2 to 20 ft. (3.6 to 6 m); spreading*

Royalty Crab Apple (M. 'Royalty'); *Zone 2; 15 to 20 ft. (4.5 to 6 m); spreading*

Dogwood

(Cornus)

Dogwood attains true tree form only in the warmest parts of Canada. Elsewhere, it tends to be grown as a large shrub. Its entrancing and long-lived blooms are irresistible. The lovely star-shaped blooms of the Pacific Dogwood grace autumn as well as spring. However, when they are planted out of their zone, members of the Dogwood family may not bloom, or even survive.

Flowering Dogwood (C. florida); *Zone 6; l0 to 25 ft. (3 to 7.5 m); spreading*

Red Dogwood (C. florida rubra); *Zone 7; 10 to 20 ft. (3 to 6 m); spreading*

Japanese Dogwood (C. kousa); *Zone 6; 15 to 30 ft. (4.5 to 9 m); upright*

Pacific Dogwood (C. nuttallii); *Zone 8; 20 to 50 ft. (6 to 15 m); conical*

Silverleaf Variegated Dogwood (C. alba 'Elegantissima'); *Zone 5; 6 to 8 ft. (1.8 to 2.4 m); rounded*

Red Twig (Native) Dogwood (C. stolinifera); *Zone 4; 8 to 10 ft. (2.4 to 3 m); rounded*

Pagoda (Blue) Dogwood (C. alternifolia); *Zone 6; 8 to 15 ft. (1.4 to 4.5 m); shrub-like*

Cornelius Cherry (C. Mas); *Zone 3; 12 to 25 ft. (3.6 to 7.5 m); small rounded*

Elm

(Ulmus)

American Elm, among the grandest and most picturesque of all shade trees, is making a come-back in rural areas after it was nearly wiped out by Dutch Elm disease. The condition can be prevented by controlling the Japanese beetle which transmits it. The small-leafed Chinese Elm is a good ornamental tree on country properties, or ideal for use as a hedge. It is too aggressive for most suburban or city lots.

American Elm (U. americana); *Zone 3; 70 to 100 ft. (21 to 30 m); umbrella*

Chinese Elm (U. parvifolia); *Zone 5; 20 to 40 ft. (6 to 12 m); rounded*

Camperdown (Umbrella) Elm (Ulmus glabra 'Camperdown'; *Zone 3; umbrella-shaped*

Ginkgo

(Ginkgo)

A survivor of the ice age, Ginkgo (Maidenhair Tree) is a reliable, hardy tree. It tends to grow slowly. It has a conical shape when young, but spreads out to become a rounded, handsome shade tree. Leaves are an unusual fan shape and are produced in clusters. Fall foliage is bright yellow. Purchase only male Ginkgoes to avoid having to clean up the disagreeable fruits produced by females. Ginkgo trees tend to grow extra-long branches. Shape the tree when it is in the 8 to 10 ft. (2.4 to 3 m) height range.

Maidenhair Ginkgo (G. biloba); *Zone 4; 40 to 100 ft. (12 to 30 m); spreading*

Hackberry

(Celtis)

Hackberry is another native tree known for its pest-resistance and tolerance to varied growing conditions. A distant cousin to the Elm, Hackberry is similarly used for shade and boulevard plantings.

Common Hackberry (C. occidentalis); *Zone 2; 25 to 65 ft. (7.5 to 19.5 m); rounded*

Hawthorn

(Crataegus)

There are several hundred species of Hawthorn. Most are hardy native trees and plant breeders have improved on

In most of Canada Dogwood is grown as a large shrub.

that natural advantage. Hawthorn is small and attractive, and has pretty flowers, edible fruit and brilliant fall foliage. Its sharp, hard thorns also make it useful as a barrier plant. Hawthorn is not fussy about soil but is difficult to transplant once it is grown higher than 6 ft. (1.8 m). It is prone to scab disease and some insect pests, and it is impossible to grow in a wet year.

Arnold Hawthorn (C. arnoldiana); *Zone 2; 20 to 25 ft. (6 to 7.5 m); rounded*

Toba Hawthorn (C. mordensis 'Toba'); *Zone 3; 10 to 15 ft. (3 to 4.5 m); rounded*

Washington Hawthorn (C. phaenopyrum); *Zone 5; 20 to 30 ft. (6 to 9 m); rounded*

Hickory
(Carya)

Hickory resembles a small Horse Chestnut. It casts light shade and bears edible nuts. Hickory is difficult to transplant and its yields will be diminished in colder regions.

Pecan Hickory (C. pecan); *Zone 5; 60 to l00 ft. (18 to 30 m); rounded*

Shagbark Hickory (C. ovata); *Zone 5; 50 to 90 ft. (15 to 27 m); irregular*

Honey Locust
(Gleditsia)

Honey Locust is a useful shade tree. It adapts well to transplanting and accepts most soil conditions, but it requires full sun for maximum growth. The varieties named below are thornless. Sunburst is useful in settled areas because it is both smaller and slow-growing. Its juvenile foliage is tinted yellow and gradually darkens. This is an open-branched tree that filters the shade but permits lawns to establish underneath.

Moraine Locust (G. triacanthos 'Moraine'); *Zone 4; 40 to 70 ft. (12 to 21 m); rounded*

Sunburst Locust (G. triacanthos 'Sunburst'); *Zone 5; 25 to 50 ft. (7.5 to 15 m); spreading*

Shademaster, (G. tricanthos 'Shademaster') *Zone 4; 35 to 40 ft. (10.5 to 12 m); rounded*

Skyline; (G. tricanthos 'Skyline') *Zone 4; 30 to 35 ft. (9 to 10.5 m); broad vase shape*

This Sunburst Honey Locust has a spreading habit. Its attractive gold-tinged foliage emerges in early spring.

Hornbeam
(Carpinus)

Noted for its resilient wood, Hornbeam (also called Blue Beech) is small and slow-growing, and lends itself to pruning. This makes it a good choice in urban settings. The pyramidal form of the European Hornbeam is especially attractive. The American variety requires light shade. Hornbeam can be difficult to transplant, so purchase saplings less than 6 ft. (1.8 m) tall.

American Hornbeam (C. caroliniana); *Zone 3; 15 to 35 ft. (4.5 to 10.5 m); rounded*

European Hornbeam (C. betulus); *Zone 6; 35 to 55 ft. (10.5 to 16.5 m); conical*

Ironwood
(Ostrya)

Ironwood is a slow-grower that dislikes being transplanted. Hence, it is seldom offered at nurseries. However, Ironwood closely resembles Elm, rarely outgrows its setting, and seldom needs pruning. Ironwood produces attractive ribbed fruits over a long period and is adaptable to many settings.

Hop Hornbean Ironwood (O. virginiana); *Zone 3; 15 to 35 ft. (4.5 to 10.5 m); rounded*

Katsura
(Cercidiphyllum)

Katsura's common name reflects its Japanese origins. Katsura produces small heart-shaped leaves which turn brilliant orange in fall. It grows slowly, and needs ample moisture and full sun. Katsura can have multiple trunks or a single, upright leader. There are pendulous varieties.

Katsura (C. japonicum); *Zone 5; 20 to 50 ft. (6 to 15 m); conical*

Kentucky Coffee Tree
(Gymnocladus)

This tree produces few branches and boasts unusually large leaves composed of many tiny leaves. Its name derives from its brown seed pods, which don't resemble Coffee in either appearance or taste. Virtually pest-free, the tree adapts well to most soils but requires moisture,

The Saucer Magnolia, with its soft pink blooms make the perfect Mother's Day gift.

full sun, and wind protection. Bark is heavily ridged.

Kentucky Coffee Tree (G. dioica); *Zone 5; 30 to 70 ft. (9 to 21 m); spreading*

Laburnum

(Laburnum)

The pendulous blossoms of Laburnum (Golden Chain Tree) are Wisteria-like, but yellow. It's useful as a small centrepiece in the garden or it can be trained espalier-fashion along a wall or fence. Provide a sheltered, moist location. All parts of the Laburnum are toxic. Remove seed pods to encourage growth and improve appearance.

Golden Chain Laburnum hybrid (L. watereri or L. vossi); *Zone 5; 20 to 30 ft.(6 to 9 m); rounded*

Linden

(Tilia)

Linden is a fragrant shade tree with many uses. Its blossoms are used in perfume, soap and honey. Its heart-shaped foliage is edible and yellows in fall. Europeans traditionally used the bark to make cord. The Little-Leaved Linden, known in various forms as Cordata, produces compact, rounded or pyramidal foliage which lends itself to city planting. American Linden is larger and provides better shade but, like Silver Linden, is less inclined to tolerate city living.

American Linden (T. americana); *Zone 2; 40 to 70 ft. (12 to 21 m); pyramidal*

Little-Leaved Linden (T. cordata); *Zone 3; 30 to 60 ft. (9 to 18 m); pyramidal*

Silver Linden (T. tomentosa); *Zone 6; 30 to 60 ft. (9 to 18 m); conical*

Locust

(Robinia)

Locust, often called Black Locust, grows rapidly, with an upright, spreading form. Its fern-like compound leaves are slow to emerge in spring and are accompanied by dangling flower clusters that are quite fragrant. Locust withstands extremely inauspicious conditions and can thrive in heavy clay soils as well as dry, sandy locations. It is prolific, and will sucker in lawns. Young suckers bear thorns.

Black Locust (R. pseudocacia); *Zone 4; 50 to 75 ft. (15 to 22.5 m); spreading*

Idaho Locust (R. 'Idaho'); *Zone 4; 20 to 35 ft. (6 to 10.5 m); pyramidal*

Magnolia

(Magnolia)

Few sights are more spectacular than a Magnolia in full bloom. Magnolia flowers in early spring, before it issues leaves, and then occasionally again in autumn. Early-flowering forms need protection from late frosts. Otherwise, Magnolia is pest- resistant and will do well if provided with shelter and moist, acid soil. Plant southwest of buildings or hillsides for protection. Transplant shock is common and new saplings may refuse to bloom for a few years. Saucer Magnolia makes a great gift for a mother. In Southern Ontario it will bloom reliably every Mother's Day.

Cucumber Magnolia (M. acuminata); *Zone 5; 40 to 80 ft. (12 to 24 m); rounded*

Merrill Magnolia (M. kobus 'Merrill'); *Zone 5; 20 to 50 ft. (6 to 15 m); spreading*

Saucer Magnolia (M. soulangiana); *Zone 5; 10 to 25 ft. (3 to 7.5 m); rounded*

Star Magnolia (M. stellata); *Zone 4; 8 to 10 ft. (2.4 to 3 m); rounded*

Maple

(Acer)

Few shade species are as distinguished or as well known as the Maple. Maple is an extremely large and varied genus – nurseries commonly stock as many as 20 different species, from the miniature Japanese Maple to the mighty Sugar Maple. The selection verges on mind-boggling. Maple comes in cutleaf, variegated, silver, red, purple, pendulous, columnar, vining, striped and paper-bark forms. It tends to be hardy and pest-resistant. Though Maple is resilient and can tolerate varied growing conditions, acid rain and other forms of pollution may cause damage, particularly to larger specimens. Most species other than Sugar Maple make good city trees.

Amur Maple (A. ginnala); *Zone 2; 15 to 25 ft. (4.5 to 7.5 m); spreading*

Box Elder Maple (A. negundo); *Zone 2; 25 to 60 ft. (7.5 to 18 m); rounded*

Norway Maple (A. platanoides); *Zone 5; 45 to 85 ft. (13.5 to 25.5 m); pyramidal*

Globe Maple (A. platanoides 'Globosum'); *Zone 5; 15 to 35 ft. (4.5 to 10.5 m); round*

Silver Maple (A. saccharinum); *Zone 5; 30 to 50 ft. (9 to 15 m); spreading*

Sugar Maple (A. saccharum); *Zone 4; 50 to 100 ft. (15 to 30 m); pyramidal*

Japanese Maple; *Zone 6; 10 to 30 ft. (3 to 9 m); spreading*

Mountain Ash

(Sorbus)

The wide, white blossom clusters of the Mountain Ash, also known as the Rowan Tree, appear in late spring, followed by a cluster of attractive orange berries. Some varieties have red berries, others have whitish-yellow berries. There are upright and pyramidal forms. The Mountain Ash grows best in full sun and prefers acid, well-drained soil. It occasionally requires treatment for boring insects, and is susceptible to fire blight disease. Pruning encourages fire blight.

European Mountain Ash (S. aucuporia); *Zone 3; 15 to 35 ft. (4.5 to 10.5 m); rounded*

Korean Mountain Ash (S. alnifolia); *Zone 4; 20 to 40 ft. (6 to 12 m); rounded*

Silver Maple is just one of the many popular species of Maple available at nurseries throughout Canada.

The Weeping Mulberry's pendulous branches hang almost to the ground. This tree is tolerant of most conditions.

Mulberry

(Morus)

Mulberry winters well and withstands dry conditions. Its fruit attracts birds but can litter walks and driveways. Thus non-fruiting males are preferred. Mulberry is tolerant of most conditions, and attains maximum growth if provided with ample moisture.

Russian Mulberry (M. alba tatarica); *Zone 3; 25 to 50 ft. (7.5 to 15 m); rounded*

Weeping Mulberry (M. albus pendula); *Zone 3; 25 to 45 ft. (7.5 to 13.5 m); pendulous*

Oak

(Quercus)

Few trees endure like Oak. It provides excellent shade and brilliant fall colour for many years. Most varieties prefer acid soil and are difficult to transplant when large. Fortunately, Oak grows slowly and suffer few pests. Larger Oaks should be given ample space to spread out. The pyramidal form of the English Oak is excellent for use in compact gardens.

English Oak (Q. robur); *Zone 5; 20 to 45 ft. (6 to 13.5 m); conical*

Pin Oak (Q. palustris); *Zone 4; 40 to 70 ft. (12 to 21 m); pyramid*

Red Oak (Q. borealis); *Zone 3; 50 to 80 ft. (15 to 24 m); rounded*

White Oak (Q. alba); *Zone 4; 50 to 80 ft. (15 to 24 m); rounded*

Pyramid English Oak (Q. robur fastigiata); *Zone 4; 40 to 50 ft. (12 to 15 m); columnar*

Olive

(Elaeagnus)

The distinct slender and silver foliage of a Russian Olive (Oleaster) gives it the appearance of a small willow. It produces fragrant yellow blossoms in spring, and silver-coloured fruit in autumn, and often has hairy twigs. Olive is a hardy, adaptable tree, and an ideal size for small gardens. Provide full sun and prune as needed.

Russian Olive (E. angustifolia); *Zone 2; 10 to 25 ft. (3 to 7.5 m); rounded*

Pears

(Pyrus)

A diminutive introduction from China, the Callery Pear (*P. calleryana*) produces prolific white flowers in spring and foliage that turns from bright green to burgundy in fall. Its puny fruit is suitable only for birds. The best-known variety is the Bradford Pear (*P. calleryana* 'Bradford'). It adapts well to city gardens. Plant in full sun.

Callery Pear (P. calleryana); *Zone 5; 15 to 25 ft. (4.5 to 7.5 m); conical*

Plane Tree

(Platanus)

Plane also goes by the names Sycamore or Buttonwood. Its leaves resemble a Maple but its seed pods are contained in multiple round balls. The bark has a distinct flaking habit. Plane grows quickly and is ideal for shade in large gardens. Tolerates drought and city conditions. Insect infestations are common but controllable.

American Plane (P. occidentalis); *Zone 4; 60 to 90 ft. (18 to 27 m); round*

London Plane (P. acerifolia); *Zone 5; 40 to 80 ft. (12 to 24 m); round*

Poplar

(Populus)

Poplar has an upright, columnar form that lends itself naturally to hedges and rows. It is sometimes known as Aspen or Cottonwood. Poplar grows rapidly but many varieties are susceptible to Poplar canker disease and die off by age 25. Gardeners often use Poplars as fillers until slow-growing, more permanent, specimens become established. Poplar roots are invasive and should be kept well away from walls, paths or drains. This tree is not fussy in its requirements.

Berlin Poplar (P. berolinensis); *Zone 2; 40 to 65 ft. (12 to 19.5 m); conical*

Bolleana Poplar (P. alba 'Pyramidalis'); *Zone 4; 25 to 50 ft. (7.5 to 15 m); conical*

Lombardy Poplar (P. nigra 'Italica'); *Zone 4; 50 to 80 ft. (15 to 24 m); conical*

Quaking Aspen Poplar (P. tremuloides); *Zone l; 50 to 80 ft. (15 to 24 m); conical*

Carolina Poplar (P. canadensis); *Zone 5; 40 to 45 ft. (12 to 13.5 m); round*

Redbud

(Cercis)

Redbud, often called the Judas Tree, is undeservedly little known. It greets spring with a multitude of tiny blossoms that cling like a mist to leafless branches. Blossoms are white pink or purple. A nice specimen tree, Redbud issues large, heart-shaped leaves late in the spring. Autumn foliage is yellow. Plant in sun when young, in moist, well-drained soil.

Eastern Redbud (C. canadensis); *Zone 6; 15 to 35 ft. (4.5 to 10.5 m); spreading*

Chinese Redbud (C. chinensis); *Zone 7; 10 to 25 ft. (3 to 7.5 m); spreading*

Redbud features pink buds followed by large heart-shaped leaves.

Tree of Heaven
(Ailanthus)

A rampant grower, the Tree of Heaven is frequently associated with inner cities where its large fern-type leaves are useful for screening. It is sometimes dismissed as a weed because of a tendency to produce multitudinous suckers. Male forms have a disagreeable flower odour. Though it is short-lived, the Tree of Heaven is impervious to most pests and will tolerate varied growing conditions.

Tree of Heaven (A. altissima); *Zone 6; 40 to 60 ft. (12 to 18 m); rounded*

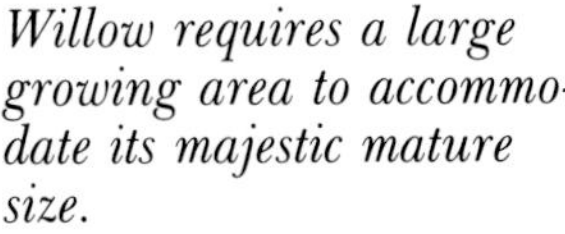

Willow requires a large growing area to accommodate its majestic mature size.

Tulip Tree
(Liriodendron)

This tree is named for its flower-shaped leaves and its yellow blossoms. Tulip Tree is native and grows to immense heights. It is an excellent choice for shade. Autumn foliage is an attractive yellow. Its cone-like fruiting heads are composed of winged nutlets. Plant in acidic, moist soil.

Tulip Poplar (L. tulipifera); *Zone 5; 50 to 90 ft. (15 to 27 m); rounded*

Walnut
(Juglans)

Walnut is planted for its fine shade and nuts. It is extremely hardy, and varieties of the Black Walnut produce good crops even where winter temperatures are very cold. Walnut emits toxins that poison nearby plants, especially Tomatoes. It is also immense at maturity. Allow Walnut plenty of space. At least two are required to produce a dependable crop. Plant young trees only as they have a tap root which grows as large as its top. Walnut requires moist and sunny locations.

Black Walnut (J. nigra); *Zone 3; 50 to 100 ft. (15 to 30 m); rounded*

English Walnut (J. regia); *Zone 7; 40 to 90 ft. (12 to 27 m); rounded*

Butternut (J. cinerea); *Zone 2; 40 to 90 ft. (12 to 27 m); rounded*

Willow
(Salix)

Willow is among the most widely admired shade trees. It grows quickly and provides an established appearance even to newly planted gardens. In late winter its branches take on a golden glow as they prepare to leaf out. The family includes the much- loved Pussy Willow. Willow is ideal for wet or moist areas, but it has invasive roots and should be provided with a very large growing area.

Thurlow Willow (S. elegantissima); *Zone 5; 25 to 45 ft. (7.5 to 13.5 m); weeping*

Weeping Babylon (S. babylonica); *Zone 7; 25 to 45 ft. (7.5 to 13.5 m); weeping*

White Willow (S. alba); *Zone 4; 50 to 75 ft. (15 to 22.5 m); weeping*

Yellowstem (S. alba vitellina); *Zone 3; 45 to 60 ft. (13.5 to 18 m); weeping*

Laurel Willow (S. pentandra); *Zone 2; 20 to 35 ft. (6 to 10.5 m); weeping*

EVERGREEN TREES

Descriptions and requirements

The tree descriptions below include a listing for the harshest climate zone, the adult size of the tree, and the tree shape.

(Previous page) Japanese Yew requires a well-drained site.

Conifers

There are seven conifer families. Four encompass all types appropriate to North American gardens. They are: Pine (*Pinaceae*), Juniper (*Cupressaceae*), Redwood (*Taxodiaceae*), and Yew (*Taxaceae*).

Within the four families are found well over 500 species. Multiple varieties of some have been developed to exploit all the colour, form and height variations that one could reasonably expect from an evergreen. Their numbers include wide-ranging types, from extreme dwarfs to the tallest, grandest trees in the world.

The family *Pinaceae*, which includes six genera, is perhaps the best-known conifer family. It includes Pine, Fir, Spruce, Hemlock, Douglas Fir and Larch. The other families have fewer subgroups and less range.

Common Cedar, or Arborvitae

(Thuja)

Thuja, known as Arborvitae or Common Cedar, is part of the *Cupressaceae* family along with Juniper. It is not really a Cedar. It is distinguished by its small, scale-type foliage and small cones. Hardy and quick growing, Common Cedar is popular for hedges. Colour is normally light green but golden and slow-growing forms are available. Its natural form is pyramidal but globe types make ideal accent plants. Alkaline soils and full sun are preferred. Arborvitae is susceptible to damage, including winterburn from drying winds. Soak the soil before freeze-up.

Eastern White Cedar, or American Arborvitae (T. occidentalis); *Zone 3; 15 to 50 ft. (4.5 to 15 m); pyramidal*

Giant or Western Red Cedar (T. plicata); *Zone 6; 150 to 200 ft. (45 to 60 m); pyramidal*

Globe Cedar; (T. occidentalis 'Globosa') *Zone 3; 2 to 3 ft. (60 to 90 cm); rounded*

Cedar

(Cedrus)

True Cedar is native to China and has a limited range in North America outside of B.C. and far-southern Ontario. It features large cones, held upright on branches that are pendulous in many varieties. Its short needles are borne in clusters. Growth is slow and it thrives only in sunny, warm sites.

Cedar of Lebanon (C. libani); *Zone 6; 40 to 90 ft. (12 to 27 m); columnar*

False Cypress

(Chamaecyparis)

Like its close relation, Juniper and Arborvitae, False Cypress has scale foliage that branches in graceful arcs. Foliage is soft and easily pruned. False Cypress' small cones are not easily noticed. Site in full sun with moist, acidic soil for the best results.

Hinoki (C. obtusa); *Zone 5; 65 to 75 ft. (19.5 to 22.5 m); columnar*

Sawara (C. pisifera); *Zone 4; 15 to 50 ft. (4.5 to 15 m); spreading*

Weeping False Cypress (C. nootkatensis 'Pendula'); *Zone 5; 7 to 10 ft. (2.1 to 3 m); mounding*

Fir

(Abies)

Most gardeners associate the fragrance and thick pyramidal shape of Fir with the traditional Christmas tree. Its whorled branches bear multiple short, flat needles which are blunt, with silver or white markings on their underside. Cones are large and held erect. Fir is quick-growing and can reach an enormous size, but it is unlikely to do so in cities. All varieties but White Fir are quite vulnerable to the effects of air pollution. Provide sun and moist, acidic soil.

Balsam Fir (A. balsamea); *Zone 1; 30 to 75 ft. (9 to 22.5 m); pyramidal*

Nikko Fir (A. homolepis); *Zone 3; 60 to 100 ft. (18 to 30 m); pyramidal*

White Fir (A. concolor); *Zone 4; 60 to 100 ft. (18 to 30 m); pyramidal*

Hemlock

(Tsuga)

A hardy native, Hemlock is useful for either specimen planting or hedges. It adapts well to shearing. Horizontal branches bear soft and short linear needles, rounded at the tip. Foliage is light green on the upper surface and silvery underneath. Cones are pendant and droop downward. Hemlock benefits from cool, moist conditions where protection is available. It will tolerate partial shade.

Canada Hemlock (T. canadensis); *Zone 4; 50 to 75 ft.; (15 to 22.5 m); pyramidal*

Sargent's Hemlock (T. canadensis pendula); *Zone 5; 5 to 15 ft. (1.5 to 4.5 m); weeping*

Juniper
(Juniperus)

The branching, mature foliage of Juniper is often accompanied by new growth in the form of sharply pointed needles. Juniper scales are arranged in tightly woven whorls grouped usually in three or four. The berry-like cones are usually a slate blue colour. Juniper foliage is often tinged gold or blue. Naturally columnar Juniper is most common but weeping and spreading forms are also popular. Tolerant of most soils, Juniper prefers a sunny, well- drained site.

Eastern Red Cedar (J. virginiana); *Zone 3; 20 to 50 ft. (6 to 15 m); conical*

Common Juniper (J. communis); *Zone 1; 6 to 12 ft. (1.8 to 3.6 m); spreading*

Mountbatten Juniper (J. chinensis 'Mountbatten'); *Zone 4; 5 to 15 ft. (1.5 to 4.5 m); pyramidal*

Rocky Mountain Juniper (J scopculorum); *Zone 2; 15 to 35 ft. (4.5 to 10.5 m); conical*

Bar Harbour Juniper (J. horizontalis); *Zone 3; 1 to 2 ft. (30 to 60 cm); spreading*

Pine
(Pinus)

The genus *Pinus* contains some of the tallest, longest-lived trees on earth. Long, sharp needles are borne in clusters of two to five. The size and placement of cones varies with the species. Some are pendant, others are borne upright. Pine comes in a range of shapes but typical forest varieties often have a pyramidal juvenile form which becomes rounded or spreads outward with maturity. Provide Pine with a sunny, well-drained site for best results. Soil type may vary. White Pine, Ontario's provincial tree, is the only species native to Canada and has a unique 5-needle cluster.

Austrian Pine (P. nigra); *Zone 2; 40 to 60 ft. (12 to 18 m); pyramidal*

Mugo Pine (P. montana mugo); *Zone 1; l to 5 ft. (30 cm to 1.5 m); spreading*

Scots Pine (P. sylvestris); *Zone 3; 50 to 70 ft. (15 to 21 m); pyramidal*

Red Pine (P. resinosa); *Zone 2; 60 to 80 ft. (18 to 24 m); pyramidal*

White Pine (P. strobus); *Zone 3; 60 to 80 ft. (18 to 24 m); pyramidal*

Spruce
(Picea)

Spruce is similar to Fir but can be distinguished by its sharper, more pointed needles and pendant cones. Foliage is thick and shaded blue in many popular varieties. Spruce does best in moist, sunny locations where it has ample room to spread. Limb development can be adversely affected by overcrowding.

Bar Harbour is a popular shrub form of Juniper.

Colorado Spruce, or Blue Spruce (P. pungens); *Zone 2; 60 to 100 ft. (18 to 30 m); pyramidal*

White Spruce (P. glauca); *Zone 2; 50 to 70 ft. (15 to 21 m); pyramidal*

Dwarf Alberta Spruce (P. glauca conica); *Zone 4; 5 to 7 ft. (1.5 to 2.1 m); pyramidal*

Norway Spruce (P. Abies); *Zone 3; 60 to 80 ft. (18 to 24 m); pyramidal*

Nest Spruce (P. Abies nidiformis); *Zone 2; l to 3 ft. (30 to 90 cm); spreading*

Yew
(Taxus)

Distinguished by its flat, sharp and bright green needles, Yew is versatile and popular for foundation plantings or as hedges. It is long-lived and its growth is easily controlled. In its native form it is low-growing and spreads widely, but it has been extensively developed to provide a multitude of shapes and growing habits. Cones resemble small nuts. Japanese female Yew produces bright red berries. Though it does well in either sun or shade, Yew absolutely requires a well-drained site.

Canada Yew (T. canadensis stricta); *Zone 3; 2 to 5 ft. (60 cm to 1.5 m); spreading*

Hicks Yew (T. media hicksi); *Zone 5; 4 to 10 ft. (1.2 to 3 m); columnar*

Japanese Yew (T. cuspidata capitata); *Zone 4; 12 to 20 ft. (3.5 to 6 m); spreading*

RULE OF THUMB

An old friend J.A. Weall often says "A hedge between makes friendship green." Evergreens make excellent permanent hedges. For sunny places try White Cedar (8-25 ft.) Hick's Yew (2-5 ft.) for shade and Hemlock for a large hedge or screen in shade (20-40 ft.)

CONIFER FOLIAGE

Many knowledgeable gardeners can't distinguish among evergreen families, let alone individual members of each family. Traditional misnomers have helped to foster confusion. For instance, the conifer most of us refer to as a Cedar is actually Arborvitae, or *Thuja*. True Cedar cannot withstand severe Canadian winters. Conifers like Larch or Bald Cypress that are deciduous add to the general confusion. Then there is the Douglas Fir, a *Pseudotsuga* more closely related to Hemlock than Fir.

But aside from a few oddities such as these, evergreens are really quite easy to sort out once you get to know them. They are a varied group, tremendously useful for landscaping purposes, so even a little knowledge is handy.

Evergreens are divided into two classes depending on their method of seed dispersal: conifers and broad-leaved evergreens.

Conifers are *gymnosperms*. They bear naked seeds, held usually by cones. Conifers also generally exhibit year-round foliage in the form of narrow needles. An exception is Larch (*Larix decidua*), a cone-bearing "evergreen" that drops its needles in autumn.

Conifers are much better adapted to Canadian winters. Their needle and scale foliage is narrow and limits moisture loss, allowing them to survive the drying winds and chill of severe climates.

Broad-leaved evergreens are *angiosperms*. Their seed is produced through flowering and encased by an ovary. Their ranks include some of the most revered and beautiful flowering plants, such as Daphne and Rhododendron.

Broad-leaved evergreens make better shrubs than trees. As a rule, they don't usually grow very large, nor do they adapt easily to typical Canadian winters.

Apart from cold tolerance, both groups of evergreens tend to favour similar growing conditions. The vast majority will tolerate a range of growing conditions but tend to prosper in typical forest conditions, on sites where moist but well-drained soil is available, in combination with filtered light. Several Pines, including Scotch Pine, prefer sandy, well-drained soil.

Hoopsie Blue Spruce: sharp, pointed needles, with a distinct blue hue.

White Spruce: sharp, pointed needles.

Juniper: flat scale-type foliage.

Hemlock: soft and short needles.

Colorado Spruce: similar to Fir, but with sharper, more pointed needles.

False Cypress: soft, scale foliage that branches in graceful arcs.

Common Cedar (Arborvitae): small scale-type foliage.

Yew: flat, sharp, bright green needles.

Spruce trees, including the Blue Spruce variety shown here, will grow in most zones in Canada.

CHAPTER 11
SHRUBS AND VINES

Someone once suggested to me that landscape design is more accurately termed "exterior design". An interior designer plans the inside of your home. A landscape designer plans your yard.

But I am tempted to consider landscape design – and in particular the use of shrubs and vines – more as an exercise in construction or renovation. Planting woody shrubs and vines is a relatively permanent commitment, like building a house or putting in a new kitchen. And if you don't believe me, ask somebody who has had to rip out established shrubs and vines. It's a lot of work.

For this reason, the use of shrubs and vines in your garden deserves special, studied attention. With the basics provided here, you can approach the job of planting a permanent landscape with some confidence. In addition, you will probably avoid some expensive and painful mistakes. Perhaps you'll save enough money as a result of reading this chapter to pay for this book several times over. At the same time, you will add substantially to the dollar value of your home.

But the real point of placing shrubs and vines in their proper place is not just to save money or make a good investment. It is to take full advantage of the colour, fragrance, form and year- round character of these plants. Shrubs and vines are the weavers in a home landscape. It is difficult to conceive an interesting or versatile landscape design without them. They connect flower borders to houses, obscure unsightly views, and increase privacy between neighbours. In my book, you can't put a price on that.

Jackman Clematis, with its deep purple blossoms, is the most reliable form of this plant for growing in a northern climate.

CARE AND MAINTENANCE OF SHRUBS

Like trees, shrubs produce thick, woody branches. But shrubs are shorter and seldom produce distinct leaders. Their stems begin to branch and develop foliated offshoots close to ground level.

Like trees, shrubs tend to have distinct shapes – rounded, weeping, upright or spreading. But shrubs offer all the advantages of trees without the size or shade. They are more easily shaped and arranged into hedges.

Deciduous shrubs make up for their autumn loss of foliage with spring and summer blossom displays. Broad-leafed evergreen shrubs differ from ordinary evergreen shrubs not just in their leaves but in their blossoms, which include some of the most beautiful and fragrant flowers in the world. A broad-leafed evergreen shrub has broad deciduous-looking leaves. Depending on the season, they will drop to the ground as they mature.

Planting shrubs

A shrub is a permanent planting. Its soil should be fully prepared as for other deep-rooted plants and amended thoroughly with organic materials, including moistened peat moss, mature compost, or composted manure. If your border incorporates several shrubs, add extra nutrients. Check moisture and pH levels and amend as required.

Ideally, shrubs should be planted when they are dormant. Fall is usually best, once foliage has begun to fade. Autumn rather than spring plantings favour maximum root development. Shrubs are less likely to suffer dehydration from heat and soil is not so inclined to be waterlogged.

The exception to the fall planting rule is a late-blooming shrub like Caryopteris or Buddleia, both of which are dormant in the spring but grow actively in the fall. In extremely cold areas spring plantings are also said to better prepare plants for the rigours of winter, especially when the plants originate in a much milder climate.

Planting dormant bushes gives you the opportunity to examine roots and start pruning even before the shrub is in the ground. Cut away soft or mushy sections, or areas that may be broken or discoloured. Root flesh should be creamy white and firm. Grey or brown portions should be promptly removed.

Prepare the site in advance by digging and marking off the space each shrub will need at maturity. To get an approximate measure of the appropriate distance between two shrubs, add the expected spread of each and divide in half. If one shrub will spread 6 ft. (1.8 m) and the next one will spread 2 ft. (60 cm), they should be planted 4 ft. (1.2 m) apart (6 + 2 = 8; 8/2 = 4).

Position shrubs so their best side faces out. Make sure they are planted at the same depth as in their nursery container, matching the soil line on the stalk with the ground level. If shrubs are planted too deeply they may be deprived of oxygen; if they are planted too near the surface the roots may send up troublesome suckers or suffer frost damage. Plant container shrubs as recommended for trees. When possible purchase stock planted in biodegradable peat pots.

As soon as your shrub is planted, water it and fertilize as prescribed by the nurs-

Planting Shrubs

1. Slit the fibre pot down the sides with a spade.

2. Remove the rim to avoid drawing moisture to the surface.

3. Amend the soil with organic matter.

4. Water generously.

Climbing Hydrangea one of my favourites for it's glossy leaves, broad creamy white blossoms and reliable hardiness in zone 4.

ery. You could also prune 1/3 of its top growth to reduce stress on the root system and compensate for potential root loss or trauma. Even shrubs planted in fibre pots may suffer root injury during potting or transportation. Some breakage of fragile rootlets is unavoidable.

To reduce the size of the top, cut out any weak or broken branches, pruning to an outward-facing bud, a strong side branch, or the base of the branch. Then take 1/3 of the length off healthy branches, again cutting to an outward-facing bud or a strong side branch.

Your efforts should create a foundation of healthy branches, evenly spaced, with no crossing or crowded areas.

Flowering shrubs require annual pruning to encourage new growth, more as well as larger flowers, and more attractive foliage. Pruning keeps shrubs in check so they fill the area you set aside for them rather than invading their neighbour's turf. Regular pruning also keeps shrubs healthier, encourages vigorous growth and makes them much less likely to fall prey to pests and disease. It can be done in only a couple of hours work twice, perhaps three times during the season. It's a pretty good investment.

SHRUB PRUNING

My rules of thumb for pruning hardy shrubs:

- Remove damaged or dead branches when you notice them at any time during the year. Use a sharp, clean saw to cut back to a vigorous side branch or right to the base. Clippers or loppers don't do as good a job on dead wood.
- Pinch off ends of branches that are growing too long.
- Remove suckers as they appear. Suckers are very strong, fast- developing shoots which grow straight up from roots or branches. Their stems are usually bigger but not as strong as ordinary branches. If suckers have different foliage, they are growing from below the graft. Follow them back to the main stem and remove them carefully.
- Remove flowers as they fade so seed production is halted. Otherwise the total number of flowers produced will be significantly reduced. This is especially true for Lilac and Viburnum.
- Beginning in the second season of growth, weak or spindly growth should be cut back by 2/3 in order to strengthen your shrub's performance.
- Remove any dead or damaged branches missed during regular maintenance. Check for crossing branches. If the bark is rubbed through where two branches meet, cut back the weaker or inward- growing branch to a side branch or base.

There are also some crucial differences in pruning requirements between spring-flowering and summer-flowering shrubs.

SPRING-FLOWERING SHRUBS

Spring flowering shrubs include Azalea, Beauty Bush, Broom, Burning Bush, Daphne, Deutzia, Elder, Forsythia, Holly, Kerria, Lilac, Potentilla, Rhododendron, Viburnum, Spirea, Weigela, Winter Jasmine, Wisteria, Clematis, Mockorange, Honeysuckle, Beautybush, Flowering Quince, and Dogwood.

Spring-flowering shrubs

Spring-flowering shrubs bloom on wood that matured during the previous growing season. By the end of summer shrubs like Viburnum and Magnolia have actually developed tiny leaf and flower buds that will lie dormant over the winter, ready to burst into bloom once spring arrives. If those branches are pruned in the fall you eliminate the flowers they will bear. Therefore, spring-flowering shrubs should always be pruned immediately after they have flowered, giving your shrub the entire summer to develop flower buds for the next season.

Follow the general pruning rules above, but also prune to remove older branches. Renew main branches by cutting off old, shaggy branches which don't produce the best foliage or flowers. Cut the old branches right to the ground to avoid overcrowding at the base.

Younger branches which have borne flowers should be cut back to a bud, or to new green growth that has started during the current year. As you trim, open the centre of the shrub to light and air by varying the length of branches, cutting some by 1/3 or less, others by 1/2 or more. This encourages the plant to grow flowers on the inner branches.

Summer-flowering shrubs

Summer-flowering shrubs generally start off the spring in slow motion. They are among the last plants in the garden to recover from winter. Many novice gardeners have dug up their Hydrangeas and Rose of Sharon convinced they were dead when no foliage had appeared by mid-May. But summer-flowering shrubs remain dormant through early spring and should be pruned at this time. These shrubs bloom on growth from the current year, and need to be pruned before new growth begins.

Follow general pruning rules above but also prune back new growth once every spring. The best blooms will come from buds on branches that started during the previous season. Newer growth is tender, with lighter, shinier bark. Prune this wood back to leave two or three buds per branch.

By pruning back a portion of young growth every year you achieve a foundation of older branches with newer growth at their tips. The shrub will keep its shape from year to year and require minimal mid-season pruning.

New branches that emerge from the roots can be pruned to the base or left during the first season in which they appear. Prune them back to the same height as the rest of the foundation of growth during spring pruning. If you encourage some base branches every year you can cut off the older and knottier foundation branches, none of which will produce vigorously beyond four years.

Rejuvenating an overgrown shrub

A grossly overcrowded deciduous shrub can be rejuvenated by cutting all the branches back. Cut the whole bush down to within 6 or 8 in. (15 or 20 cm) of the ground, then eliminate the oldest, shaggiest stumps by sawing them down to the soil. Protect wounds with pruning paint. This method is extreme and it may take two growing seasons for the bush to recover. The bush is more likely to survive drastic pruning if the process is spread out over two seasons.

SUMMER-FLOWERING SHRUBS

Summer-flowering shrubs include Caryopteris, Butterfly Bush, Hydrangea, Rose of Sharon, Silver Fleece Vine, and Trumpet Vine.

CARE AND MAINTENANCE OF VINES

Growing vines is a quick way to make a new garden look well established. Vines can provide a mast of flowers or lots of thick green foliage the first season. They can be grown on a fence or wall, as a ground cover, or over an arched support to form a cosy arbour.

When you plant vines with more than one shoot, choose the strongest two or three shoots, and cut all the others at the base. Cut the chosen shoots back to a bud, leaving two or three buds per shoot. When there is only one shoot, cut it back to four to six buds.

Maintenance pruning

Pinching encourages spreading. When you pinch the growing tips, the vine splits where growth was stopped, creating two branches instead of one.

Some vines – the Ivies, for example – are grown for foliage. These are almost indestructible. They are hardy, grow very quickly, and can usually be pruned anytime.

But flowering vines which bloom on this year's growth must be pruned at different times of the year depending on when they flower. Spring-flowering vines should be pruned as soon as they have finished blooming. Summer-flowering vines should be pruned in early spring, before the new growth begins. Spring-flowering vines which bloom on this year's growth include: *Clematis jackmanii* and Trumpet Flower. Vines which bloom on last year's growth include: Honeysuckle, *Clematis armandii*, Wisteria, and others.

Some vines have very specific needs to keep them flowering. Check with the nursery where you buy your stock, or take a cutting from your vine for advice if you're not sure what kind it is.

Here are my rules of thumb for pruning vines:

* Any time of the year, remove broken, damaged, or dead vines, or any which have torn loose from the support. Simply cut back to the nearest strong side branch, to a bud, or down to the base.
* During the growing season, you will see long, very slim vines called tendrils reaching out from the support, looking for something else to grow on. Cut back to one bud if they are in an area that is starting to fill. Cut back to two or more buds if there is lots of room.
* Remove flowers as soon as they wilt. This keeps them from going to seed, and encourages the production of new flowers.
* Remove suckers which grow up from the roots, particularly after a well-established plant has been pruned.
* Thin overcrowding, and keep vines away from windows and doors by cutting small branches back to the nearest crotch.
* Rejuvenate vines by bringing on vigorous new growth to replace the old, woody vines. Cut shaggy vines back to vigorous side branches, or let new shoots grow from the roots, removing old vines completely.
* Occasionally, when vigorous, fast-growing vines have not been cut back for some time, they may get too heavy for the support. Ivy, Honeysuckle, Wisteria, and Clematis can all be cut to the ground in early spring, letting the new growth from the roots replace the old framework.

Boston Ivy. Although used primarily as a climbing vine, Boston Ivy and it's close cousin Virginia Creeper can create an effective, fast growing ground cover.

SHRUBS AND VINES

Descriptions and requirements

For each shrub and vine description below, I have listed the light requirements, climatic zone, moisture and soil requirements.

LIGHT REQUIREMENTS

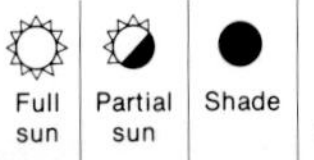

Full sun | Partial sun | Shade | No Preference

MOISTURE REQUIREMENTS

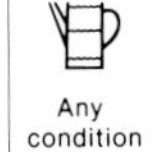

Moist | Average | Dry (well drained) | Any condition

SOIL REQUIREMENTS

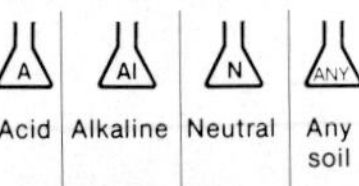

Acid | Alkaline | Neutral | Any soil

CLIMATE ZONE

Plants will grow in the climate zone numbered, and in any zone higher in number.

SHRUBS

Azalea

(Rhododendron 'Exbury' hybrids)

The Azalea family is vast, but only one species is reliably hardy and available in most regions of Canada. Exbury Azaleas will grow to 5 ft. (1.5 m) in full sun and acid soil. Dig in generous quantities of peat moss to lower pH.

Large Rhododendron-shaped flower clusters are available in vibrant colours.

Winterize with a mulch of Pine needles or Oak leaves around the root zone. This plant is hardy to Zone 5.

Beauty Bush

(Kolkwitzia)

The high arching stems of Beauty Bush carry clusters of tiny pink bell-shaped blossoms at their tips. This bush grows in the shape of a fountain, its slender branches reaching upwards of 10 ft. (3 m). Beauty Bush will stay in flower longer than most flowering shrubs.

Beauty Bush prefers full sun and well-drained soil. It seldom requires pruning.

Bluebeard

(Caryopteris)

Bluebeard is named for the sprays of delicate blue blossoms it issues beginning in August. Its flowers are unusual for their long graceful stamens as well as their colour.

Caryopteris is hardy to Zone 5. It prefers sun and average, well-drained soil. Without pruning it takes on a naturally rounded form and grows about 3 ft. (90 cm) in height. However, early spring pruning is usually recommended, especially in cold regions. It frequently dies back to the ground like an herbaceous perennial.

Boxwood

(Buxus)

The dense, dark-green, leathery foliage of this broad-leafed evergreen shrub makes an excellent low hedge. Boxwood can also be pruned as topiary. It grows slowly to a height and spread of 2 ft. (60 cm).

Plant in full sun to partial shade, in well-drained, acid soil. Hybrid or Korean Boxwood (*B. microphylla koreana*) is hardy to Zone 5. Evergreen foliage needs protection in winter.

However, English Boxwood *B. sempervirens*) is much less hardy and not recommended in regions colder than Zone 6. Even then, use only in a protected location.

Broom

(Cytisus)

Broom is a deciduous shrub featuring bright yellow or white pea-like flowers in spring. It grows to a height of 7 ft. (2.1 m) in Zone 6 with a broad spread. There are also dwarf carpet varieties.

Grow in full sun to partial shade, in well-drained soil. Broom is hardy to Zone 5, where it requires a sheltered position and winter protection.

Burning Bush

(Euonymous)

Burning Bush, or Winged Euonymous, (*E. alatus*) is primarily grown for its colourful foliage, which turns burgundy-pink in fall, accompanied by obscure reddish-orange fruit. Tiny, insignificant white flowers appear in spring. But this plant's curious jagged bark provides an interesting feature in the garden all year round. Euonymous usually produces brilliant red foliage in fall.

Plant in full sun to partial shade, in ordinary soil. This plant develops a naturally rounded appearance that requires little pruning. It grows about 8 ft. (2.4 m) high. The dwarf variety *E.a. compacta* will

(Previous page) Wisteria, a vine, produces pea-like flowers in shades of mauve, beginning in early May.

Burning Bush is primarily grown for its foliage, which turn burgundy-pink in fall.

grow to only about 5 ft. (1.5 m).

Two other forms of Euonymous are the Purple Winter Creeper (*E. fortunei*), which form vines or ground carpets, and Spindle Tree (*E. europaeus*), a hardy upright form of the smaller *alatus* shrub variety.

Butterfly Bush
(Buddleia)

Another August bloomer, Butterfly Bush sends forth arching flower spires in pinks or purple. Bushes tend to form rambling clumps. Much to my surprise, this colourful bush actually does attract butterflies.

One species, the Orange-Eyed Butterfly Bush (*B. davidii*) blooms on current year's growth and can be safely pruned in early spring. Another, Fountain Butterfly Bush (*B. alternifolia*), cannot. The two differ slightly in leaf and flower form. The Orange-Eyed species grows wild in areas of British Columbia.

Butterfly Bush prefers full sun and moist, well-drained soil. It is hardy to Zone 5, but usually dies back to the ground in Ontario. Gardeners, especially in cold areas, should give it the benefit of the doubt in spring: Butterfly Bush often doesn't even begin to issue leaves until June. But it is fast-growing.

Daphne
(Daphne)

There isn't a more lovely-scented flower in spring than Daphne. It is one of the smaller broad-leafed evergreen shrubs, seldom growing above 3 ft. (90 cm). Blossoms are usually pink or white. Two forms are deciduous, and their foliage often emerges after flowering is complete.

Daphne prefers full sun and rich, moist soil. But unlike most broad-leafed evergreens, Daphne likes near neutral soil. Some forms are hardy to Zone 4, but I still like to protect this plant over winter with boughs of Pine (cuttings from your Christmas tree are useful). This is not an especially easy plant to grow, but gardeners who take the trouble are well rewarded for their efforts. Popular species include *D. burkwoodi*, *D. Mezereum*, and *D. cneorum*.

Butterfly Bush (Buddleia) produces arching flower spires in pinks, purple and white.

Deutzia
(Deutzia)

Deutzia is a quick-growing shrub which bears clusters of white flowers on last year's wood. It stays in bloom for a long time. The bark of this deciduous plant is interesting in winter. *D. lemoinei* grows to a height of 4 ft. (1.2 m) and a spread of 3 ft. (90 cm). *D. gracilus* grows only to 2 1/2 ft. (75 cm) and a spread of 1 1/2 ft. (45 cm).

Both varieties tolerate some shade but grow best in full sun. Provide an even water supply and fertilize for abundant flowers. Deutzia is hardy to Zone 5.

Elder
(Sambucus)

Elder has everything going for it: colourful foliage, showy, creamy white flowers, and red or black fruit. It is a fast-growing deciduous shrub which grows to a height and spread of 10 ft. (3 m). Provide ample space. Elder makes a great screen or informal hedge. It provides edible fruit which can be used in pies and wine-making. Red Elder (*S. pubens*) is very hardy, and has plume-shaped flowers. Common Elder (*S. canadensis*) has flat clusters of flowers.

Forsythia
(Forsythia)

The deciduous shrub Forsythia is best known for its brilliant yellow flowers, which appear in early spring. It grows to a height and spread of 8 ft. (2.4 m), and can be used as an attractive informal

RULE OF THUMB

Holly (Ilex) fruit clusters are popular Christmas decorations. To ensure pollination, touch female flowers with pollen from male flowers using a fine paint brush. One male plant will pollinate several female plants.

hedge or for massing on banks and in spacious areas. It is also great for forcing indoors during late winter months.

Plant in full sun to partial shade, and provide an even water supply. Forsythia is normally hardy to Zone 5, but some varieties are hardy to Zone 4. These include *F. ovata* 'Ottawa' and 'Northern Gold', both hardy introductions developed by Agriculture Canada. A weeping cultivar, *F. suspensa*, is not so hardy.

Holly

(Ilex)

Both deciduous and evergreen forms of Holly grow in Canada. Leaf forms vary significantly but white flowers and red berries are common to both. Evergreen forms like English Holly (*I. Aquifolium*) are generally not considered hardy outside of Zone 7, but Blue Holly, a relative newcomer, is hardy in most regions of Canada. All Hollies require a male and female plant within several feet of one another to ensure cross-fertilization and the production of berry clusters.

Like other broad-leaved evergreens, Holly prefers sun or light shade and rich, moist, acid soil. Apply acidic mulches for best results. Treat as an evergreen.

The native Winterberry, or Black Alder, (*I. verticillata*) is a deciduous Holly with bright orange berries, which are considered poisonous.

The white flowers of Double Mock Orange have an orange-blossom fragrance.

Hydrangea

(Hydrangea)

Hydrangea is a deciduous plant which ranges from a 3-ft. (90-cm) shrub to a 15-ft. (4.5 m) tree.

Hydrangea features snowballs of white flowers, which appear in midsummer (*H. arborescens* 'Annabella') or elongated Lilac-shaped flowers of cream white, which appear in early summer (*H. paniculata grandiflora* or 'Peegee'). Annabella, which is hardy to Zone 2B, is one of my favourite shade-tolerant flowering shrubs. Peegee, which is hardy to Zone 4, grows to 4 ft. (1.2 m) or 15 ft. (4.5 m) as a standard and is more sun-loving. *H. petiolaris* is a climbing Hydrangea which is outstanding as a slow-growing vine.

Plant in full sun to partial shade.

Kerria

(Kerria japonica)

Small golden yellow balls of petals appear on Kerria for several weeks in spring and then periodically thereafter until fall. Kerria grows to about 5 ft. (1.5 m) tall. This is an excellent shade-tolerant flowering shrub, with striking glossy green foliage. The variegated form is equally popular.

Plant Kerria in a moist, shaded site.

Lilac

(Syringa)

The striking flower clusters of Lilac range in colour from white to blue to deep purple. This deciduous shrub, also known for its strong fragrance, grows as high as 20 ft. (6 m) and as wide as 12 ft. (3.6 m). Taller tree Lilacs are also popular.

Lilac needs full sun to partial shade and well-drained soil. Add a handful of crushed limestone each year to maintain alkalinity. It is hardy to Zone 2. Remove spent blooms to encourage flowering. Some popular species include Chinese Lilac (*S. chinensis*) and the French hybrids. *S. prestoniae*, developed by Isabella Preston of Agriculture Canada, blooms about two weeks after other Lilacs are finished.

Mock Orange

(Philadelphus)

Most forms of Mock Orange, sometimes called Orange Blossom, produce a striking display of white flowers with intense orange- blossom fragrance. It is a deciduous shrub which can be grown as an informal hedge. *P. coronarius* 'Aureus', or Golden Mock Orange, reaches a height and spread of 6 ft. (1.8 m). *P. virginalis* reaches a height and spread of 10 ft. (3 m). Prune every three years. Otherwise they become open at the bottom.

Grow in full sun to partial shade in well drained soil. *P. coronarius* grows best in full sun, which brings out the striking gold colour most intensely. Hardy to Zone 3.

Potentilla

(Potentilla)

Potentilla in the form of a woody shrub is often called Bush Cinquefoil. It's a wonderful addition to any sunny garden where season-long flowering can be appreciated. Depending on the variety, it usually grows less than 4 ft. (1.2 m). Blossoms range from the traditional yellow (sun-loving) to the recently-introduced white (sun-loving), and pink (which prefers partial shade).

Potentilla prefers average soil, and will tolerate dry conditions. It is one of the most cold-resistant shrubs. Recently-introduced cultivars include Gold Drop, Goldfinger, and Red Ace.

Privet

(Ligustrum)

In Canada, Privet is a deciduous shrub which produces small white flowers and inconspicuous black fruit. Its dense foliage grows as high as 7 ft. (2.1 m) and as wide as 4 ft. (1.2 m), making an excellent hedge. Amur Privet (*L. amurense*) is useful as a hedge, while *L. vulgare lodense* makes an excellent low hedge. *L. vicaryi*, with its golden foliage, makes a popular contrast shrub for foundation plantings.

Much larger species of Privet grow in warmer climates. Evergreen forms grow in Zone 9. Privet tolerates city conditions. Plant in full sun to partial shade.

Rhododendron

(Rhododendron)

The great beauty and colour choice available among this group of plants makes it one of the world's most popular shrubs. Rhododendron is a broad-leaved evergreen with several forms that are hardy in Canada. They range from small dwarf types to varieties that, in Zone 9, are easily mistaken for small trees. Check zone information and growing requirements carefully before you buy.

Rhododendron prefers light shade, especially in areas subject to intense heat. It requires moist, acid soil, rich in leaf mould and peat moss. Mulch often and fertilize early in the season with evergreen fertilizer. Treat as an evergreen.

Rose of Sharon

(Hibiscus)

The distinct three-lobed, upright-growing leaves of Rose of Sharon begin to emerge in late spring. They are eventually followed by dramatic, often bicoloured blossoms in August through September.

Rose of Sharon (*H. syriacus*) prefers sunny sites with rich, well-drained soil. It grows as high as 12 ft. (3.6 m) naturally and is hardy to Zone 5. Tree forms and double-flowering cultivars are also available.

Bridalwreath Spirea produces generous clusters of showy white flowers in mid-June.

RULE OF THUMB

Some popular shrubs that attract birds include Russian Olive, Honeysuckle, Elder, Sumac.

Weigela is also available in forms with white, pink or variegated blossoms.

Snowball
(Viburnum)

Viburnum is an extremely varied genus but its members all have one common feature: large clustered balls of white flowers, often called Snowballs. Depending on the variety, Viburnum shrubs vary in height, fragrance and fertility. The famous Cranberry Bush (*V. Opulus*) has large, broad, red flower clusters in June. Late season berry clusters attract many birds. European Snowball (*V. Opulus roseum*) has maple-like leaves which turn red in fall, but it doesn't set fruit. *V. Opulus nanum* is a popular low-growing, small-leafed form, ideal in rockeries, foundation-planting, and hedges. Several Viburnum are native, including the Highbush Cranberry (*V. trilobum*), the Arrow-Wood (*V. dentatum*), and the Nannyberry (*V. lentago*). Spicebush or Fragrant Viburnum (*V. carlcephalum*) is aptly named for its pleasant fragrance.

Viburnum prefers full sun but will tolerate partial shade and average, well-drained soil. Most species are hardy to Zone 2.

Spirea
(Spiraea)

Spirea is a deciduous shrub which bears white, pink or red flowers, and makes a good informal hedge. Plant in full sun. Many varieties are hardy to Zone 2, but some will not grow well outside of Zone 4. Check labels carefully. Some, like *S. vanhouttei*, grow taller than 5 ft. (1.5 m). Others, like *S. bumalda* 'Froebelii' and *S. b.* 'Goldflame', won't grow above 3 ft. (90 cm).

Bridalwreath Spirea (*S. vanhouttei*) is a very popular shrub for a screen, or in yard planting. It produces generous clusters of showy white flowers in mid-June. It is hardy to Zone 4 and will tolerate partial shade. Garland Spirea (*S. arguta*) is a little shorter, and produces flowers along the stem.

Froebel's Spirea (*S. bumalda* 'Froebelii') is invaluable as a hardy foundation planting. It grows vigorously, producing a mass of cerise flowers from mid-June through July. It is hardy to Zone 3.

Goldflame Spirea (*S.b.* 'Goldflame') is a dwarf flowering shrub most suitable in small yards and rockeries. It produces golden yellow foliage in spring, followed

by masses of light crimson flowers through July. Hardy to Zone 3.

Spirea ranges from 3 to 6 ft. (90 cm to 1.8 m) high, depending on form.

Sumac

(Rhus)

Sumac is a deciduous shrub which features a distinctive pyramid of red fruit and compound leaves which provide brilliant red colour in fall. Sumac grows as high as 15 ft. (4.5 m), and spreads rapidly by suckers. Several strains are useful as ornamentals. Wild or Staghorn Sumac (*R. typhina*) produces fruit clusters which are an important food for wildlife.

Sumac is an excellent choice where a fast-growing shrub is required to control erosion (e.g. embankments and hills) or for sandy or gravelly soils.

Plant in full sun and light soil.

Weigela

(Weigela florida)

The flowers of Weigela are blue, white, pink, red, or variegated. This deciduous shrub grows to a height of 10 ft. (3 m). The 'Bristol Ruby' variety bears flowers in spring and summer. There are several outstanding ornamental strains.

Plant in full sun to partial shade, in well-drained soil. Hardy to Zone 4.

Winter Jasmine

(Jasminum)

The delicate, graceful stems of Winter Jasmine (*J. nudiflorum*) are lovely arranged on a trellis or arbour. They are covered in fragrant, sunny yellow blossoms for intermittent periods throughout the year when grown in warm regions.

Winter Jasmine is hardy to Zone 5 but doesn't flower dependably in climates harsher than Zone 7. Plant it in full sun in average, well-drained soil.

VINES

Bittersweet

(Celastrus scandens)

Bittersweet is a gorgeous native vine which climbs by twining. The fruit appears in terminal clusters of yellow which later ripen to display masses of bright orange-red berries. These are excellent for winter bouquets. In autumn, Bittersweet turns a striking yellow. It reaches a height of 25 ft. (7.5 m), and will grow in Zones 2 to 4. Lower stems become woody.

Cinnamon Vine

(Dioscorea)

Cinnamon Vine (*D. batatas*) produces immense heart-shaped leaves on vines that grow 10 ft. (3 m) or more by early summer. Its ability to cover a porch completely within a few weeks is remarkable given that it dies to the ground in winter.

Cinnamon Vine is hardy to Zone 4 and prefers sun or light shade in combination with moist soil.

Clematis

(Clematis)

One of the most lush-flowering vines to grow in the north, Clematis produces beautiful large blossoms for several weeks in summer. Hybrids produce the largest flowers but the Jackman Clematis (*C. jackmanii*), with its deep purple blossoms, is the most widely grown, reliable type.

Pruning Clematis is tricky because some hybrids set bloom on growth from the previous season. However, many of the best hybrids, as well as Jackman, bloom on current season's growth. Ask your nursery the exact name of your Clematis and when it should be pruned.

Buy the most mature Clematis you can find. Growth sometimes hesitates for a year following transplanting.

Provide Clematis with rich moist soil in a lightly shaded location for best results. An eastern exposure is best. Its

roots grow close to the surface. Protect from heat with a good mulch and don't overcrowd or cultivate soil in the vicinity. Apply a small handful of crushed limestone to the root zone twice yearly to keep soil alkaline.

Honeysuckle

(Lonicera)

When in bloom, Honeysuckle is a real eye-catcher. It's a beautiful twining vine with trumpet-shaped flowers produced abundantly in early summer. Some flower periodically until fall. Honeysuckle retains its foliage late into winter, growing as high as 12 ft. (3.6 m).

Dropmore Scarlet Honeysuckle is a hardy hybrid developed by Skinners Nursery north of Winnipeg. It provides an excellent display on a trellis. Hardy to Zone 2.

Goldflame Honeysuckle (*L. heckrottii*) produces clusters of trumpet-shaped buds and fragrant flowers from late spring until midsummer. Attractive bicolour flowers show brilliant flame pink on the outside of the petals and creamy golden yellow inside. Hardy to Zone 4.

Kudzu

(Pueraria)

A hardy, rugged vine which will produce light purple, pea-type flowers in Zone 8 or warmer, Kudzu is an ideal, fast-growing vine. It can completely cover house walls in a single season. It is hardy to Zone 3.

Plant Kudzu where it can enjoy sun and average soil. Do not fertilize.

Silver Lace Vine

(Polygonum)

The shrub-like tangles of Silver Lace Vine (*P. aubertii*), or Silver Fleece Vine, are most appreciated for the airy clouds of white blossoms they produce. Silver Lace Vine is hardy to Zone 4, though some growth dies back during the winter. Since it flowers on new wood this is not a problem. Silver Lace can grow as much as 15 ft. (4.5 m) in one season.

Plant in full sun and average soil.

Trumpet Vine

(Campis Radicans)

The lovely orange trumpet blooms of Campis Radicans adorn many homes in July. Campis is a perennial vine with the deciduous habit of losing its foliage in autumn. It climbs more than 20 ft. (6 m) and is hardy to Zone 5. It may take up to two years from transplanting to establish itself. Don't expect any substantial top growth for some time.

Trumpet Vines prefer full sun and rich, moist soil. Provide them with mature compost and mulch well.

Virginia Creeper

(Parthenocissus quinquefolia)

Virginia Creeper is a hardy native plant which climbs by progressively twining its distinctive 5-lobed leaves. Once established, it will often become self-clinging. This high climbing vine grows very quickly, reaching as high as 50 ft. (15 m). It requires very little care. Foliage turns brilliant red early in the fall.

Virginia Creeper also provides an excellent ground cover. It is hardy to Zone 2.

Boston Ivy (*P. tricuspidata*) belongs to the same family but bears sharply cut single leaves and tends to be slightly less hardy. It is self-clinging to almost any surface and growth is vigorous. It withstands dense urban conditions. Autumn colouring is a spectacular scarlet.

Wisteria

(Wisteria)

The gnarled and twisted wooden vines of Wisteria hang with pendulous racemes of pea-like flowers in shades of mauve, beginning in early May. Fragrance, colour and hardiness varies depending on type. Forms hardy to Zone 5 tend to attain less height. Wisteria must be pruned in warm climate regions to keep it in check and encourage flowering.

Plant in full sun and provide with strong support and ample compost or fertilizer. It is sometimes available as an attractive standard.

The trumpet vine (Campis Radicans) is a vigorous climbing plant with beautiful orange flowers that bloom throughout the summer.

SECTION IV

Vegetables and Fruits

MOST OF US LIKE TO EAT. WE especially like to eat vegetables and fruits from our own gardens.

This section provides advice about fruit and vegetable gardening to maximize the fruit-bearing potential of each plant. It also gives special consideration to such factors as taste, keeping quality, insect and disease resistance, drought resistance, space requirements, and maintenance requirements.

Like other sections of *A Greener Thumb*, this section dispenses with hocus-pocus and needless technicalities, and concentrates on the how-to of successful food gardening.

Perhaps more than any other kind of gardening, fruit and vegetable culture is surrounded in lore. Pick up a copy of the *Old Farmer's Almanac* sometime, and you'll see what I mean. Some of these tales are based on fact, and I have experimented successfully with many of them.

Let me suggest that, after you have read through this section, including my own Rules of Thumb, you take an experimental approach to food gardening. Who knows, you may rediscover some century-old secret to growing the perfect Apple or Tomato.

CHAPTER 12

VEGETABLES

While the vegetable garden at my house takes up a relatively small portion of our yard, it is the most rewarding. The kids go to the vegetable garden more often than any other part, and they are now old enough to take some responsibility for their own little area. Carrots, Radishes, Cherry Tomatoes, and Green Beans – these are just some of the wonderful crops our children enjoyed fresh from the garden. And they eat them. Another bonus!

Our vegetable garden generates more dinner table conversation than the rest of our yard.

"We've got three Cucumbers in the fridge. Would you like to take some to work?"

"These Beans are the pits! Should have kept last year's variety."

"But I like to experiment."

By some standards, this is mundane stuff. But this kind of conversation makes dinner a family event. And it's home-grown, home-cooked meals from our garden that make a house a home.

If I have learned anything about vegetable gardening since childhood it is that there is little hocus-pocus involved. Just common sense and some effort. Providing you start with good, deep soil. Begin there and you are 90 per cent on your way to success.

RULE OF THUMB

Large, four-legged pests and birds are a particular problem for vegetable gardeners. Before you declare chemical warfare against groundhogs and other unwelcome dinner guests, consider physical barriers, like fences, live traps, nets, and electrified fences.

CARE AND MAINTENANCE OF VEGETABLES

Preparing your vegetable bed

The best time to prepare your vegetable bed is in the fall or very early spring. Determine roughly what you'd like to plant and measure out the appropriate space, allowing room for walking paths and adequate space between rows. Consult Chapter 2 for further details on bed preparation.

If you rototill or dig deeply in the fall and apply plentiful organic matter, the soil need only be lightly turned and raked over once spring arrives. This type of thorough advance preparation has several advantages for vegetable gardeners: it eliminates or retards the development of insects and perennial weed seeds; it reduces labour in spring heat; it helps to ensure that your soil has been adequately nourished, thereby reducing dependency on chemicals; and it allows you a quick start in spring.

If you have provided enough time for the breakdown of organic fertilizers you can directly seed cold-hardy vegetables like Lettuce, Spinach, Peas, and Beets (see Cold-Hardy Vegetables box) as soon as the ground is dry. They don't mind the occasional cold snap and can be planted as early as mid-April throughout much of Canada.

You'll know if the soil is adequately dry by squeezing a handful of it. If it turns to muck or water runs from your fist, the ground is still too wet for planting or digging. Soil is very vulnerable to damage when waterlogged. Walking on it reduces oxygen content, making it tough and compacted.

Eager gardeners should hold off on planting until the spring run-off has truly run off. Ground that is excessively wet is also unlikely to grow anything other than mould.

Sowing Vegetable Seeds

Most vegetables can be grown from seed in your outdoor garden. However, the short growing season in Canada requires that some vegetable plants, such as tomatoes and pepper, be planted as seedlings which you can either purchase or grow yourself indoors.

1. After amending the soil and raking smooth, mark the rows with garden string to ensure straight lines.

2. Make a furrow with a hoe using the string as a guidline.

3. Place the seed in the furrow at the density recommended on the soil packet instruction.

4. Cover over the seed and smooth the surface. It is now ready for the frequent waterings required for the seed to germinate.

Fertilizer

Most vegetables can be fertilized if needed with mixtures of 6-12-12. The list includes Asparagus, Beets, Broccoli, Brussels Sprouts, Carrots, Celery, Corn, Onion, Peppers, Potato, Spinach, Tomato, and Turnip. The exceptions are Cabbage, Cauliflower, Lettuce, and Radish, all of which are fertilized with 20-20-20, and Squash, which is fertilized with 20-20-20. Peas and Beans, I have found, produce equally well without fertilizer, providing the soil has been well prepared.

Pests and diseases

Protecting crops against predators and disease is a major concern for vegetable gardeners. As I outline in the appendix of this book, the best strategy is to garden defensively: clean up refuse, weed regularly and ensure that your plants have what they require in the way of space, sun and water. These factors are 95 per cent of the battle.

Hang tinfoil pie plates, strips of colourful cloth, old nylons or plastic from trees and poles, even Corn stalks, in order to detract predators. Nylons filled with hair – dog or human – are supposed to be most effective. They need replacing after a good rain.

Battery-operated devices that emit high frequency sound can repel rodents like rabbits and groundhogs. Wind chimes and radios are also used by many gardeners to good effect.

VEGETABLES

Descriptions and requirements

GOURMET GARDENING

There is a popular image of vegetable gardeners as earthy folks interested primarily in wholesome, traditional fare. But vegetable gardeners are also likely to be *aficionados* of fine food in all its forms. As any gourmet gardener can tell you, pesto prepared from freshly picked, home-grown Basil and Garlic has it all over pesto served in any restaurant.

What's the difference between regular fare and gourmet cooking or *nouvelle cuisine*? Piquancy. Piquancy can be defined as flavour and presentation that is pleasantly stimulating to both the palette and mind. It relies on freshness, variety and novelty. Your garden can provide all three.

Nothing is fresher than home-grown produce. For variety and novelty you need only consult the most recent catalogues of the leading seed houses or well-stocked nurseries or garden centres. You will find such oddities as variegated green and purple Lettuce, red Chard, tiny Cherry Tomatoes and a multitude of other hybrids of unusual colour and form. In this chapter I have incorporated some lesser-known gourmet or international varieties together with their more common relatives.

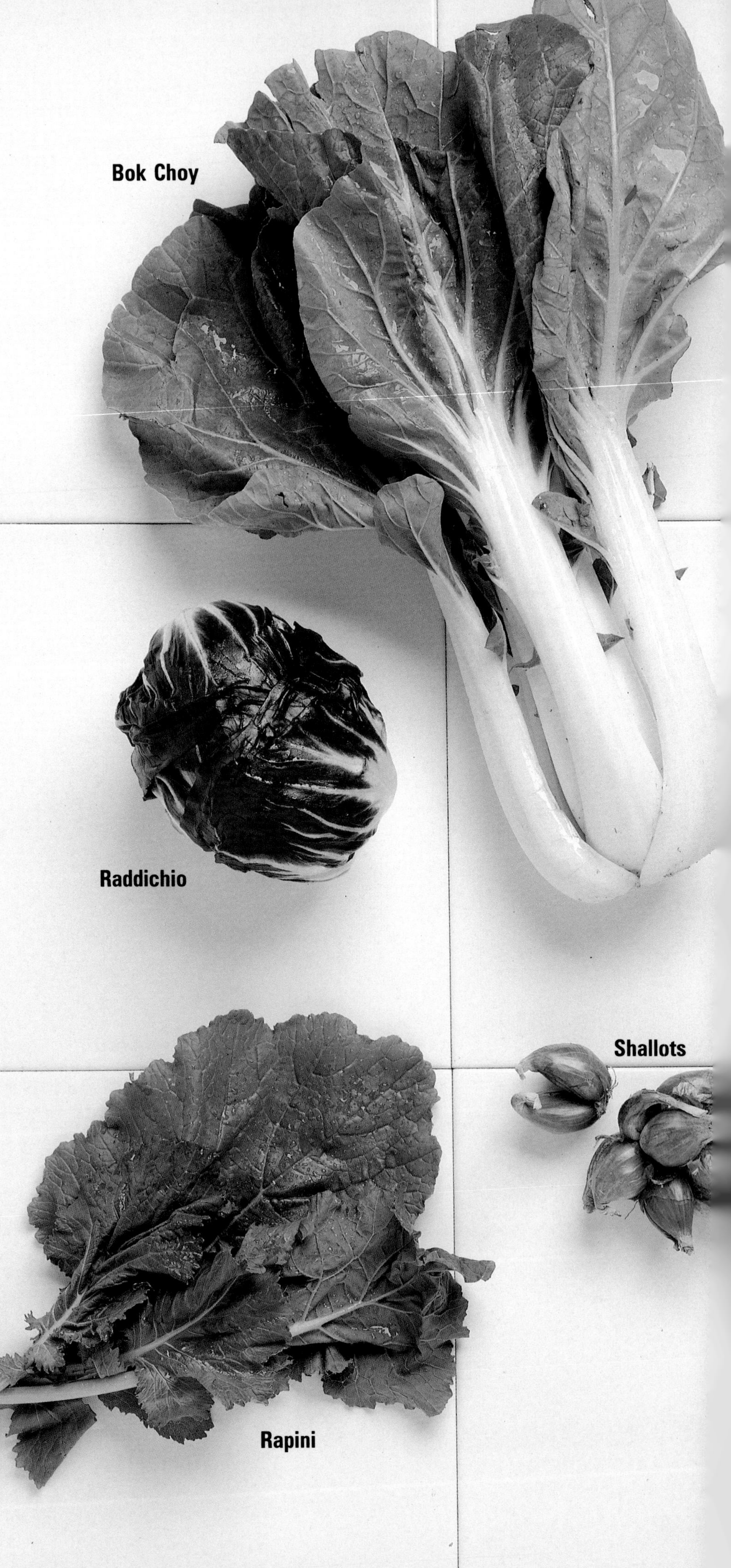

(Previous page) Peppers should be planted in a bed where family members, including Tomato, Potato and Eggplant, were not grown during the previous season.

Kohlrabi
Hot Peppers
Snow Peas
Fennel
Fava Beans

Tomato

(Lycopersicum esculentum)

Two hundred years ago, people shunned the Tomato. They thought it was the fruit that got Adam and Eve kicked out of Eden. Today, the Tomato is the most popular vegetable in the garden. Like many stars, however, it can be temperamental.

Choose a spot where you have not grown Tomato, Potato, Pepper, or Eggplant for a year or two. Amend soil as required, neutralizing pH. Use plentiful amounts of mature compost.

In spring, eight weeks before the last expected frost, sow Tomato seedlings indoors. Give potted seedlings plenty of light. If you grow them in artificial potting mixtures, fertilize with water-soluble 20-20-20 four weeks after sowing, and again when you transplant into the garden. You should end up with sturdy green Tomato seedlings, 8 in. (20 cm) tall and 8 in. (20 cm) wide to the outer tips of their leaves. Buy seedlings this shape if you don't raise your own.

Transplant the seedlings into the garden when temperatures are warm throughout the day and overnight, usually by the end of May in most regions of Canada. Plant them deep – at least up to their first true leaves, and deeper if seedlings are long and leggy. Roots

PRUNING TOMATOES

Early Tomatoes don't need pruning, but main season varieties do. The approach differs, depending on whether Tomatoes are staked or caged:

Staked

Tie the Tomato plant to a 4- or 5-ft. (1.2- to 1.5-m) stake as it grows. Allow side shoots to develop three leaves, then pinch out the growing tip of the branch. The remaining two or three leaves provide photosynthesis and shade the fruit. six weeks before the first frost is expected, pinch the growing top of the plant, to direct growing energy into ripening fruit.

Caged

Place a cage over each Tomato plant after it has been set in the ground. Then pinch back any growth which extends much above or beyond the cage.

will form along the buried stem. Space 2 ft. (60 cm) between plants.

Top-dress with compost or apply a solution of liquid 20-20-20 to get them off to a good start. Go easy on Nitrogen or Tomatoes will grow, but delay bearing fruit. Wet weather followed by drought will often cause Tomatoes to split.

Generally speaking, early season Tomatoes do not need support. But main season varieties need stakes, cages, or scaffolds. These should be set up as you plant. The kind of support you provide affects your harvest. Plants trained and pruned to a stake will bear earlier, but the fruit is more likely to suffer growth cracks. Tomatoes in cages tend to mature later but they have more attractive fruit.

Fences or covers made from plastic sheets attached to a lath frame can extend the growing season into the fall. But if you still have green fruit on the vine when hard frost is expected, there are many green Tomato recipes for relishes and chutneys.

Before frost, dig up whole Tomato plants and hang them upside down in a basement or shed. Within a few weeks green fruit will colour up nicely. If space is limited, place them on newspaper on shelves or in baskets. Green fruit that has grown to mature size can be ripened in a cool dark place. Place an Apple among the Tomatoes. The Apple will give off ethylene, hurrying the ripening process.

The selection of Tomatoes is almost endless, ranging from Cherry Tomatoes to giant Beefsteak, from fleshy Plum Tomatoes to yellow varieties. If premature frosts are a problem in your area, select early-maturing varieties or mid-season types. Winter-keepers are the best Tomato for long storage. New forms include improved small cherry varieties (my favourite is Sweet 100 – with more vitamin C per ounce than an orange), low acid Tomatoes, and some that sport yellow or pink fruits.

Buy Tomato varieties resistant to verticillium wilt, fusarium wilt, and nematodes. Look for the letters VFN after the variety name on seed packets or when ordering from a seed catalogue. Watch for cutworms, Tomato hornworms, aphids, flea beetles, and whiteflies. Also watch for late and early blight, and blossom end rot.

Asparagus

(Asparagus officinalis)

Few gardeners start Asparagus from seed because it takes years to grow to harvest size. Asparagus root sections, called crowns, are available. Crowns need only two years to grow before harvest.

To plant crowns, dig a trench about 1 ft. (30 cm) deep and 1 ft. (30 cm) wide, spacing 2 ft. (60 cm) between plants and 4 ft. (1.2 m) between rows. Soil should be fertile and well-drained, with a pH of 6.5. Fill within 6 in. (15 cm) of the top with well-packed organic material. Place crowns in the trench and barely cover. As the shoots grow, gradually fill in the hole with loam. Mulch, and water normally. This process may take a whole season – be patient!

Asparagus is a heavy feeder. Weed well to eliminate competition. Fertilize or work in mature compost as spring growth begins, and again at the end of the harvest.

In the third season, thick spears appear. Pick when they are 6 to 8 in. (15 to 20 cm) long, breaking them off below ground. After a few weeks, thinner spears appear. Very thin spears should be left to develop foliage. Apply compost or fertilizer and a thick blanket of mulch.

For white European-style Asparagus, hill earth over the spears as they grow in the spring. In the absence of sunlight, they remain white. The fern-like tops turn yellow in the fall and should be removed at this time. It is important to allow some foliage to mature in this way, to help build up the Asparagus roots for next year's crop. Mulch the bed again with 3 in. (7.5 cm) of composted manure and 6 in. (15 cm) of leaves.

Watch for asparagus beetle. Plant varieties which are resistant to rust and fusarium wilt, such as Viking and Mary Washington.

Beans, Snap

(Phaseolus)

Snap Beans, also called String Beans, Green Beans, or Wax Beans, need no special soil preparation, providing your garden is friable, but they will not germinate until the soil reaches 60 degrees F (16°C) or warmer.

Sow in furrows to a depth of 1 in. (2.5 cm) in spring, 2 in. (5 cm) in summer. Space 2 to 3 in. (5 to 7.5 cm) between plants. Cover with a light soil mixture, or mulch with peat moss. This

RULE OF THUMB

"Hot" crop love heat. The more sun & natural heat they receive, the sooner the harvest. These include tomatoes, peppers, eggplant and summer squash (e.g. zucchini.)

prevents the formation of a clay crust which can hinder seedling growth. It also prevents excessive damp, which invites fungal growth.

Beans benefit from a side dressing of mature compost or fertilizer when they are 6 in. (15 cm) tall, but that's all they need. Too much nitrogen discourages the setting of pods.

Water routinely. Drying out causes underdeveloped pods called pollywogs.

Beans require about 60 days from seeding to harvest. Harvest when pencil-thick. Check every two or three days. Once seed shape becomes visible, pods are too tough for good eating, but remove them from the plants anyway, to encourage future production of Beans.

Harvest lasts about three weeks. Depleted Bean plants are rich in nitrogen and should be added to the compost.

Pole Beans are similar to Bush Beans, but they need to be staked or trained on string. A simple wooden frame with one string for each plant will suffice. If placed to the north, the frame can form a wall to protect the other plants from cool winds.

Bush or Pole Green Snap Beans freeze well as do Bush, Yellow or Wax Beans. Unusual varieties include purple cultivars which turn green when cooked, stringless and dwarf forms. Broad or Fava Beans are cultured like Snap Beans, but can be planted earlier since they thrive in cool weather. Pinto and Black Beans require over 100 days of frost-free weather. Enterprising gardeners often try their hand at raising these field Beans and others, like Kidneys and Limas.

Watch for aphids, Japanese beetles and Mexican bean beetles. To prevent blight or fungus, water early in the day, keep spray off foliage, and avoid touching the plants when they are wet, which can spread virus.

Beet

(Beta vulgaris)

Beets need to be planted as soon as the soil can be worked in early spring. Prepare your bed, removing stones and other debris, and check the pH to ensure it is not below 6. Beets prefer a rich, sandy loam. Rake over in spring.

Sow Beets intensively or in furrows, spacing seeds well apart. Plant to a depth of 1/2 in. (1.5 cm) in spring, 1 in. (2.5 cm) in summer. Each seed sprouts several Beets, which will later need thinning. Plant at intervals until about ten weeks before hard frost is predicted. But skip midsummer sowings, which can be damaged by heat.

When Beets are 2 in. (5 cm) tall, thin to 1 in. (2.5 cm) apart. Thin again to 3 in. (7.5 cm) when they reach 4 in. (10 cm). Larger winter-keeper types need to be thinned even more.

Hybridizers have produced early or late canning and bunching beets in red, white and yellow. Sizes range from miniature to cylindrical or large Potato-sized types. One novelty variety, Chioggia, boasts concentric red and white rings.

Beets are also raised for their edible foliage, which is especially tasty in early summer. Purplish red veins decorate green leaves.

Watch for leaf miners and leaf spot diseases.

In a quarter century, Canadians have increased their Broccoli consumption seven times.

Broccoli

(Brassica oleracea italica)

Recently Broccoli has been hailed in the medical community as a good food source for preventing cancer. Maybe that helps explain the tremendous surge in popularity. Canadians now eat over 700 per cent more Broccoli than in 1964.

Plant Broccoli in well-prepared soil two weeks before the last expected spring frost. Check the pH – acid soil can bring on disease. Sow two or three seeds 1/4 in. (6 mm) deep at 2-ft. (60-cm) intervals. Remove all but the hardiest shoots when 2 in. (5 cm) tall.

For an earlier start, sow seeds indoors six weeks before the last expected frost. Set out seedlings once the danger of hard frost has passed.

Start a second crop in June for fall harvest, either indoors or in the garden. Before setting out this crop, check the pH again.

After five weeks of growth, side dress Broccoli with a handful of mature compost or fertilizer per plant. Pinch out the growing point as soon as sprouts begin to form.

Harvest by cutting stems just above where leaves join the main stem. Smaller flowers at the leaf axil should be left to grow to harvest size. The fall harvest tastes better after a light frost.

Plant early varieties in spring and cold-resistant types for fall. Attractive yellow, red and purple forms have recently been introduced. Raab or Rapini, used in Italian dishes (mainly stir fries), is a sprouting type of Broccoli that does not form heads. Broccoli generally bolts rapidly and cannot be neglected. Romanesco Broccoli features multiple heads that are closely packed and resemble flowers.

Watch for cutworms, root maggots, aphids, cabbage worms, clubroot, and blackleg diseases.

Brussels Sprouts

(Brassica oleracea gemmifera)

Prepare the soil as you would for Broccoli, avoiding areas where members of the Cabbage family (*Brassica*) grew last season. Test and adjust the pH, which should be slightly alkaline, or at least neutral.

Sow in the garden in late April, or start seedlings in early April to set outdoors after May 20. Plant to a depth of 1/2 in. (13 mm), leaving 2 ft. (60 cm) between plants.

When the first sprouts begin to develop on the stem in early August, side dress each plant with mature compost or a handful of fertilizer. As the sprouts grow and surround the leaf stems, twist off the lower leaves. When the sprouts are about 1 in. (2.5 cm) around, start harvesting.

Brussel Sprouts are one of the hardiest, longest-lasting fall vegetables. Recent new varieties include a beautiful wine-red form.

Control pests and diseases as for Broccoli.

Brussels Sprouts is one of the hardiest, long-lasting fall vegetables.

Cabbage

(Brassica oleracea capitata)

Cultivate Cabbage as you would Brussels Sprouts, Broccoli and Cauliflower (all members of the *Brassica* family). Unless you have a very long growing season, start Cabbage indoors six to eight weeks before the last expected spring frost. A cold frame provides ideal protection for hardening off. Otherwise, set out when the danger of frost has passed, spacing 18 in. (45 cm) between plants.

Cabbage has a shallow root system, which makes it particularly sensitive to weeds and uneven water supply. Give plants 1 in. (2.5 cm) of water each week. Weed by hand, not with a hoe. Mulches are ideal for keeping down weeds and retaining moisture. Apply mature compost or fertilizer.

Early-, mid-, and late-season varieties are available in both red, green and Savoy types. Adventurous gardeners should try tall-growing oriental forms like Mi-

Rule of Thumb

Keep Cabbage from splitting in hot weather by cutting off some roots. Insert a shovel into the earth to one side of the stem and give the roots a pop. A farmer friend of mine simply pulls his Cabbage straight up while applying pressure with both hands. He continues to pull until he hears a pop – indicating that the tap root has been torn and his Cabbage will not bolt to seed.

chihli, Celery Cabbage, Napa, or Bok Choy. Many are bolt-resistant, immune to common Cabbage pests or diseases, and great in salads or stir-fries. Michihli and Napa are head-formers and mature in two months or more. Bok Choy grows like Chard and is ready for harvest in about 40 days.

Protect from pests and diseases as you do other *Brassica*.

Cantaloupe and Melon

The Melon family includes Cantaloupe (*Cucumis melo reticulatus*), Honeydew Melons (*C. melo inodorus*), and Watermelon (*Citrullus vulgaris*). Cantaloupe are the earliest-maturing member of this family, which generally need as much as four months of warm weather from germination to harvest. You can hurry them along by starting early, as with Squash or Cucumbers.

Prepare hills as for the other gourds, leaving 10 ft. (3 m) between hills. Soil should be rich, fertile, organic and well drained, with a pH of 6.8. Cover with a black plastic sheet or an old rubber tire to capture the heat of sun and warm the earth.

When the soil reaches 80°F (27°C), cut slits in the plastic and plant two seedlings 1/2 in. (13 mm) deep in each hill, peat pots and all, making sure the pot rims are below the soil surface.

Protect seedlings with newspaper or plastic if the temperature falls below 70°F (21°C). Where spring warms early, plant four seeds per hill and leave the strongest 2 to grow.

Side dress with a handful of fertilizer when the vines are about 1 ft. (30 cm) long, and again when the first fruit appears. Water well, long and slow, so the deep taproot gets wet.

Harvest Cantaloupe when the garden smells Cantaloupe-ish, when the stem slips easily off the fruit, and when the area between the raised net pattern on the skin changes from green to tan. Cover with netting just before they are ripe or birds will be there first. Other Melons are ripe when they smell sweet. Watermelon is ready when it sounds hollow. Hills should yield about 10 lbs. (4.5 kg) of Melons.

See Cucumbers for information about pests and diseases affecting vine crops.

Carrot

(Daucus carota sativa)

Carrots demand light, friable soil that is well-worked, stone-free and able to accommodate long tap roots. Rocky soil or crowding causes forked or misshapen Carrots. Adjust pH to 6.5.

Sow 1/2 in. (13 mm) apart, planting every three weeks until about 60 days before hard frost is expected. Thin Carrots to 3 in. (7.5 cm) apart in early summer.

Uneven water supply causes splitting, sow water Carrots once a week – more often when it's hot and dry, especially later in the season. Weed regularly. Top-dress with mature compost or fertilizer at mid-season.

Don't compact the soil. Lay a board between rows to distribute your weight. If your friable soil is shallow, plant miniature gourmet Carrot varieties.

Harvest when Carrot tops are about 3/4 in. (2 cm) in diameter.

Watch for two mid-season problems, Carrot rust fly larvae and Carrot beetle. Rodents and rabbits consider Carrot tops a delicacy.

Cauliflower

(Brassica oleracea botrytis)

Cauliflower needs the same attention as the rest of the *Brassica* (Cabbage) family. Start indoors 6 to 8 weeks before the last expected spring frost and plant when all danger of frost has passed. Space 2 ft. (60 cm) between plants.

For a second crop in the fall, sow seeds outdoors approximately ten weeks before the first expected frost.

Water thoroughly once a week.

As soon as the heads or curds begin to grow, tie the top leaves loosely around to shade them and keep them white. Blanching is unnecessary for purple-headed varieties, which turn a light green when they are cooked, and for self-blanching varieties now listed in popular Canadian seed house catalogues.

New varieties feature purple colouring forms with multiple mini-heads, and self-blanching hybrids.

Celery

(Apium graveolens)

Celery requires about 100 days of optimal weather to grow from seed outdoors. Thus, most Canadian gardeners start it indoors, putting seedlings out when all danger of frost is passed. Prepare a trench 1 ft. (30 cm) deep, working in 3 in. (7.5 cm) of organic material. Space 6 to 8 in. (15 to 20 cm) between plants.

Shade seedlings with a newspaper tent for the first few days. As they grow, fill in the trench with mulch. Celery requires lots of attention to produce good specimens.

Keep Celery well watered, with at least 1 in. (2.5 cm) of water per week. Apply lots of mature compost or fertilize with a half concentration of water-soluble fertilizer every two weeks if you wish.

Harvest by twisting the whole plant off its root, or by pulling off outside stalks as you need them.

Celeriac is a member of the Celery family resembling a knobby Turnip. It is prized by French and Oriental cooks who use it grated raw or in cooked dishes. It stores very well.

Start Celeriac indoors and transplant with Tomatoes in late May. It should be hardened off in a cold-frame before being set in the ground. Plant in a rich, moist site in full sun. Space Celeriac 8 in. (20 cm) apart. Crowns should be flush with the soil surface.

Watch for fungus diseases and aphids.

Chicory

(Cichorium)

Chicory, which looks like a cross between Lettuce and Cabbage, is an ethnic European vegetable used primarily in salads but also in cooked dishes.

Chicory comes in several different forms. Some, like the crimson- coloured Raddichio, form definite heads. Witloof or Belgian Chicory grows upright like Romaine Lettuce. Various Endive Chicories produce smooth Bibb-type or scalloped loose leaves.

Like Lettuce, Chicory is relatively easy to raise. But it is much more cold resistant. Many Chicory varieties resist light frosts easily. Some, like Radicchio, even winter over when provided with adequate protection in Zone 6. In milder zones it can be fall-planted for spring harvests.

Most Chicory varieties should be direct-seeded. Like Lettuce, they resist transplanting. Sow in well-prepared soil that is rich and moist, with full sun exposure. Heading types should be spaced 8 to 12 in. (20 to 30 cm) apart.

Radicchio is prized for its lovely burgundy colour, while Witloof's interior white foliage is considered a great delicacy. To obtain the best colour from these varieties keep them blanched or covered. Grow them as trench vegetables. Keep them at least partially covered with friable organic material.

Corn

(Zea mays)

The flavour of home-grown sweet Corn is so much better than store-bought, it's worth making room to grow it yourself. Sow seeds two weeks before the last expected spring frost, planting at two week intervals until ten weeks before the first fall frost. Or plant early and late varieties. Usually, the later the variety the larger the ear. Sow Corn in blocks instead of rows for better pollination, leaving 1 ft. (30 cm) between plants.

Soil should be rich, with a pH of 6.5. Corn likes mid-season side-dressings of mature compost or 2 tbsp (30 mL) of fertilizer per plant, an even water supply, and diligent weeding. Harvest when the tassels are completely brown, when the ear feels firm and the kernels look right. Peeking doesn't hurt. Remove the stalks when you pick the last ears, and put them on the compost heap after you

FLOWERS FOR EATING

When's the last time you filled up on Nasturtium sandwiches or a Viola salad? Bees know something gardeners don't – flowers are often edible. It may sound odd, but remember that one of the world's most popular beverages, tea, consists of Camellia blossoms and leaves.

Cooks who serve flowers are not soon forgotten. Blossoms can make superb garnishes, and they are ideal in salads, soups, stuffings, beverages, ice cream and almost anything else you can think of. Let your culinary imagination run wild. Serve flowers in party drinks frozen in ice cubes. Use large flowers like Lilies, Gladiolus, Hollyhock, or large single Rose blooms to make exotic bowls for dips or salads. Sugared petals can be served as candies, or used to decorate deserts.

Cook with flowers wisely.

Never, use blossoms from plants that have been chemically treated. Grow your own – organically – to ensure safety and freshness.

Blossoms are fragile and need careful handling if they're to look their best on a plate. Trial taste tests are recommended. Remove stamens and pistils unless you like the bitter flavour or colour they may provide. Don't serve blossoms to anyone with plant allergies.

Many plants are extremely poisonous. If you don't know, don't guess. Saffron Crocus is edible but ordinary Crocus is not. Vegetable Pea flowers are edible, but Sweet Pea, which comes from a completely different family, is not. Use only those plants recommended in the following list of vegetable, fruit and ornamental flowers that may safely be consumed by most people:

Apple blossoms, Snap Bean blossoms, Bergamot, Borage, Calendula, Chrysanthemum, Clover, Fuchsia, Geranium, Gladiolus, Hibiscus, Hollyhock, Impatiens, Jasmine, Viola, Lavender, Lilac, Lily (including Daylily), Mallow, Marigold, Nasturtium, Orange blossoms, Pea, Primrose, Rose, Saffron Crocus, Snapdragon, Sunflower, Tulip, Squash.

have broken them up into small pieces.

Corn can be yellow, bicoloured, or white. There are multicoloured Oriental varieties. For novelty's sake, grow some popcorn. Be selective when you purchase seed. There is a great difference in flavour and keeping qualities.

Watch for large, four-legged pests, corn borers, and fungus diseases. Until recently, all Corn seed was treated with fungicide. Untreated seed is now available.

Corn Salad

(Valerianella)

Corn Salad, also called Mache or Fetticus, is a great salad green that has recently become quite popular.

Culture like Lettuce. Sow seed direct in average soil with full sun. Sow thickly and then thin periodically so that plants are eventually spaced about 6 in. (15 cm) apart. Mulch in late fall with finely-ground bark and you will likely be successful in overwintering some plants.

Plants form small rosettes that can be served whole or broken up in salads.

Watercress

(Nasturtium officinale) and Garden Cress (Barbarea)

Nasturtium officinale is the well-known peppery Watercress. Watercress grows only in a wet, warm environment. It is an aquatic plant and must be continually soaked. Gardeners in freshwater coastal areas should try it. Plant only in a pure stream or other clean water body. Otherwise, raise Watercress indoors.

Germinate seeds indoors regardless of where it is being grown. Transplant, using wet peat moss to lightly mulch the seed bed. Watercress flowers in spring and can be harvested year round where it is established.

Garden or Dryland Cress, which belongs to the genus *Barbarea*, is quite a different plant. It produces loose heads with foliage similar to Cabbage family members, only thinner and more succulent. Plants bolt easily, so lightly shaded sites are best. Cultivate as for Lettuce, spacing rosettes about 8 in. (20 cm) apart.

Cucumber

(Cucumis sativus)

Dig a hole 6 in. (15 cm) deep and 2 ft. (60 cm) around and fill it with well-rotted manure. Mix a handful of 6-12-12 fertilizer with the soil you removed from the hole and put it back on the manure-filled hole, planting the Cucumbers on this hill. Plant three to five seeds per hill and space 6 ft. (1.8 m) between hills.

Cucumbers can also be grown on upright supports like Beans. As Cucumbers develop, cradle them in plastic netting or used pantyhose.

Cucumber is a warm-weather crop that cannot be sown *in situ* until all danger of frost has passed. Get an earlier harvest by starting seedlings indoors four weeks before warm weather arrives. Plant three seeds in each peat pot. When you transfer the seedlings outdoors, remove all but the strongest vine in each pot and plant three per hill. If the pot is biodegradable, plant it too. If it isn't, carefully lift out the plant.

Water deeply and often. A plastic mulch over the hill will help conserve moisture and warm the soil.

Harvest pickling Cucumbers when they're about 3 in. (7.5 cm) long, slicing varieties at 6 in. (15 cm), and the long English seedless type at 14 in. (35 cm) or more. All should be picked before they turn yellow. Any left too long will inhibit production of new Cucumbers, so pick even overripe Cucs to encourage fruiting.

Newer forms include lemon, white, and long gourmet greenhouse varieties. Burpless Cucumbers tend to be mildest and thinnest-skinned. Try Kee Chi, the Oriental Cucumber that produces burpless thin fruits up to 3 ft. (90 cm) long, which is great raw or in stir-fries.

Watch for scab, mosaic, mildew, Cucumber beetles and aphids. Squash vine borer can kill a whole vine. It's easy to spot – a whole vine will wilt from one day to the next. Check along the vine for the borer's hole, and carefully dig it out with a knife. Bury the part of the stem you split open, and water it well.

Eggplant

(Solanum melongena)

Eggplant has many fans among European and Oriental cooks. Its Melon-like fruit is thin skinned and completely edible. The common European form has beautiful purple colouring. Oriental Eggplant lives up to the name Eggplant

– fruits are often white or yellow, and about the size of an Apple.

Eggplant is a tender plant that should be started indoors. Set out after all danger of frost, in well-worked soil that is moderately acid. Space plants about 2 ft. (60 cm) apart.

Eggplant is vine-like and resembles its cousin the Tomato in growth habit. Cages or staking are needed to support each plant. Pinch growing tips to promote side growth and better fruit production.

Fennel

(Foeniculum vulgare)

Fennel, often classed as an herb, looks like a cross between Celery and Caraway. Its thick rootstalk inspires the common name Italian Celery. Like Caraway, its feathered foliage has a distinct licorice flavour.

Germination requires cool temperatures. Plant outdoors or, for more controlled germination, start indoors. Set plants outdoors in early spring in a site with full sun and average soil. Seedlings should be planted in a shallow trench. Once the base of the stem thickens, backfill around the plant to keep it blanched. This will result in milder flavour.

Harvest stalks or leaves before they begin to flower, as you require them. Fennel is great in salads, soups or on its own.

Fennel may attract rodents and slugs.

Kohlrabi

(Brassica oleracea caulorapa)

Kohlrabi is a member of the Cabbage family that closely resembles Turnip. It can be substituted in any recipe that calls for Turnip. It's nice eaten in salads, stuffings and soups as well. Best of all, it's extremely easy to grow. It matures so quickly you can grow two crops in a single season.

Sow seed directly, in soil where no other member of the Cabbage family has grown. Provide neutral well-worked soil in full sun. Space young plants 4 in. (10 cm) apart. Kohlrabi is a typical root vegetable: it appreciates ample, regular watering.

Kohlrabi is available in white and purple forms. Its greens can be eaten.

Harvest Kohlrabi when bulbs are less than 3 in. (7.5 cm) wide as thicker roots are less tasty. Harvest carefully as Kohlrabi produces widely extended roots and immature produce may be pulled up at the same time.

Control pests and disease as for other members of the Cabbage family.

Lettuce

(Lactuca sativa)

Lettuce is ever popular and most often successful in backyard gardens. It has become even more popular with the introduction of exotic red and slow-bolting varieties.

As soon as the earth can be worked in the spring, sow seeds in rich soil with a pH of 6.5. Every week, sow as much as you can eat in an average week. Stop sowing in the middle of May, then start again in mid-July. Lettuce which matures in hot weather tends to bolt.

Spacing depends on the variety. Leaf Lettuce can be sown in closely spaced rows or blocks. Iceberg and Butterhead should be thinned 8 to 10 in. (20 to 25 cm) apart. If you let Lettuce plants grow too close together, they won't shape up.

Harvest by tearing off the outside leaves as they mature. Cut off Romaine (*L. sativa longifolia*) when it's about 1 ft. (30 cm) tall, and Butterhead when it's 10 in. (25 cm) across. Harvest and store Lettuce in the fridge. Lettuce left too long in the garden gets bitter and loses nutritional value.

Watch for slugs, aphids, earwigs, leafhoppers, and green worms (Cabbage worms).

Onion

(Allium cepa) and Leek *(Allium porrum)*

The Onion family includes globe types, giant Spanish, tiny pickling, red, bunching or green, perennial Shallots and Scallions.

Shallots and Scallions are prized by gourmets for their delicate, mild flavour. Shallots resemble miniature cooking onions, except that they are better keepers and they need to be planted in sets. Scallions such as the Welsh Onion are extra-large bunching onions that, like a green Onion, do not form bulbs, and multiply spontaneously.

Sow seeds directly into the garden, 1/2 in. (13 mm) apart, as soon as the soil can be worked in the spring. Soil should be rich and well drained. Keep seeds moist.

Bunching Onions and Scallions can be planted in groups in trenches. Gradually fill in the trench as they grow, mounding soil over the lower portion to keep them white. Pickling Onions should be planted deeper than other types. If left too long in the ground they become large, flat-topped white Onions.

Large onions need to be thinned when stalks reach 8 in. (20 cm). Pull every other Onion. Repeat the process three times for Globe and Spanish Onions. Thinning is the secret to good Onion harvests. For an earlier harvest, start indoors in February and set out seedlings when the soil can be worked. Thin as you would rows seeded directly.

If your growing season is short, plant larger Onions from sets. Onion sets are small bulbs that should be planted 5 to 8 in. (12.5 to 20 cm) apart and deep enough that their tops crown at or just above thc soil surface. Some types, like Shallots, are difficult to raise from seed and should only be grown from sets.

Weed and water regularly, and side-dress with lots of compost or apply 1/2 lb. (227 gm) of 6-12-12 fertilizer per 20-ft. (6-m) row in July.

Harvest Green Onions by pulling them up as you need them. Harvest storage onions by waiting until the tops turn yellow, then digging them up and letting them dry in the sun for two days. Store your harvest in a cool, well-ventilated place.

Onions suffer from relatively few pests. But watch for root maggots and thrips.

Leek is a member of the Onion family with an appealing mild flavour. Start Leeks indoors six weeks before your garden is workable. When the ground thaws, dig a trench 12 to 16 in. (30 to 45 cm) deep and work 3 in. (7.5 cm) of compost into the bottom of the trench. Plant Leek seedlings 1 1/2 to 2 in. (4 to 5 cm) deep in the bottom of the trench. Fill it in as they grow. This blanches the plants so you get more of the usable white stem portion. I confess a weakness for my mother-in-law's home-grown, home-made Leek soup.

Parsnip

(Pastinace)

Parsnips are sweet root vegetables that are cultured much the same as Carrots. They look like an albino Carrot. Allow more than 100 days for Parsnips to mature.

Parsnip seed should be soaked to spur germination. Plant seed directly in double-dug, well-worked soil about 1/2 in. (13 mm) deep. To avoid problems with germination cover seed with a moistened, friable medium like peat moss.

Parsnips are prolific. If given rich, moist organic soil they will produce much heavier crops than Carrots. They prefer moderately acid soil and should be spaced about 5 in. (12.5 cm) apart as they can grow quite large.

Keep Parsnips well watered and weeded. They have few natural pests but are sometimes afflicted by root maggots or Carrot rust fly. They can be overwintered in the ground and harvested first thing in the spring.

Pea

(Pisum sativum)

Peas need rich soil with a pH of 6.5. As soon as the soil is dry enough to work, amend as required. For an earlier start, work the soil in the fall, or plant Peas in a raised bed before the snow has melted.

Peas like cool, moist roots, so plant them in a trench 4 in. (10 cm) deep and cover them with 1 in. (2.5 cm) of soil. As the plants grow, fill in the trench as with Leeks and Celery. Space 2 in. (5 cm) between plants.

While some edible-pod varieties set pods all summer, most Peas stop producing when temperatures rise above 75°F (24°C). You can plant a second crop in August to mature in cool fall weather. Plant the seeds 2 in. (5 cm) deeper in the trench.

Two adjacent rows of Dwarf Pea vines will support each other. Taller standard varieties need to be trained on a fence, chicken wire, or strings tied to a wooden frame.

When Pea vines have grown to 10 in. (25 cm), side-dress with extra compost or two handfuls of 6-12-12 fertilizer for every 20 ft. (6 m) of row. Keep Peas evenly moist all season with mulch and soak weekly.

they form visible lumps in the pod. Check vines for ready pods every two or three days. Pods toughen quickly, and if you leave them too long on the vine, Pea production stalls.

Pick edible pod Peas (*P. sativum macrocarpum*) while they are flat. Use both hands to harvest – one to hold the vine and the other to pull off the pod. Otherwise, vines have a tendency to snap off.

Watch for aphids, which help to spread mosaic disease. Also watch for Pea weevils and mildew. Very early plantings may be particularly subject to fungus.

RULE OF THUMB

Among the choicest table delicacies are the succulent baby greens culled by the thinning process. Don't discard those tender and tasty Beets, Lettuce, Onion, Radish, Turnip or Spinach leaves. They're ideal for salads, stir-fries and garnishes and a good source of nutrients.

RULE OF THUMB

"Bolting" is a gardening term used in reference to the fast production of a flower head on cold weather crops like cabbage, brocolli, cauliflower, radish and rhubarb.

Pepper

(Capiscum frutescens)

Peppers like hot weather. Wait until June to plant outdoors, or start seedlings indoors eight weeks before constant warm weather arrives. Plant several seeds in each 4-in. (10-cm) pot and place in a warm, sunny spot. When shoots are 1 in. (2.5 cm) long, remove all but the strongest.

Harden off gently. Place Peppers in a closed cold frame for at least a week, unless the temperature is very hot. Cover the glass with newspaper on cool nights.

Most home gardeners purchase established plants in mid to late May and set them out.

Plant Pepper seedlings, pots and all, in a prepared bed where no members of the Pepper family grew in the past season. Pepper family members include Tomatoes, Potatoes, and Eggplant. Soil should be rich, with a pH of 6.0. Space 2 ft. (60 cm) between plants.

Shade newly transplanted Peppers for the first few days and keep them evenly moist throughout the entire growing season. Dryness can cause blossom drop. Apart from this, I have found the secret to successful pepper growing is to plant them in a sunny, warm spot in well-prepared (and warmed) soil.

Harvest Bell Peppers anytime, but for sweeter, more tender Peppers, wait until they turn red or yellow. Hot Peppers should be left on the plant until they are fully mature, and turn completely red or yellow. Hot Peppers are less hardy and may need some frost protection in fall.

Pepper plants which are slow to set fruit may need an extra dressing of 2 tbsp (30 mL) of muriate of potash per plant.

Watch for cutworms, aphids and white flies.

Potato

(Solanum tuberosum)

Prepare the Potato patch in the fall for early spring planting. Amend the soil until it is light and friable to a depth of 1 ft. (30 cm) or more. This may require as much as 6 in. (15 cm) of moistened peat moss over the entire bed. Avoid manuring a Potato patch just before planting; it invites diseases such as scab.

Soil should be acid, with a pH of 5.0 to prevent common Potato diseases. The peat moss will probably lower pH sufficiently, but check it and amend if necessary. 5 lbs. of peat moss per 100 sq. ft. (1 kg/4 sq. m) lowers pH by 1 point.

Buy certified disease-free seed Potatoes. Commercial potatoes are often treated to prevent sprouting, and they may carry blight. Plant whole seed Potatoes, or cut them into egg-sized chunks with at least one eye apiece. Leave them to dry overnight.

Lay seed Potatoes in a trench 6 in. (15 cm) deep and 6 in. (15 cm) wide. Cover with 3 in. (7.5 cm) of earth. As plants grow, fill the trench. Hill it above ground. The Potatoes will grow at the base of each plant. Space 1 ft. (30 cm) between plants.

Always keep developing Potatoes covered with earth or straw or they will become green and inedible.

If you have very heavy soil you can work the surface and place the seed Potatoes on top, covering with straw or a heavy mulch. Keep the mulch moist but not saturated. At harvest time, lift the straw or mulch with a fork and remove the Potatoes.

Watch for Potato blight, and leafhoppers, which help to spread this disease. Also watch for scab, Colorado Potato Beetle, and aphids.

Radish

(Raphanus)

Standard Radish matures before other garden crops, making it ideal for interplanting with larger, slow-growing members of the *Brassica* family. It can also be used to mark rows of slow-germinating vegetables such as Carrot. It's a great crop for children or beginning gardeners and should be planted early in the season, 2 weeks before the first frost free date.

Soil should be fertile and light, with a pH of 6.0. Sow seeds 1 in. (2.5 cm) apart in the furrow, then thin to 2 in. (5 cm). Space 6 in. (15 cm) between rows. Water regularly and weed diligently. Regular salad Radish has a shallow root system and does not stand up to competition, drying, or temperatures above 72°F.

Harvest when Radishes reach mature size. Check the seed packet for the maturation time of the variety you choose. Radishes that mature before hot weather are milder.

Fall and winter Radish varieties include Oriental hybrids, like the Daikon or Serpent Radish, which mature over two months or longer. 'April Cross' or 'Chinese White' varieties are white, with a long, cylindrical form like a Carrot. These types need to be planted 1 in.

(2.5 cm) deep in well-dug soil and later thinned to a minimum spacing of 5 to 12 in. (12.5 to 30 cm), depending on variety.

Watch for root maggots and Cabbage moth larvae (green worms).

Squash

(Cucurbita)

There are two main groups of Squash: Summer (*C. pepo melopepo*) and Winter (*C. maxima* and *C. moschata*). Summer Squash, including Zucchini, grow on low, sprawling bushes and mature early. Winter Squash, a broad category which includes Pumpkin, Hubbard Acorn, and Butternut, usually grow on spreading vines which need lots of room and a long growing season.

Otherwise, the needs of summer and winter Squash are the same. Prepare hills as you would for Cucumber, spacing 4 ft. (1.2 m) between hills for summer Squash and 8 ft. (2.4 m) between hills for winter Squash. When the weather turns warm, plant six seeds per hill. Thin to the three most vigorous when shoots are 6 in. (15 cm) long.

You can start Squash vines indoors four to six weeks before warm weather arrives. Transplant vines, peat pot and all, when it's warm. This is necessary in areas with a short growing season for late-maturing Squash like Hubbard.

Give Squash a plentiful, slow watering once a week. Drying can stop production.

Harvest summer Squash when young and tender. Pick Zucchini when it is 6 to 10 in. (15 to 25 cm) long and its skin can be easily pierced with your fingernail. If you have never grown Zucchini, two plants will show you why there are so many Zucchini cookbooks around. Summer Squash plants mature quickly, so check them every couple of days.

Leave winter Squash on the vine until its skin is hard. It will stand a light frost. When you pick, shear the connecting stem, leaving a 2-in. (5-cm) stem on Squash. Do not break it off. The wound leaves the Squash vulnerable to pests and diseases.

Control pests and diseases as you would for Cucumber.

Spinach

(Spinacia oleracea)

Sow in early April – Spinach needs to mature before the weather gets hot or it bolts. Plant a second crop in August for a fall harvest.

Sow seeds 1 1/2 in. (4 cm) apart. Thin to 3 in. (7.5 cm) when the tops touch. Thin to 6 in. (15 cm) when they touch again, dressing with mature compost, or apply two handfuls of 20-20-20 fertilizer per 20-ft. (6-m) row.

Harvest as you thin. Small plants are quite tasty. Pick the outside leaves of the plant when they are 2 or 3 in. (5 to 7.5 cm) long, not including the stem. When buds form, harvest the whole plant. Bolting can be postponed if you pinch out initial seed heads.

For heat-resistance, try ever-bearing varieties or Malabar Vine Spinach, which can be grown in pots.

To avoid mosaic virus, buy resistant strains. Watch for aphids and leaf miners.

Turnip

(Brassica rapa)

Turnip allowed to mature in cool weather is less bitter. Sow your first crop as soon as the soil can be worked in the spring. When you pull up Peas or early Beans, you can also sow a second Turnip crop, timed to mature in the fall.

Sow seeds 1/2 in. (13 mm) apart, in light organic soil. Thin to 1 in. (2.5 cm) when seeds sprout, 2 in. (5 cm) when tops touch, and 4 in. (10 cm) when they touch again. As you thin, save the greens for eating. Young Turnip greens are quite tasty.

Keep Turnip weeded and well watered. Size and sweetness are affected most by two factors: adequate moisture and cold. The best fertilizer for Turnip is a top-dressing of compost and wood ash. If you want to use a prepared commercial fertilizer, buy a 5-10-5 formula. Start harvesting when roots are 2 in. (5 cm) across. Roots larger than 3 in. (7.5 cm) are not as tasty.

Rutabaga or Swede Turnip (*B. napobrassica*) is a large Turnip that stores well. Like its smaller cousin, Rutabaga will have a better, sweeter flavour if exposed to autumn cold. Sow 90 days before the first hard frost is expected. Cultivate as you would Turnip, thinning to a minimum of 6 in. (15 cm). Large root growth is dependent on ample watering. Rutabaga keeps for months in cool, moist sand, or coated with wax.

Watch for root maggots, aphids, and flea beetles.

RULE OF THUMB

Provide 1 in. (2.5 cm) of water weekly. Uneven water supply causes knobby and hollow-heart Potatoes. Start harvesting when flowers bloom. Dig into the hill with your hands and pick some thin-skinned new Potatoes. To harvest mature Potatoes, wait until plant tops die. Lift out the whole plant, Potatoes and all, with a spading fork.

CHAPTER 13

BUSH FRUITS AND FRUIT TREES

If you have ever reached high into the branches of your own fruit tree and plucked from it the sun-ripened fruit, you have experienced a feeling unique to the group of gardeners we loosely refer to as orchardists, fruit growers, and berry-pickers.

If you haven't, then you're in for a big treat. Growing your own fruit and berries is not difficult, and the road to success is not strewn with deadly chemicals or labour-intensive non-chemical pest control methods – especially if you lower your expectations for the picture-perfect specimen and concentrate instead on taste and nutritional qualities.

This chapter offers advice and information that will lead you down a garden path lined with fruit-bearing trees and shrubs that produce healthy, tasty food – food that will give you growing satisfaction as the years go by.

Take special note of the hardiness zone symbols listed with each plant name. The Rules of Thumb are particularly useful for the home orchardist who wants to maximize the fruit-bearing potential of her fruit trees and berry bushes.

My approach to fruiting plants includes three steps:

Firstly, choose fruit trees and berry bushes that suit your tastes.

Secondly, match your favourites to the hardiness zone, light availability, and soil requirements in your garden.

Thirdly, stop dreaming and start planting. In just a couple of years, you'll be telling your neighbours how it's done.

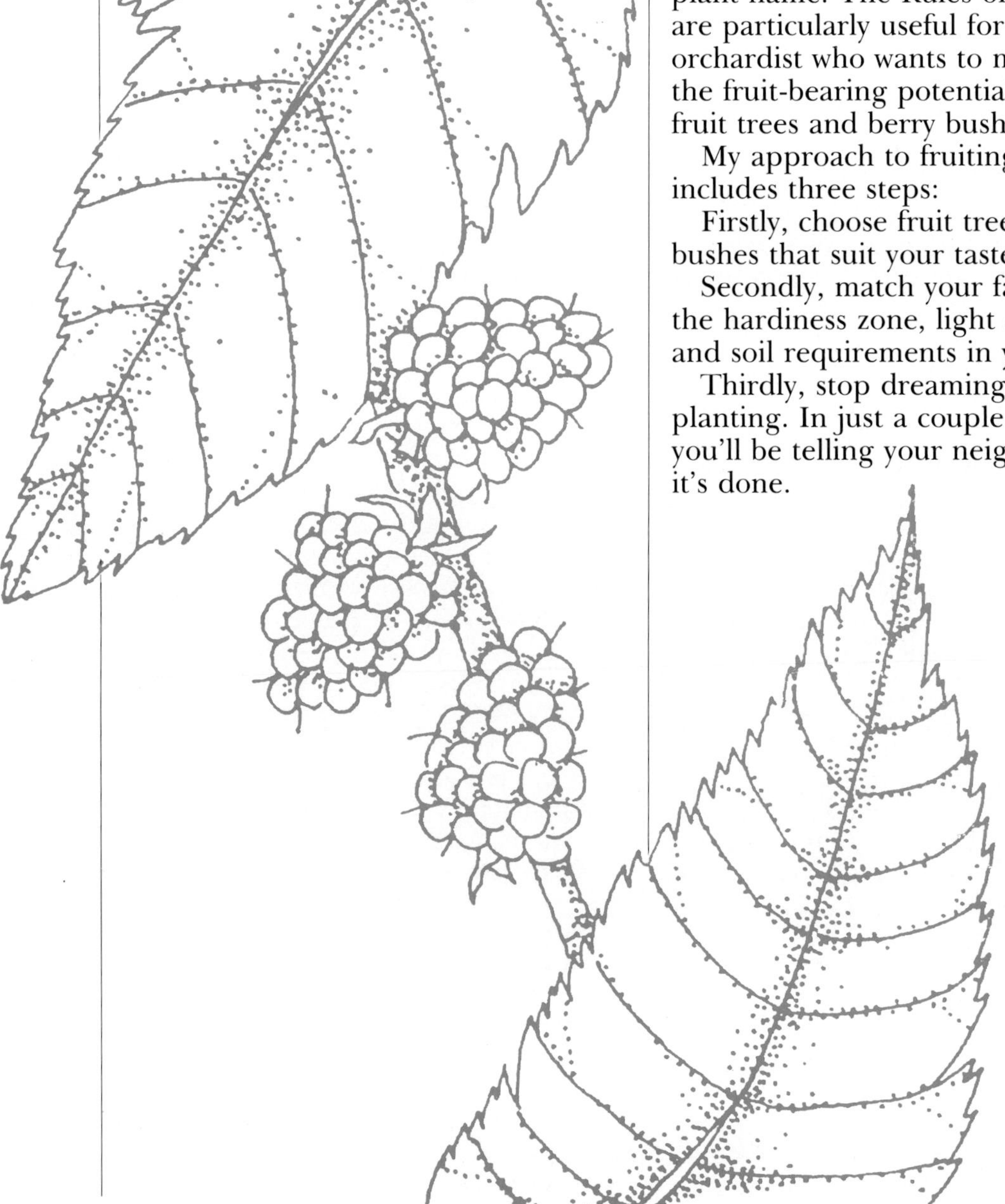

CARE AND MAINTENANCE OF BUSH FRUITS

Fruiting plants, whether trees or bushes, share a love of sun and rich, moist organic soil that registers acid on the pH scale. Only members of the *Prunus* family – Cherries, Peaches, Plums, Apricots, as well as some Pears and Grapes – prefer neutral or more alkaline soils. For all the rest, if you supplement with generous amounts of organic mulch and provide plenty of sunshine and water, you are nearly assured of producing overflowing baskets of luscious, juicy fruits. Many fruit trees and bushes appear to thrive in moderate shade or near-neutral soil, but they will not perform to their potential unless planted in full sun and acid conditions. A range of pH from 5.5 to 6.5 is optimal for fruit, depending on variety and unless otherwise specified. The same is true of feeding and watering. The fullest, best- developed fruits are produced by trees and bushes that are neither thirsty nor lacking in nutrients.

Fertilizer requirements

Top-dress with matured compost and heavy organic mulches. Leaf colour should be a healthy green if your fruit plants are obtaining enough nourishment organically. If you choose to use chemical supplements, most bush fruits require 12-18-9 or 6-12-12 fertilizer mixtures. These include Blackberry, Blueberry, Melon (Cantaloupe), Grape, Raspberry, Gooseberry, and Strawberry. The exception is Rhubarb, which requires a 20-20-20 mixture, and Blueberry, which favours an evergreen fertilizer like water- soluble 30-10-10.

Pests and diseases

The pests and diseases that attack bush fruits have been listed in the descriptions below. For more information, including methods of control, see the section on weeds, pests, and diseases in the appendix of this book.

Descriptions and Requirements

Blackberry

(Rubus)

The Blackberry group includes Loganberry and Boysenberry, which remind us of wine or jam. Blackberry should not be confused with Black Raspberry. Here's a simple way to distinguish them. The Blackberry core stays in the fruit when it is picked, while the Black Raspberry core stays on the cane.

Plant berries in an established bed to minimize cutworm problems. Soil should be well drained and very organic. It should also be quite acidic – at least pH 6.0 or less, and preferably 5.5. Amend as required.

Plant in fall or early spring when canes are dormant. Set out rooted canes, spacing 3 ft. (90 cm) between plants, and 8 ft. (2.4 m) between rows. Leave 10 ft. (3 m) for trailing varieties. Match soil level to the soil mark on the cane. Tamp and water well. Cut the canes back to the bud nearest a point 1 ft. (30 cm) above the soil surface.

Use a long stake and a wire hoop to surround and support each plant. Alternatively, set up three wooden Ts for each 20-ft. (6- m) row, stringing a heavy wire between the ends of the crosspieces. When canes reach 3 ft. (90 cm), pinch or prune the tip to force side branches. If you remove flowers in the first season, it will help to establish strong canes and better crops in future years.

For the first three years, side dress with a handful of 6-12-12 fertilizer for each plant when you mulch in the spring. Water only during long dry spells.

Blackberry bears fruit on the previous

With each description, I have included symbols indicating light requirements, most northerly climate zone, and soil requirements.

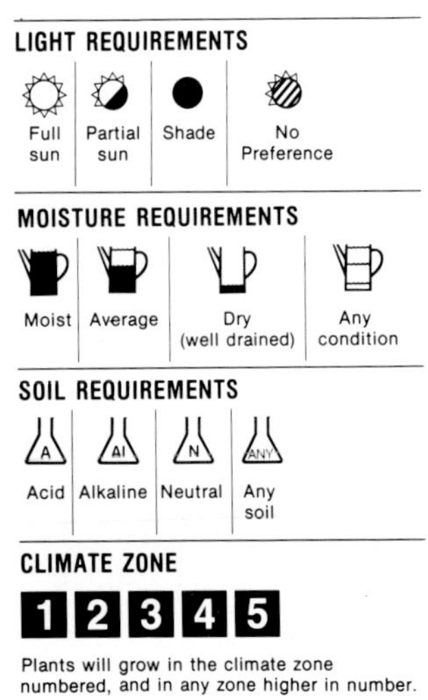

year's canes, so when harvest ends, immediately remove all the canes which had berries on them. In the fall, when the plant is dormant, trim the long branches and cut the main stalks back to about 4 ft. (1.2 m) in height. Remove any suckers which grow between plants or rows.

Harvest begins in the second year and lasts for two or three weeks, regardless of the weather. Wear leather gloves with the fingertips cut out of them to protect yourself from the sharp thorns. Blackberries bruise easily, so be gentle. Plants yield about 3 pints (1.5 L) each.

Most pests and diseases can be controlled by selecting highly resistant varieties, choosing stock that is certified pest- and disease-free, and following a programme of good cultivation. Keep the bed clean, mulch well, and check regularly for problems.

A preparation of lime sulphur and dormant oil spray will take care of many pests. Check the pests and diseases chapter in the appendix for solutions to other problems. If a section of the plant wilts, look for signs of cane borer in the top portion of the plant, and cut off and destroy the affected section of the cane. Cheesecloth or garden netting will keep birds away during harvest.

Blueberry

(Vaccinium)

Blueberries need acid soil with a pH below 5.0, ideally 4.0 to 5.0. Soil should also be highly organic and well-drained. Amend as required, adding aluminum sulphate. Prepare in summer to plant in the fall, which is preferable, or in the fall for spring planting.

The main species are High-Bush Blueberry (*Vaccinium corymbosum*) and Rabbiteye Blueberry (*V. ashei*). Some popular cultivars are Berkeley, Blueray, and Bluecrop.

Blueberries need cross-pollination, so choose two or more varieties and alternate them in a row. Many professional growers insist on at least three varieties for maximum cross-pollination. For this reason, some nurseries sell Blueberry bushes in threes. Space 3 to 5 ft. (90 cm to 1.5 m) between plants and rows, 5 or 6 ft. (1.5 or 1.8 m) apart, depending on the variety.

Dig a hole big enough to hold the roots comfortably, and match the soil line on the trunk to the soil surface. Fill the hole with water and let it drain. Meanwhile, soak the soil removed from the hole. Place the bush in the hole, replace the soil, and tamp well, watering periodically to eliminate air pockets as you fill the hole. Mound soil in a 4-in. (10-cm) high circle around the plant, the diameter of the rootball, and fill the moat with water. Fertilize about a month after planting with a balanced fertilizer such as 20-20-20.

When growth starts in spring, keep Blueberries evenly moist but not soggy. Mulch with acid organic material. If the leaves develop yellow patches, correct pH with a tablespoon of cider vinegar in a cup of water for each bush.

Patient gardeners remove flowers in the first year, letting the plant conserve its energy to establish itself. In the next two years, prune only dead or damaged branches. From the fourth year on, remove one to four of the oldest shoots so they can be replaced by new ones.

If you want to prune new growth to shape the bush, do it early in the growing season. This allows the pruned branches to set buds for the following year's fruit.

Keep birds away from ripe berries by throwing a net over the bushes. Protect from rabbits. Cover with chicken wire in winter. Plants yield as much as 5 quarts (5.5 L) each.

Currant

(Ribes)

Currant produces clusters of red, white or black small fruit that hang like grapes. It makes a good hedge, and grows 3 ft. (90 cm) or higher, with an equal spread. Other than annual pruning and some 6-12-12 annually and some lime sulphur to keep the mildew at bay, it requires little or no care and will live 30 years or more.

moist clay soil or mulch on sandy loam. Plant bushes in fall or spring, spacing them about 4 ft. (1.2 m) apart. Prune when planted to 6 in. (15 cm) above ground level the first season. Wait four years to prune again. Prune mature bushes thereafter in autumn, removing all but six healthy canes.

Like other members of the *Ribes* family, Currant may help to spread fungal diseases to White Pine. If your evergreens break out in a blistering rust disease, Currant bushes may be responsible.

Gooseberry

(Ribes)

Gooseberry fruits are greenish-yellow, pink or red and resemble striped grapes. The green Pixwell type is quite sour and best for jam-making. They are also the hardiest. Other types can be eaten fresh.

Gooseberries grow on thorny, 3-ft (90-cm) high canes that tend to ramble. They like rich, moist soil and slight shade. Water only when summers are dry. Mulch with matured manure or compost in fall and spring. Harvests can usually be obtained when plants are three years old.

Gooseberry is quite hardy and seldom needs winter protection. Plant bushes approximately 5 ft. (1.5 m) apart in the fall. Prune to ground level. After the first summer, prune out all but four to six of the healthiest branches. Cut these above a bud about 6 in. (15 cm) above the root stalk. Thereafter prune annually in the same manner, ensuring that a few healthy older canes are left. Fruit is produced on new canes or new shoots on old canes. Cut back branches to 6 in. (15 cm), making sure a bud remains. This encourages necessary new growth on older stalks. Cut back more severely on poor producers.

Protect from birds, aphids, sawfly and mildew. Gooseberry can spread fungus disease among evergreens, especially white-pine blister rust. Also susceptible to mildew.

Grape

(Vitis)

Grape needs a long, hot summer and a mild winter. But with protection in winter and a well-chosen site, it can be grown in Zone 5. American or free skin varieties (*V. labrusca*) are generally hardier than European kinds (*V. vinifera*). Hybrid seedless Grapes tend to be less hardy than self-rooted seed varieties. Agriculture Canada recommends Himrod, Seneca, Buffalo, Delaware, and the old favourite, Concord.

Choose a site with good protection from the north. Create your own ideal site by building a wall to the north of the bed. Soil needs to be well drained, even sandy, and moderately fertile, with a relatively high pH. A range from 6.0 to 7.0 is usually adequate, depending on the variety.

Plant rooted cuttings in the fall or

spring (spring is safer), deep enough to let one bud show above the soil surface. Space 6 ft. (1.8 m) or more between plants, and 8 ft. (2.4 m) between rows. Tamp down and water well as you backfill the hole, then mound the earth up to cover the cutting. Mulch with straw in the fall.

Each growing season, mulch around Grape vines with rotted manure or compost enriched with a handful of 6-12-12 fertilizer. Water well. When plants are dormant, mulch with straw or leaves. You can apply a white rodenticidal paint to discourage mice. Wrap the vines with tree wrap in cold areas.

Harvest when Grapes are ripe. Unlike other fruit, Grapes do not continue ripening after they are picked. Choose a dry day and cut the bunches from the vine, handling with care. Plants yield 10 to 15 lbs (4.5 to 6.8 kg) of Grapes each.

Watch for downy mildew, black rot, and anthracnose. Dead arm, which enters the vine through pruning cuts or winter kill, is a progressive fungus disease which affects leaves first, then stems. It can be controlled only by cutting the vine down to ground level and spraying the new growth with garden sulphur as it comes up in the spring.

Grape shade

Grapevines can be trained to cover and shade a patio with a lattice roof. They will provide shade in summer and let light through in winter. Don't try this with hybrid seedless varieties, though, unless you live in Zone 8. They're not hardy enough. In Zones 5 and 6 stick with types like Concord, Niagara, and New York Muscat.

PRUNING GRAPES

Pruning Grapes is a major task – it takes three or four years to train them properly. The idea is to provide a strong root system and a sturdy trunk. two of many available methods are described here:

Spur training

Spur training, used for European Grapes, is easy in the first year. Place an arbour, trellis or other support beside the cutting when you plant it and let the Grapes grow unpruned. When the vines are dormant in the fall, remove all but one sturdy upright branch and cut that one back, leaving only three buds.

In year two, let only those three buds grow, rubbing off any others that develop. When the three branches from those buds are 1 ft. (30 cm) long, choose the most vigorous and remove the other two. When this branch grows above the place on the support where you want it to branch out, cut it at that point, and let two branches grow. Tie the two branches horizontally to the support. Branches which grow up from these two horizontals should be pinched when they are 8 in. (20 cm) long.

In year three, let the shoots grow up from the two horizontal branches, spaced about 8 in. (20 cm) apart. Rub out any buds that develop closer than that. In the fall, prune these upright shoots to two buds.

In year four, you finally get some Grapes. From each of the two buds on the upright shoots, a bearing vine will grow. Pinch back these bearing vines to leave three or four branches of Grapes. In the fall, prune the stronger of the two bearing vines back to the two buds, removing the other completely.

From those two buds, two bearing vines will grow in the fifth year. These you do not pinch back. Let them bear as many Grapes as they want. When they are dormant, remove the weaker and prune back the stronger branch to two buds. Repeat this process each year.

The Kniffin system

The Kniffin system is designed for American Grapes. Set two 8-ft. (2.4-m) posts 10 ft. (3 m) apart and drive them 18 in. (45 cm) into the ground. String two heavy wires between the posts, at 3 ft. and 6 ft. (90 cm and 1.8 m) above ground level.

In the first year, let the Grapes grow. Train one vigorous vine to grow upright by tying it to the two wires. In the fall, when the vines are dormant, cut off all but this one vine, which will become the trunk.

In the second year, choose four sturdy side branches which will grow from this trunk, and train them along the wires on either side of the trunk. Tie them to the wires. Do not prune during the season, but pinch back any long vines apart from the four you are training. In the fall, remove all but the four main branches.

In the third year, the four trained branches should bear fruit. Rub off any buds that form on the trunk except two near the wire and two near the top. These will grow to replace this year's bearing vines. In the fall, remove the vines which bore Grapes and tie the four replacements to the wire.

In subsequent seasons, repeat Year 3 activities.

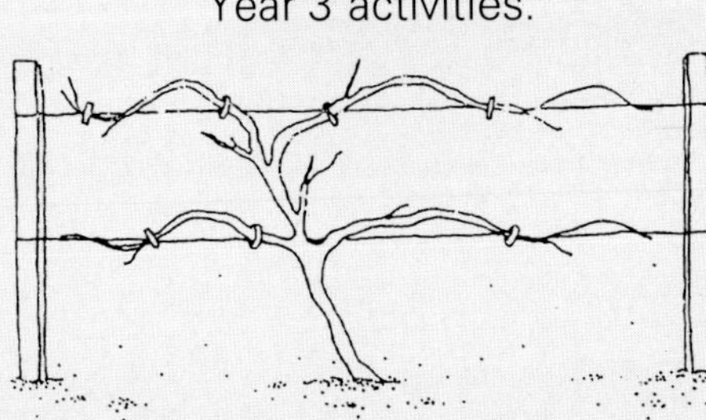

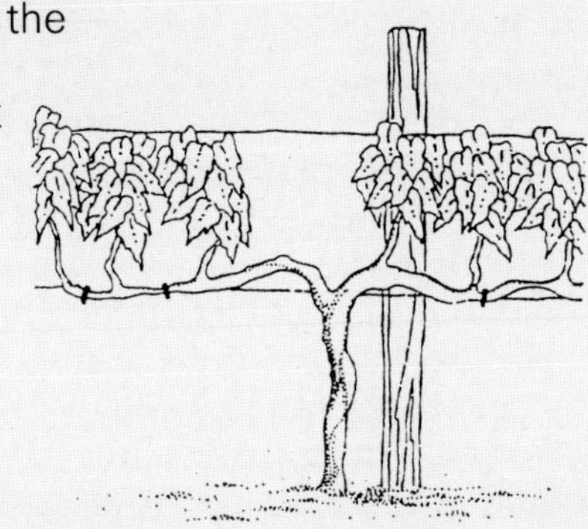

Raspberry

(Rubus)

Like Blackberry, Raspberry prefers established beds. Soil should be fertile, organic, and well drained, with a very low pH of 5.5. Amend as required.

Plant spring or fall, spacing 18 in. (45 cm) between plants and 6 ft. (1.8 m) between rows. Set the rooted canes deep enough to match the soil line. Tamp down and water as you back-fill.

Erect supports when you plant. Pound in T-posts as for Blackberry, with foot long cross-pieces at each end of the row. Rows longer than 20 ft. (6 m) will need a third support mid-row.

Mulch in spring with straw or shredded bark. Weed by hand, and water during long dry spells.

In the first year, remove all flowers. In the second year, harvest gently, and do not pile the berries too deeply in the basket. Raspberries are fragile. Each plant yields 2 to 3 pints (1 to 1.5 L).

After the harvest, remove canes that bore fruit and cut back suckers that grow between rows or established plants. Prune fall- bearing varieties in October or November; prune July-bearing varieties right after the harvest in midsummer.

See Blackberry for pests and diseases.

Rhubarb

(Rheum rhaponticum)

Nothing could be easier to grow – except maybe Mint. Plant in fall or spring, spacing 3 ft. (90 cm) between plants and rows. For each, dig a hole 2 ft. (60 cm) deep, fill it halfway with composted manure, and amend the soil removed from the hole as required. Soil should be organic, fertile and well drained, with a pH of 6.8. Spread Rhubarb crown roots in the hole, positioning so the crown is covered by 2 to 3 in. (5 to 7.5 cm) of topsoil. Tamp and water as you back-fill. Cover with shredded bark or straw mulch.

When growth begins, remove the mulch to amend with composted manure or 20-20-20 fertilizer, then replace the mulch. Water during hot, dry weather.

In the first year, don't harvest stalks. In the second year, take only the thick stalks that grow in the first two weeks. In succeeding years, you will get strong, thick stalks for six to eight weeks, and you can harvest them all.

When Rhubarb starts to thin out, let stalks grow to nourish the roots for next year. If it bolts, remove the seed stalk immediately to retain the leaf- and stem-bearing potential of the plant.

Every five years, Rhubarb should be divided to encourage production. Separate established clumps into three or four crowns, and begin anew. Note that Rhubarb leaves are poisonous.

RULE OF THUMB

Strawberries, like blueberries and raspberries do not continue to ripen after picking. Always pick when at peak of ripeness.

Strawberry

(Fragaria)

Soil that grows good Potatoes grows great Strawberries. It should be fertile and organic, with a pH of 5.7. To minimize problems with white grubs, always start with an established garden rather than claiming one from the wild.

Double-dig the bed in the fall, amending with lots of mature compost or composted manure. Set out Strawberry plants, spacing 20 in. (50 cm) between spring-bearing plants, and 8 in. (20 cm) between ever-bearing types. Leave 30 in. (75 cm) or more between rows.

The extra space between spring-bearing plants provides room for runners to develop. In the first year all runners should be removed. They can be placed in a nursery bed and allowed to mature.

Plant Strawberries in holes that allow generous space for root expansions. The crown of each plant should meet the soil surface.

Water newly planted Strawberries well, then mulch. Remove all flowers from spring-bearing varieties in the first year. Ever- bearing Strawberries should have their initial blossoms removed, but they will flower again and produce a light midsummer crop.

For a consistent, abundant harvest of Strawberries, plant two beds one year apart. One will flourish while the other is making ready for the next year. Runners from two-year-old plants can provide next year's fruit. Stem layering encourages runners to establish a mature root system. Select the strongest healthy runners from your most productive plants for the best results.

Clean up Strawberry plants when the tops die in the fall. Some gardeners burn the tops off. Others raise their lawnmower as high as it will go and mow the tops off. Mulch with clean straw when the cold weather arrives.

To control diseases, buy certified disease-free stock and resistant strains, and practice crop rotation. If any disease gets through your defences, remove the whole plant right away and burn it. Wash your hands immediately after handling a diseased plant to avoid contaminating any others.

Strawberries may need protection from a variety of insects, including aphids, Japanese beetles, leafhoppers, leafrollers, slugs, thrips, mites, weevils, spittlebugs, and earwigs. Mulch heavily with straw or use plastic matting to keep berries raised off the soil. If you keep the beds clean and practice crop rotation, insects are unlikely to become a serious problem.

If you use chemical fertilizer, be careful to keep it off leaves or fruit.

Keep birds off berries with netting, or suspend tin plates over the row on strings. Yelling is effective.

During harvest, check daily. Strawberries become overripe very quickly and are vulnerable to grey mould. Strawberries harvested when wet should be eaten right away. Fruit should not be washed until the moment you are going to eat or process it.

CARE AND MAINTENANCE OF FRUIT TREES

Before you plant a fruit tree consult the following checklist:

Suitability

Is the variety best for your eating or cooking needs? Many fruit trees have been hybridized to accentuate characteristics suitable to one use or another. If you have limited space but want to grow more than one type of fruit species consider a dwarf tree.

Bloom period

Different varieties of the same species may also blossom at separate times. Period of blossom affects both hardiness and pollination. In very cold regions, look for trees that blossom later. Flowers that are nipped by cold seldom set fruit. If your trees require cross-pollination ensure that the varieties you plant bloom simultaneously.

Hardiness

It is sometimes difficult to gauge hardiness where fruit trees are concerned. Local conditions are extremely important. Consult your local nursery about the latest developments in fruit trees hardy to your region. Provide ample winter protection and select a good site. Shelter fruit trees from wind. Planting on a south- facing wall is also recommended. For vulnerable early bloomers, like Peach or Apricot, choose a north-facing slope to reduce the risk of premature flowering.

Pollination

Self-pollinating trees includes Peach, Apricot, Sour Cherry, and Stella Sweet Cherry. Others (e.g. Apple, Pear and Plum) need another variety to cross-pollinate. Both should be in bloom at the same time.

Pollination can sometimes be tricky. Even fruit trees listed as self-fertile require intervention by helpful insects or humans. Bees are not as abundant as they should be since the advent of chemical lawn and garden treatments. Some fruit trees blossom before bee populations have revived from winter. In either case, gardeners often need to pollinate manually. Shake small trees. Dab each blossom with a soft brush every few days. Pollination works best if the brushing is done when blossoms are dry. When in doubt about whether a tree is self-pollinating, plant two.

Thinning

Fruit trees have an evolutionary design flaw – they often produce more fruit than they can support. Overcrowded fruit trees are more prone to breakage and disease. Thinning fruit promotes longevity and vigour in tree stock and encourages plump, healthy fruit.

Pests and diseases

Human beings have to compete with a wide array of predators and diseases in order to obtain their rightful share of juicy, plump fruits. Fruit trees share genes and several growth characteristics. Thus, an organism that attacks one fruit species will often attack another. If Plum weevils attack your Plums, your Peaches and Cherries need protection.

Good cultural practices can help to control insects and diseases. Discard clippings after pruning. Remove and destroy any diseased fruit. In late fall, rake and remove leaves from fruit trees that have been attacked by disease. Many organisms overwinter in leaves and debris.

In the descriptions of individual fruit trees below, I refer to common pests and diseases, leaving the reader to check the listings in the appendix of this book for further information, including methods of control.

Descriptions and Requirements

Apples
(Malus)

Although Apples are grown widely and appear to thrive under a variety of growing conditions, they require care and pruning for maximum fruit production.

In cold climate regions, spring is the best time to plant a new tree. Apple appreciates cold winters but it can be shocked if freezing temperatures develop soon after a fall planting. Cold hardy forms that blossom late in spring are best in Zone 4 or colder. Miniature and dwarf forms are not as cold-resistant

RULE OF THUMB

Considering the similarity between peaches, apricots and nectarines, pay close attention to hardiness when planning your tree purchase. The hardiest of the three is apricot (zone 4) nectarine (zone 5) peach (zone 6) though peach will grow in zone 5 with protection.

and should always be given protection where winters are severe. Even a spring that combines high daytime temperatures with night frosts is damaging. Blossom development suffers and branches split.

Plant Apple trees in pairs, no more than 50 yds (45 m) apart. Pollen has to be transferred from one tree to another to facilitate fertilization. The spacing of trees in your orchard depends on the type you plant. Dwarf forms require less space and are most popular among urban gardeners. Plant them about 12 ft. (3.6 m) apart. They can be trained on wires similar to grape culture. Otherwise stake them individually.

It pays to coddle young Apple trees. After planting, water well and mulch for several years running, applying matured compost, manure or fertilizer below a cover of straw or other organic material. Apples prefer well-drained, moderately acid to neutral soil, and a sunny site. Don't allow new trees to fruit for a couple of years. Rub out their large conspicuous fruit buds.

Trees often take between four to ten years to reach maturity. Restrict fruit production until then to avoid stress, which ultimately damages limbs and retards root development, and to allow the development of healthy roots necessary for mature harvests.

Thin Apple crops for the same reason. Reduce fruit clusters in early summer to one or two immature Apples to reduce stress on branches and encourage maximum fruit production. Wait until after mid-June, when the diseased and deformed fruit usually drops. Thin again in mid-season to remove all but the healthiest specimens. Ideally, Apples should be spaced at least 6 in. (15 cm) apart.

Pruning technique depends on the age and type of tree. A well- trained tree consists of a central leader and three to five main wide-angled branches spiralling up the trunk, 1 ft. (30 cm) apart. A one-year-old tree usually has a single leader (main trunk). It will send out several branches in its second summer if it is cut back to 2 ft. (60 cm) high. For the next two years, prune young, non-bearing trees so that their branches point upward and tips are spaced 1 ft. (30 cm) or more apart. Take care to ensure that each cut is made above a bud.

Sometimes Apple trees become larger than anticipated. Weigh down individual branches or train them to droop by tying them to stakes. This will moderate growth. Late summer pruning rather than fall pruning also helps restrict growth in the following season.

Apricot

(Prunus armeniaca)

The sweet but tart fruits of Apricot develop following lovely displays of pink, spring blossoms.

Apricots originated in warm areas of Asia and still prefer moderate climates. Some forms promise to produce in Zone 4, though, they may grow as dwarves or produce meagre crops. They grow best on the west coast, in southern Ontario, southern Nova Scotia and the north-east section of Prince Edward Island.

Once they are established, Apricots are ideal trees for urban gardeners. They can live as long as 40 years and need little pruning, other than thinning or removing deadwood. Most are self-fertile but you may have to provide assistance. Fruits appear in late summer and should ripen on the tree.

Apricots, especially those suffering from cold, may produce less fruit and fall prey to many of the pests that afflict other fruit trees in your area. Some popular varieties are Goldcot, Alfred, and Veecot.

Cherry

(Prunus)

Cherries are categorized as Sweet (*P. avium*), Sour (*P. cerasus*), or Bush form (*P. besseyi*). Sour and Bush Cherries are hardiest and most flexible in their requirements. All will grow in Zone 5, but Sour and Bush types can be grown in Zone 3 with adequate protection. More than one Sweet Cherry tree is required for successful pollination, with the exception of 'Stella' sweet red Cherry. Look for types that flower simultaneously.

Allow Cherries to ripen naturally. Harvest carefully to avoid damaging the thin spurs that will produce more fruit in consecutive years. Cherries keep better with their stems left on.

Cherries prefer well-drained, sandy, neutral soil. Give them a sunny site and plant in early fall for best results. Water only under extremely dry conditions. Mulch with straw and add mature com-

post in fall and again in early spring. Fertilizer (6-12-12) can be applied with the mulch in spring.

Cherries produce fruit on old wood and begin active growth in early spring. Thus excessive pruning carried out in spring could cause damage. Prune mature trees moderately in the fall to remove deadwood or to thin.

Cherries may attract many pests, especially birds. I have found large pieces of bird netting to be an effective control. Montmorency is an old favourite Sour Cherry. Popular sweet (black) varieties are Viva, Bing, and Stella, which is self-fruitful. White sweets include Vega and Victor.

Peaches and Nectarines

(Prunus persica)

Nectarines are really radical Peaches. Their thin, fuzz-less skin is the result of a genetic accident. For unknown reasons a Peach tree may suddenly sport a hybrid branch that bears smooth-skinned fruit. Both Peach and Nectarine trees are available as standard trees and are less hardy than Apricot.

Peaches and Nectarines mature early and often begin producing large crops within five years. They are self-pollinating, but planting two trees provides good insurance. Peaches and Nectarines seldom live beyond two decades.

Supply a good, sunny site and well-supplemented, neutral soil. Water well as fruit begins to develop fully in early summer.

Winter-hardy Peach varieties are now commonly available, but wise gardeners provide a sheltered location to protect early blossoms. Avoid applying fertilizer with high nitrogen content beyond early summer, which would stimulate growth of new wood vulnerable to cold. This is especially true with new saplings. Use more mature compost or fertilizer as the tree ages and increases in size, but never apply after the first of August. Some popular varieties are Redhaven, Redskin, and Vivid.

Peaches and Nectarines may attract boring insects, aphids, mites and many others.

Pear

(Pyrus)

Pear is considered by many to require the lowest maintenance of all full-sized fruits. Pear produces wonderful fruit, and it is also beautiful to look at, with its billowy white spring blossoms, glossy green foliage and fall colouring. Pear is ideal for urban lots because it grows no larger than the average ornamental tree. Growth can be easily kept in check with annual pruning. Most Pear trees grow upright, and occupy relatively little space in lawns and gardens.

Like Apple, Pear is usually not self-pollinating. Plant at least two different varieties to ensure fruit production. Cultivation of Pear and Apple is similar in other respects.

soil and moister conditions than Apple. Plant in well-supplemented soil with a pH no higher than 7.0. Keep well watered. Generally, Pear does not respond well to pruning. Prune only when trees get out of hand.

Unlike Apples, Pears need to be harvested when slightly immature. Otherwise, they become soft and mealy. You know they're ready to be picked when their stems begin to thicken. Simply twist upward to remove fruit and then store it in cool, dark surroundings for two weeks. Popular Pears for the home garden include Clapp, Favourite Anjour, and Bosc.

Watch for aphids and fire blight. And watch for sawflies or weevils, which may be attracted to your Cherry and Plum trees.

Plum

(Prunus domestica)

Plums and Prunes are ideal for British Columbia gardeners because they prefer moderate temperatures and dry environments. But it is also relatively easy to raise Plums for eating or cooking throughout Canada, in Zone 4 or warmer. There are also hardy plums which will grow in the prairies.

Some varieties are self-pollinating, but you are safer to plant more than one. Plums do *not* do well in acid soil. They prefer a sunny site and soil with a pH as high as 8.0. Fertilize or apply extra compost only in spring. Plum prefers a well-drained site but will tolerate damp soil conditions better than most fruit trees.

Prune annually to remove deadwood and to keep leader growth in check. Prune in late summer following harvest. Plums can be left to ripen on the tree.

Those intended for cooking should be picked when slightly immature.

Plums may attract wasps, and a score of other pests, including bacterial, viral and fungal disorders. Beware of black knot, which attacks Plum and Cherry. It causes black swelling on branches and outer twigs. Prune afflicted branches.

Quince

(Chaenomeles)

Quince, formerly called Cydonia, is most often grown in North America for its striking, salmon blossoms, which appear in late spring. But many gardeners are more attracted by its scented leaves and yellow fruit. Some varieties produce peach or white- shaded blossoms. Quince rarely grows above 3 ft. (90 cm).

Quince bushes are easy to raise. They are not fussy about soil, so long as they receive full sun. Prune current season's growth after flowering, as required. Quince, especially Japanese Quince (*C. japonica*), makes a colourful low-growing hedge. Quince fruit is used often in preserves. Slices of Quince placed in the refrigerator absorb food odours while imparting a soft pleasant odour of their own.

REVIVING AN OLD FRUIT TREE

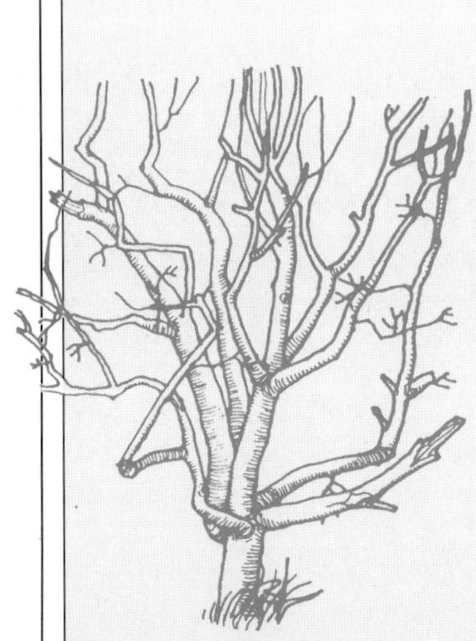

A fruit tree that has gone untended for a few years can be quite a mess.

A fruit tree that has gone unattended for a few years can be quite a mess of broken branches, dead twigs, and tangles. However, unless the damage is severe, and the tree has several large broken branches, or is split down the trunk, it is certainly worth trying to bring back. At the very worst you will have wasted a little time and energy.

Step One: Start early in the spring, before the buds have begun to swell. Remove all dead branches, any with split or badly damaged bark, and any broken branches. When you cut, remove the branches completely, at the trunk of the tree, or a vigorous lateral.

Step Two: Remove all suckers. These are vigorous branches which grow vertically, straight up from main branches, the trunk, or the tree roots. They do nothing but rob the tree of nutrients and should be pulled off. Pulling them discourages the growth of more suckers from the same spot, but on an old tree, this might be difficult. Cut them off right at the branch, trunk or root, and file any leftover bumps down flush.

Step Three: Remove any branches which cross or rub together. Unless the damage to the bark is severe on both, remove only one of the two. Choose the one growing in an outward direction, away from the trunk.

Step Four: Let the sun shine in. To stimulate growth on the inner portions of the branches, you have to open up the centre of the tree. This is accomplished by removing laterals, paying particular attention to the very top of the crown. This is the part where the branches end directly above the main trunk. By thinning the number of branches that terminate in this area, the center of the tree is opened up to let more light in. Any other crowded areas of the crown should be thinned as well.

Look for the laterals which end in the crowded areas, and remove them. Cut them off right at the branch, angling the cut along the branch so you do not leave a stump. This method is described more thoroughly in the section on Thinning the Crown of mature trees.

Step Five: Thin any crowded twiggy growth at the ends of the branches.

Step Six: Paint all wounds larger than one-half inch in diameter with tree-wound dressing. Pick up all the branches you have removed from around the tree. Take them well away from the tree because they often harbour pests. Remove all grass and weeds from around the tree from the trunk right out to the drip line under the ends of the branches.

Step Seven: Stand back and admire your handiwork, and wait for the warm weather to see how much good it did.

APPENDICES

THE WELL-STOCKED TOOL SHED

How to buy tools

If you are just starting out in the gardening game, resist the temptation to buy cheap tools. Cheap tools break, rust and rot, and then you have to replace them. That's no saving.

Buy tools made of tempered steel, and forged rather than stamped. Bargains may be had at auctions or contents sales held when people move out of their houses into apartments or condominiums. You can clean off rust with rust remover, and sharpen the tools yourself or have them sharpened at a hardware store.

Care of tools

Give wooden handles a couple of coats of oil-based paint or spray. This makes them easier to find in the garden, and protects them if they are left out in the rain. Store your tools in a garage or shed accessible to the garden, hanging them on nails or pegs to save space.

To keep tools clean, place a bucket of sand mixed with oil close to the storage area. Just before you put your tools away, dunk them in the oily sand. This will take off any dirt, and prevent your tools from getting rusty.

File

Keep a good metal file handy to sharpen spades, trowels, lawnmowers, hoes, etc.

Rotary tiller

You can rent one of these in the spring and fall for major cultivation jobs, but if you have one of your own you can also use it to dig in soil additives like manure or compost. You can get weeder blades for some tillers and use them on long rows.

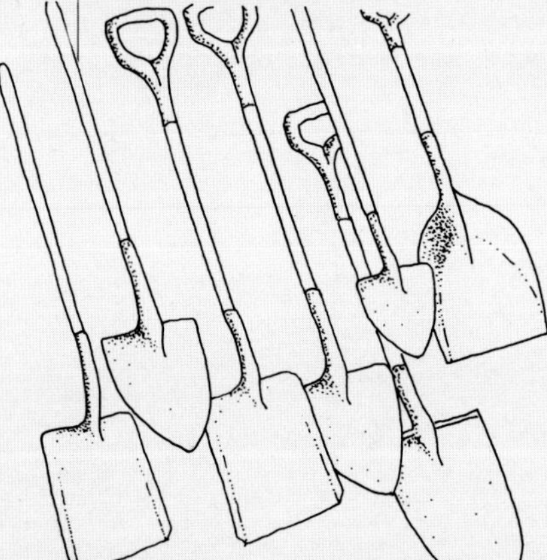

Shovels and spades

A D-handled pointed spade is best for digging down and turning hard soil in early spring, applying peat moss and mulch, and carving out new garden beds. A long-handled shovel gives good leverage when digging post holes or planting perennial vegetables and fruits like asparagus and rhubarb. A short-handled scoop, with a wide blade and sides, comes in handy for picking up debris like a dustpan.

Trowel

You will use a hand trowel constantly to dig small holes and mix in amendments when setting out bedding plants. It's a good idea to keep two or more. Choose trowels which are relatively heavy, yet comfortable to grip. They should be smooth and strong where the steel joins the handle. If this joint is composed of two pieces welded together it will probably weaken and break with use.

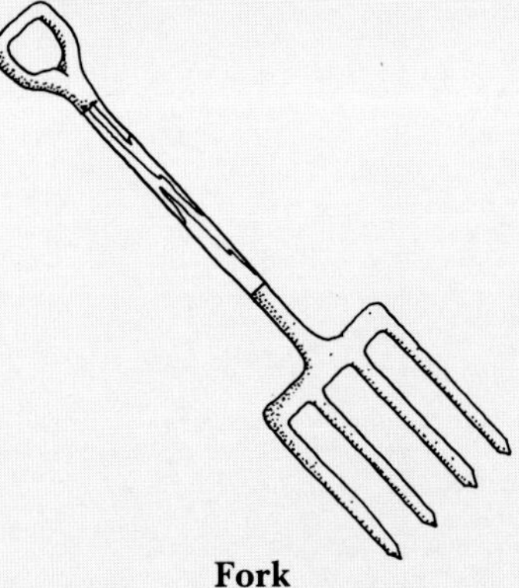

Fork

A garden fork is handy for turning the earth in the early spring and breaking up large clumps. A fork is also useful for mixing in amendments like peat moss, compost, and manure, forking compost, or lifting and spreading mulch. Buy one with tempered steel tines, which are less likely to bend.

Rake

Use a rake to smooth the earth and give it a finely textured surface, particularly before planting seeds. Use the bottom of the rake's tines to tamp down a light sprinkling of soil covering the planted seeds.

Cultivator

Cultivators have three curved prongs which are wonderful for breaking up the earth. Use a small hand cultivator to loosen soil around plants without damaging roots. Hand cultivators are also useful for low-growing plants and raised gardens. Use a long-handled cultivator for the areas between rows and around large sturdy plants. Buy tempered steel.

Hoes are indispensable. A small hand hoe can clear away the weeds from tender seedlings, and clean up the earth in raised gardens. A large hoe is the best tool for removing weeds and grass between the rows of a picking garden. Keep the blades sharp. Buy forged steel.

Knife

When you are gardening, carry a knife with a rounded tip and a sharp, smooth blade. It will be useful for a variety of purposes, including cutting out bedding plants from flats and digging out errant weeds.

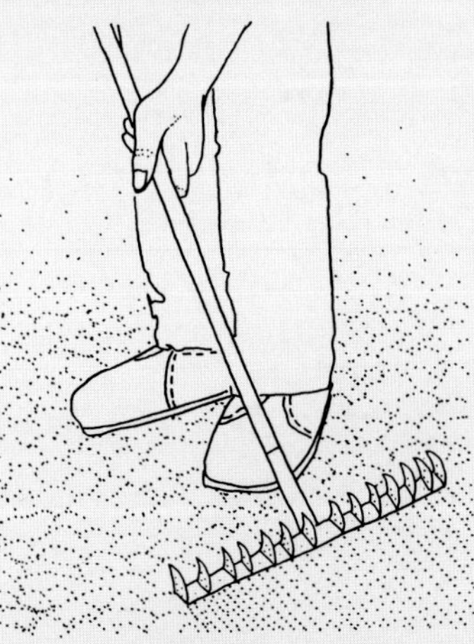

Scissors

Use scissors to prune flowers and take cuttings. Get a pair with blunt ends so you can safely carry them with you in a pocket.

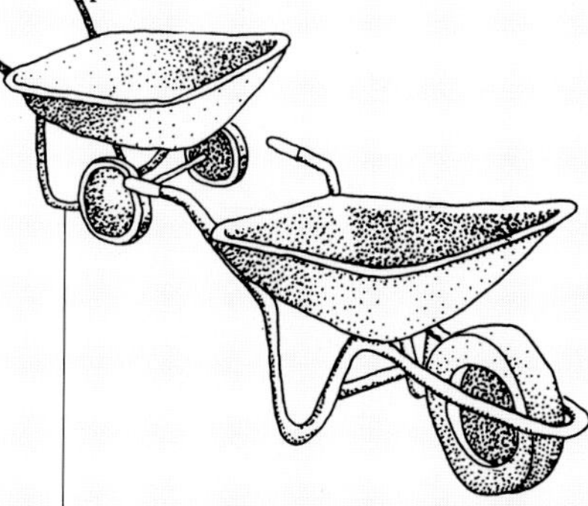

Wheelbarrow

Use a wheelbarrow to transport tools, mulch, compost, peat moss, plants and anything else that needs to be moved from one place to another in the garden. A wheelbarrow can also be used to mix amendments like peat moss and manure before putting them in planting holes. Plastic wheelbarrows are lighter and won't rust, but might not stand up to heavy work like building a rock garden. To prevent rust on a steel wheelbarrow, paint with a non-toxic oil-based paint. Consider a large two- wheeled cart for large properties, especially with uneven terrain.

Hose

A 3/4 in. (19 mm) hose carries double the water of a standard 1/2 in. (13 mm) hose. Unlike plastic hoses, rubber hoses stay flexible and won't cramp up, even in cool weather. Buy quality. Cheap hoses kink, break, and crack.

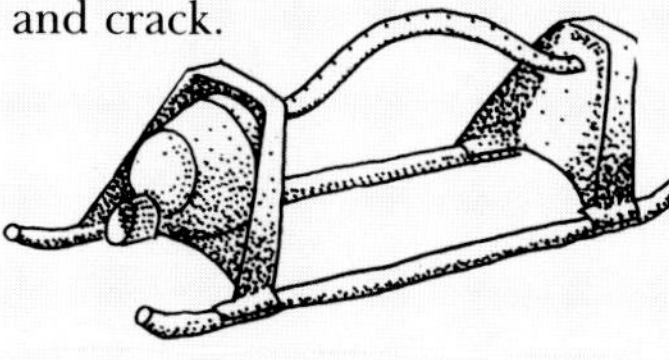

Water sprinklers

Sprinklers come in many shapes and sizes, including the popular fan or oscillating type. Impact sprayers are directional but cover only a small area at a time. Oscillators and fan sprinklers cover larger areas but apply water unevenly. Tripod sprinklers look state-of-the-art, but they don't apply water at the root zone, where it is most needed. To ensure gentle watering of seedlings and young bedding plants, attach a spray on the end of the hose, which will give a fine mist.

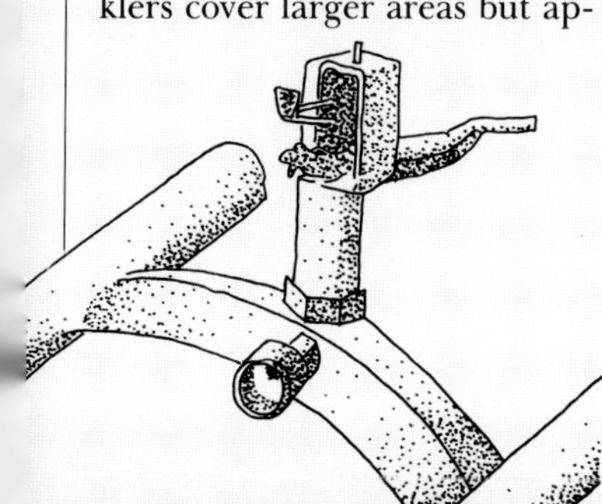

Soil soakers and perforated hoses

A soil soaker or perforated hose attached to the end of your hose puts the water right where it's needed. Mulch and earth get an even amount of water, leaves don't get wet (causing mildew and spotting in some plants), and flower heads don't get heavy with water and break off. Perforated hoses can even be permanently installed, exactly where they are needed. Use a mulch to hold them in place and protect them from the sun's rays. Some models withstand ultraviolet radiation better than others.

Bug sprayer

By far the best sprayer I have ever used is the new Dial-a-Spray sprayer that fits onto the end of your hose. It is simple to use, lasts for years, and is inexpensive.

Plant supports

Use 1 in. or 1 1/2 in. (2.5 cm or 3.8 cm) square stakes of cedar, redwood or pressure treated lumber, 4 or 6 in. (10 or 15 cm) fence posts and 10 gauge galvanized wire to support grapes and raspberries, chicken wire for Peas, cages for Tomatoes, etc., strips of old sheets or nylon stockings for tying, green bamboo stakes for support.

Gauges and testers

Rain gauge, pH tester, thermometer (for burying in squash hills to check if soil is warm enough to germinate seeds for warm weather crops), soil test kits, soil sampler to test for pH and to check what's under the topsoil.

Frost protection

Plastic 4-qt. (5 L) jugs can be placed over new seedlings in the spring. Wash them well and cut the bottoms out with a sharp knife. To keep a row of plants warm, use a sheet of opaque white or clear corrugated fibreglass, bent like a croquet hoop and held with a lath frame at each end and in the middle. Lay old newspaper on top of the soil for insulation. Build a lath or pipe frame to be left permanently over raised beds. When it gets cold, drape a sheet of heavy plastic over the frame.

Miscellaneous extras

Plastic mulch, 2-in. (5-cm) paper cups, gloves (leather provides a combination of protection and flexibility), twine, watering can, bucket to mix water soluble fertilizer, board or foam to kneel on, black string to repel birds, harvest baskets, a board to lay between rows, stakes and twine to lay out rows, a square of canvas or heavy cloth to pick up leaves or to hold dirt when you dig holes.

Reel Type hand mowers

Here's a way to beat the noise and fumes of power mowers. Keep the mower clean, greased, and oiled. Sharpening the blade can be tedious and tricky. You may want to have it done professionally.

Rotary power mowers

It has been said that rotary mowers are so dangerous they should be banned entirely. That's an extreme view, but caution is certainly called for. Keep the mower clean and the blade sharp. New models will automatically shut off if unattended, a good safety feature.

Electric rotary mowers

These are easy to use and maintain. Just watch you don't run over the cord, and don't use them in wet weather.

Drum mowers

These are more expensive, but they mow longer, with fewer repairs and less sharpening than other models. Hence their popularity with professional lawn service companies.

Sit-down mowers

Watch that you don't sacrifice lawn-cutting effectiveness in return for a free ride. Ask for a try-out before you spend the big money. The best of the sit-down mowers is a lawn tractor, with a drum mower, rototiller, snowplow, and other attachments.

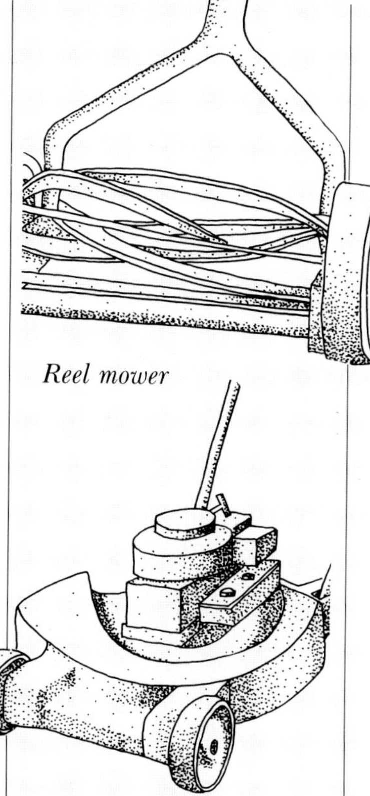

Reel mower

Rotary power mower

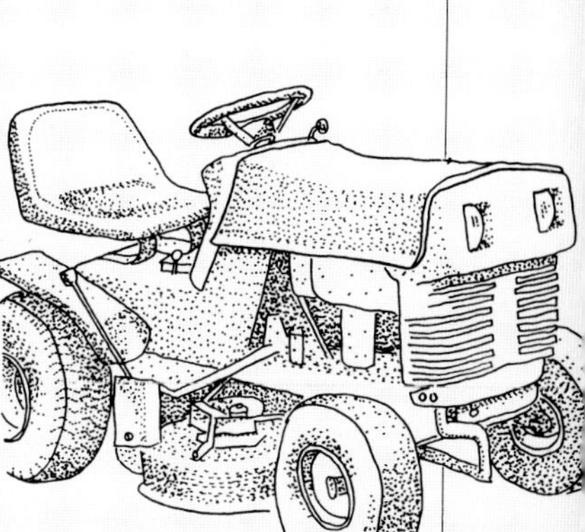

Sit-down mower

Lawn clippers

Springed, one-handed clippers are best for trimming grass around trees, beside gardens, and along fences. Keep the blades clear to avoid sticking. Larger two-handled clippers will do the job if they're in good shape, but they double as hedge clippers and shrub trimmers so they are heavier than necessary to cut grass. Powered string trimmers are easy to use, but can flay the bark off trees if you're not careful, and they're noisy.

Spreaders

Of the two main types of spreader for fertilizer or weed and feed, broadcast spreaders and drop spreader, the broadcast type is better for most purposes. Hose it out after use and store it in a dry place to avoid corrosion. A small, hand-held cyclone is great for fertilizing small and hard-to-get-at areas.

Sprayers

You can use air pressure or tank sprayers to spray pesticide, herbicide, or fungicide. But be sure to wash out the sprayer thoroughly when you are finished to avoid mixing chemicals. Or use separate sprayers for each. Another option is Dial-a-Spray, which can be attached to the end of your garden hose.

Edgers

Options for edging lawns include a half-moon edger, a square shovel, and a sod shovel.

Hand clippers or pruners

Use hand clippers on small branches up to 1/2 in. (13 mm) in diameter. Of the available varieties, I like the cutter-and-hook type, which is lighter and more manoeuvrable among crowded branches than either the scissors type or the cutter-and-anvil type. The scissors type makes the cleanest cut. Choose clippers that are small enough to fit your hand comfortably. Check to ensure there is a clean fit along the length of the blades. If the blades are "sprung" or bent apart, they won't cut properly.

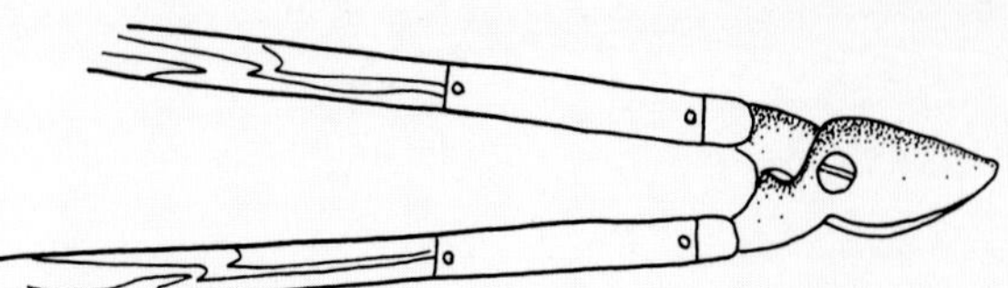

Loppers

Loppers are long-handled cutters for use on branches up to 1 in. (2.5 cm) in diameter. Like hand clippers, they come in three types. Again, I prefer the cutter-and-hook type.

Small pruning saws

Small pruning saws, 12 to 14 in. (30 to 35 cm) long, are used to cut branches up to 2 in. in diameter. I prefer a small 12-in. (30-cm) saw with a curved blade and a fixed wooden handle for strength.

Large saws

Large saws, 18 to 24 in. (45 to 60 cm) long, are used to cut branches up to 4 in. in diameter. I prefer an 18-in. (45-cm) large-toothed saw with a straight blade, which is useful for cutting branches from below.

Extension pruning saws

These consist of a small, curved saw blade on a handle 8 ft. (2.4 m) or longer, often combined with a lever-action cutter operated by pulling a long rope. The saw is for branches up to 2 in. (5 cm) and the cutter is for branches up to 1/2 in. (13 mm). These are useful as a safer alternative to climbing a ladder.

Swede saws

These consist of a thin, flexible blade attached to the ends of a tubular steel handle bent in a "D" shape. They cut efficiently but are awkward for use in crowded locations.

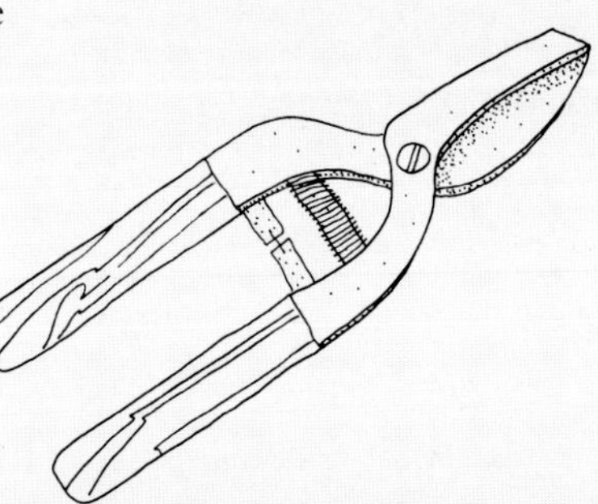

Hedge shears

Hedge shears or clippers are used to prune small, twiggy growth, particularly on small-leafed shrubs and hedges. Serrations on one of the two blades hold the twigs in place during a cut. Take care not to cut too many branches at once, or branches that are too big. As with hand clippers, check to make sure the blades are not sprung. Aluminum handled shears are lighter. Electric shears will do the job, but they are unnecessary if you prune regularly, and they can be hard to control.

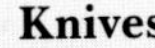

Knives

Pruning knives have a hooked end, like a linoleum or rug-cutting knife. If they are kept sharp, they are useful to clean up the raw edges of saw cuts, or to cut new, small branches up to 1/4 in. (6 mm) in diameter.

Ladders

Buy a good quality ladder for pruning. Compare the thickness of metal used in aluminum ladders before buying. When using an extension ladder, place it within easy reach of the branch you want to cut, make sure it is set securely on the ground, and tie it to a strong branch or the tree trunk for safety. The combination of a 6-ft. (1.8-m) step ladder and a 20-ft. (6 m) extension ladder is usually adequate for pruning requirements

WEEDS, PESTS AND DISEASES

Chemical-free gardening is a phenomenon in Canada. Organic gardening is no longer endorsed strictly by a narrow group of fringe gardeners. It seems to me that every Canadian with a conscience for the future needs to pause and consider the consequences of using chemical pest controls. My reflections on the topic over recent years have lead me to the point where I no longer recommend their use when an effective biological (i.e. organic) solution will suffice.

Since the Second World War, science has developed an armoury of chemical preparations for use in controlling weeds, pests, and diseases in our gardens. But in recent years, we have learned more about the environmental costs of manufactured chemical pesticides, and their effectiveness has sometimes been challenged. These pesticides are not the "magic bullets" we once thought they were.

Chemical pesticides tend to be *non-specific* – if we develop a poison to kill a particular pest, it will almost certainly be harmful to other living organisms, including beneficial insects, which are far more numerous than the destructive ones we call pests. What's toxic for the potato beetle is often toxic for a praying mantis or a honey bee, or even a dog or a child.

Reliance on pesticides can damage the complex ecosystem which breaks down organic matter in the soil – the protozoa, nematodes, mites, springtails, earthworms, millipedes and other decomposers which are necessary to naturally healthy soil. They can harm bees and other insects necessary for plant pollination.

Pesticides can damage the natural enemies of the pest you are trying to control, resulting in a resurgence of the target pest in greater numbers than before treatment. Spider mites are the classic example. Insecticides often kill mite predators, allowing spider mites to multiply unchecked.

Alternatively, pesticides may eliminate one pest, clearing the way for an infestation of another which is less affected by the treatment. Some herbicides create spaces for invasion by herbicide-resistant weeds.

Chemical pesticides can be addictive. Once you start using them, your garden becomes dependent on them. You have to keep using them regularly or the pest will return.

Scientists and government agencies often support claims by the pesticide industry that its products are not dangerous to human beings when used properly. But pesticides are toxic. They are made to kill living things. In my opinion, it seems wise to avoid the unnecessary stress on people and the environment due to chemical pesticide use when it is practical.

I must admit that we had to have a baby before I made the decision to divest myself of all garden chemicals. And then it took me five years. But I recommend you go cold turkey, if you share my concern for the real quality of the food we eat and the ultimate condition in which we will leave the environment for the next generation.

PREVENTION

Instead of viewing pests as enemies to be vanquished with chemicals, we should take an outbreak as evidence we are doing something wrong. *The problem isn't the pests; the problem is the way we garden.* If we understand our gardens as complex ecosystems, we can design and manage them to keep pests within acceptable limits through relatively natural or organic means.

Proper care

The best way to control pests without manufactured chemical pesticides is to ensure healthy plants. Study the needs of the individual plants in your garden. Some have very specific requirements. Others are more flexible. But all can be put under stress if they are exposed to inappropriate conditions of moisture, light, soil nutrients.

Gardeners are sometimes the biggest pests in their own gardens. Heavy-Handed Havocs kill their plants with kindness, by over- watering, over-fertilizing, over-pruning, and taking other excessive measures. Procrastinating Pests go to the other extreme. They neglect plant needs until it is too late, giving pests an opportunity to flourish.

Soil, water, and light requirements for individual plants are discussed throughout this book. A number of other preventive measures also nurture healthier plants and help to control pests naturally. Together, they add up to good cultivation practices:

Competition

Make sure each plant has the room and the resources it needs to grow. Annuals and vegetables always do better when they are thinned to reduce competition for nutrient elements and moisture. Grass and other plants need extra water and nutrition when growing near the roots of thirsty shade trees.

Ventilation

Problems with fungus and mildew are reduced by providing adequate ventilation. Ventilation, which can often be improved by removing lower tree limbs and leaving adequate space between plants, allows foliage to dry and warm earlier in the morning, and much sooner after a rainfall.

Resistant varieties

Look for plant varieties which have been bred for resistance to fusarium wilt, verticillium wilt, rust, and other diseases. Potato seed is a good example.

Certified stock

Especially in the case of vegetables, buy only seed stock which is guaranteed free of fungus spores, viruses, and insect eggs to which the plant is susceptible.

Rotation

When you plant the same crop in the same place two or more years in a row, you make it easy for pests and diseases to find their prey. Eggs or spores winter in the soil and attack plants the following season. Rotation minimizes this problem. Avoid planting members of the same family in succession. For example, members of the Brassica family, including Cabbage, Brussels Sprouts, and Cauliflower, should not be planted in the same location in consecutive seasons. The same prohibition applies to members of the Tomato family, including Potato, Eggplant and Pepper. (Rotation also helps to vary and balance the nutritional demands on the soil from one year to the next.)

Companion planting

Onions and Carrots planted together are said to repel one another's major pests. Chives, Dill, Nasturtium, Geranium, Thyme, Basil, Celery, Mint, Garlic, Onion, Parsley, and Broccoli keep away certain species of insect. Basil protects Tomato from all kinds of infestation. Savory protects Beans. Plants with small flowers such as Parsley, Dill, and Queen Anne's Lace attract small insects that will parasitize and kill many pests.

Careful planting

Minimize stress when transplanting and provide optimum conditions for seeds. Arrange planting times to avoid pests. If you delay planting Carrots by two or three weeks you can avoid an attack by carrot rust fly.

Cleaning up

Keep your garden free of debris during the growing season. Spent flowers, fallen leaves, and ripened fruit can harbour pests and diseases which spread. At the end of the growing season, clean up the leftover stems, leaves and roots. Discard and compost all extraneous material, returning it to your garden as mature compost. Don't dig it in. Mulch and other soil amendments should be taken from clean, uninfected sources. Keep weeding to minimize problems in the next season. Don't give weeds a chance to seed.

Support

Keep fruit and vegetables off the ground with trellises, stakes, or mulch. This protects them from pests like slugs and snails, and diseases which thrive in damp earth.

RULE OF THUMB

To control aphids, leaf hoppers, and other small insects, spray with a garlic solution. Chop one whole bulb of garlic and soak it for a day in 4 tbsp (60 mL) of vegetable oil. Add 1 qt. (1.14 L) of water and 1/2 tbsp (7.5 mL) of biodegradable soap. Dilute 1 part of this solution to 4 parts water before spraying on plants. For extra kick, boil two hot peppers in 2 qt. (2.28 L) of water until the liquid is reduced to half its volume. Add to the garlic/vegetable oil mixture along with a 1/2 tbsp (7.5 mL) of biodegradable soap. Dilute with water as above before spraying. This mixture is harmless to all plants, including edibles, but most undesirable in the opinion of many garden pests.

ALTERNATIVE PEST CONTROL

Before you panic at a minor infestation, ask yourself whether the problem warrants drastic action. Do you really need an absolutely weedless lawn, or fruit or vegetables entirely free of blemishes? Our society is somewhat obsessive about pests, often far out of proportion to the damage they cause. In fact, most insects are either neutral in their effects or beneficial as pollinators, decomposers, predators of genuine pests, and food for animals such as fish and birds. I feel we will be better off learning to live with limited levels of pests than attempting to eliminate them altogether, which is usually destructive and ultimately impossible. My Grandma ate many Apples with worms in them and she lived to a ripe old age.

To keep pests and diseases under control, you need to know the problems most likely to affect the plants in your garden. Then you can recognize the first signs of trouble, and catch it at an early stage, when it is easier to prevent an outbreak without the use of manufactured chemicals.

Hand picking and pruning

Often insects can be hand picked. Check daily – cutworms can destroy a whole row of cauliflower seedlings within a few hours of transplanting and slugs can strip all the new blooms off your mums over night. Pick caterpillars and other large insects off leaves and drop them into a can of water with a film of oil or kerosene on top.

As soon as you notice a leaf, flower or plant with signs of disease or insect damage, get rid of it so it doesn't infect the rest of your garden.

Pests such as mining insects and many caterpillars often lay their eggs directly on or in the food source. Birch trees and Columbines are subject to miners that deposit eggs within their leaves. Egg-infested leaves sometimes bear rings or blotches that are a tell-tale symptom of an impending invasion. The eggs produce larvae that will devour or disfigure your plant.

Remove all suspect foliage. Your plant's growth may be slowed, but at least it won't die. Don't go overboard. Prune only the affected parts.

When you discard an infected plant or part, don't put it on the compost heap. Burn it, if you can, or put it in a plastic garbage bag.

Physical barriers and traps

Earwigs and slugs can be trapped in grooved boards laid on the ground at night. Brush them out of the grooves into soapy water in the morning. A shallow bowl of beer will attract and drown slugs. Tins filled with a sticky bait, like honey and bran, are ideal traps for earwigs. Set them amid the insects' preferred foods – Lettuce, Tomatoes, and Corn. Cover with a ventilated cover of cardboard or tar-paper to keep the varmints inside. Some gardeners mix appropriate poisons with their bait.

Protect seedlings from cutworms with a 4-inch (10 cm) cardboard collar or a tin can cut in half. Protect members of the *Brassica* (Cabbage) family from root maggots by encircling the stem before transplanting with a square of tar paper or cardboard softened in water.

Insecticidal soap

A hard jet of plain water dislodges insects from trees and shrubs. Insecticidal soap, available in various preparations under the Safer's and Fossil Flower brand names, controls pests such as aphids, mealybugs, whitefly, spider and mites. It's safe to beneficial insects. Make your own insecticidal solution by mixing two tbsp (30 mL) of biodegradable soap (sold in natural food stores and grocery stores) with a quart (1.14 L) of water.

Sticky strips

Yellow strips attract insects, which stick to the surface. They're effective traps for whiteflies, leaf miners, fungus gnats and others. These are available commercially, or you can make your own by coating a yellow ribbon or sheet of yellow plastic with honey or some other sticky substance.

Tree Tanglefoot

This is a sticky paste, available under several brand names, which is applied as a barrier around tree trunks. Prevents insects from reaching leaves, buds, and fruits. Controls ants, caterpillars, cankerworms, and other crawling insects.

Dormant oil spray

This product, available under various brand names, is applied to dormant fruit trees and ornamental trees and shrubs. An extremely thin layer of mineral oil suffocates overwintering mites, mealy bugs, scales, and other insects. It is non-poisonous to warm- blooded animals. Not for use on leaves. (N.B.: Never apply any insecticide when fruit trees or garden plants are in bloom. You may kill pollinating insects such as honeybees.)

Lime sulphur spray

This combination is used as both an insecticide and a fungicide on fruit trees, bush fruits, and ornamentals.

Garden sulphur

This is a fungicide, available in varying strengths, which attacks mildew, rust, black spot, scab, black knot, and certain mites. Useful for flowers, fruits, and vegetables. If watering the soil, take into account the impact on soil pH.

Bacillus thuringiensis (*B.t.*).

B.t. is a parasitic bacteria which controls cabbage worms, tomato hornworms, tent caterpillars, gypsy moths, and many other pests. Apply at sunset, directly to the underside of the leaf or on the soil. Sold in garden centres under trade names such as Dipel and Thuricide.

Diatomaceous earth

This is a non-toxic powder consisting of pulverized remains of fossilized sea creatures called diatoms. Diatomaceous earth scratches the wax off insects' bodies, causing them to dry up and die. It is safe to warm-blooded animals, but it kills all insects indiscriminately. Use with caution. DE is ineffective if it gets wet. Sold under brand names such as Puroguard and Fossil Flower.

Rotenone

This botanical insecticide is made from the derris root. It is available commercially under several name brands as a dust or spray, for use on bush fruits, grapes, vegetables, or flowers. Rotenone wards off spittle bugs, aphids, etc.

Pyrethrum

This botanical insecticide, derived from plants in the Chrysanthemum family, kills aphids, white flies, leafhoppers and thrips. It is relatively safe, but harmful to cold-blooded creatures such as fish. Avoid using it near bodies of water.

Borax

This is a relatively non-toxic cleanser which kills moulds and fungus. Sprinkle liberally, and let sit overnight. Available in the detergent section of any grocery store.

Insect predators

Some insects can be used to control other insects. They either prey on them or parasitize them, destroying them in the process. Insect predators work very well in a greenhouse, but in the garden you may have trouble convincing them to stick around long enough to attack your pests. You may need to make a special effort to provide them with a good home, including plenty of food, and attractive plants.

The following may be available on special order from your garden centre. Or they can be ordered from Better Yield Insects, 13310 Riverside Dr. E., Tecumseh, Ontario N8N 1B2.

Trichogramma wasps

These tiny parasitic wasps attack over 200 species of insect pests, including fruitworm, cutworm, tent caterpillar, codling moth, and spruce budworm. Eggs are laid in the insect, and develop there, destroying their host when they emerge as adults. Can be bought as eggs.

Praying mantis

Young praying mantis eat aphids and leaf-hoppers. Adults eat chinch bugs, beetles, crickets, caterpillars, etc. But they don't have the appetite you might expect for such a large and fierce-looking insect. Buy 16 egg cases per acre.

Mite predator
(Phytoseiulus persimils).

These are good at controlling two-spotted spider mites or red spider mites. Introduce predators only once a season. Two predators are needed for each infected plant, or two per leaf if the plant is large.

Lady beetles

Adult ladybugs eat 50-100 pests a day, including aphids, mites, scale insects, mealybugs, leafworms, leafhoppers, and stinkbug eggs. Use 500 ladybugs to patrol an average garden; use 4000 per acre. Order in spring from a supplier. Lady beetles are very likely to wander if they are not carefully established in your garden.

Aphid predator
(Aphidoletes aphidimyza).

This is a predatory midge that feeds on the green peach aphid and other aphid species. Place at the foot of plants, five predators per sq. yd. Repeat in two weeks for best results.

Green lacewings

Lacewings are among the best insect predators, because of their appetite and their tendency to stay put in your garden. Lacewing larvae prey on aphids, red spider mites, thrips, mealybugs, and worm eggs. Release into the garden as eggs begin to hatch.

SYMPTOMS AND CAUSES – A DIAGNOSTIC CHART

The following chart will help you diagnose pests, diseases, or other problems afflicting your plants. It has been divided into four sections – fruit, flower, leaf, root – according to the plant part where the damage appears.

Leaf

SYMPTOMS	POSSIBLE CAUSES
Pale or yellow.	May be natural, particularly on older leaves or lower leaves of tropical plants; low light, cool temperatures; nutrient deficiency, particularly when accompanied by contrasting veins; early signs of too much light.
Black areas, sometimes surrounded by yellow.	Black spot.
Large brown patches at leaf margins.	Too much fertilizer; uneven water supply.
Large brown patches on exposed surfaces.	Too much sun; sucking insects under leaf, such as whiteflies, aphids, or scale.
Small brown spots.	Flea beetles (leaves will also have small holes); leaf miners (leaves will also have trails); diseases such as anthracnose, fungus, mould, rust.
Yellow patches.	Insects such as whiteflies, leaf miners, aphids, mites under leaf; early stages of sunscald; diseases such as clubroot, virus, mildew, aster yellows.
Silver spots or mottling.	Thrips, leafhoppers.
Purple blotches.	Blight (particularly on Potatoes and Tomatoes)
Wilted leaves.	Too little (or too much) water or fertilizer; poor root action from disease; frost; sucking insects under leaf, such as whiteflies, aphids, or scale; stem borer (when the whole vine or shoot wilts); verticillium wilt; fusarium wilt.
Holes or pieces cut from leaf margins.	Insects such as Japanese beetles, earwigs, caterpillars, tarnished plant bugs, weevils, leaf-cutting bees, slugs, snails.
Bronzed or silvery specks.	Leafhoppers (severe infestations cause dead areas in leaf), spider mite, thrips.
Curled leaves.	Drought; herbicide damage; insects such as whiteflies, aphids, scale; leaf rollers (if there is a web on the leaf); early stages of wilt (see "Wilted leaves" above).
Irregular trails in leaf.	Leaf miners.
Powdery deposits.	Fungus diseases, mildew, botrytis.
Under-sized leaves.	Insufficient light, fertilizer; virus disease.

Fruit

SYMPTOMS	POSSIBLE CAUSES
Holes in skin, sometimes surrounded by brown castings.	Slugs, snails; corn borers, corn ear worms, fly larvae; curculio; tarnished plant bugs on Apples.
Cracks, open or covered with scar tissue.	Fruit may contain insects or slugs, but the cause is usually stress from uneven water supply, such as a flood following a dry spell.
Leathery patches.	On the bottom of Tomatoes, blossom end rot; on tree fruit, scab, or if patches are raised, insects such as surface-feeding caterpillars, apple maggot, or tarnished plant bugs; on top of soft fruit and Tomatoes, sunscald (patches can also be shrunken and soft in this instance); on Beans, anthracnose.
Soft brown areas, white powdery deposit.	Rot or blight; mildew, botrytis, advanced stages of rot.
Misshapen.	Mildew, botrytis, rot, poor cultural practice.
Small "nubby" Strawberries with hard seedy tips.	Tarnished plant bugs.

Flower

SYMPTOMS	POSSIBLE CAUSES
Dropped flowers.	Sudden change in growing conditions, particularly temperature and water supply; poor pollination due to cold or lack of pollinating insects; insufficient light.
Misshapen flowers.	Slugs, snails; caterpillars, insect adults such as Rose chafers, Japanese beetles, aphids.
Small flowers.	Stress caused by poor cultural practice; too little or too much light, water, or fertilizer; insufficient pruning.
Non-existent flowers.	Poor cultural practice, including excessive nitrogen, poor drainage, improper preparation of spring-flowering bulbs, or late pruning of spring-flowering shrubs.
Powdery white or grey deposit followed by rotting.	Botrytis, brown rot, downy mildew (more on leaves than flower).

Roots

SYMPTOMS	POSSIBLE CAUSES
Black, grey, or brown spots, often with soft areas.	Diseases, such as botrytis, rot blight, or poor drainage.
Holes.	Root maggots, slugs; borers (particularly in Peach, Flowering Almond, Purple Sandcherry, Lilac).
Cracking and splitting.	Poor cultural practice, usually uneven water supply.
Distorted shape.	Poor soil filled with rocks or debris; clubroot; crown gall disease.

Stems

SYMPTOMS	POSSIBLE CAUSES
Long and spindly	Insufficient light, fertilizer
Bent near end, which eventually dies.	Stem borer; canker.
Deposit like soap suds where leaf joins stem.	Spittlebugs.
Scaly deposit, cut at ground level.	Aphids, scale insects; cutworms; damping-off disease, mildew, fungus.
Chewed bark.	Mice, rabbits, deer.
Bark cracked or split.	Whipped by wind; dehydrated over winter; sunscald in winter; too much or too little water or fertilizer; disease on roots; diseases such as scab, canker, botrytis, anthracnose.

WEEDS

Many weeds can be prevented through non-chemical means, principally by pulling or digging them up. A strong, well-groomed lawn will compete most weeds out of existence. An annual overseeding helps to keep aggressive lawn weeds at bay.

Bladder Campion

Bladder Campion has a very long root, and will grow back from root sections left in the ground. It spreads by seeds and rhizomes. Dig out the root, or hoe repeatedly.

Canada Thistle

Canada Thistle spreads by seeds, and by rhizomes which are resistant to pesticides. Dig out all the rhizomes you can find, and watch for new shoots in the same area.

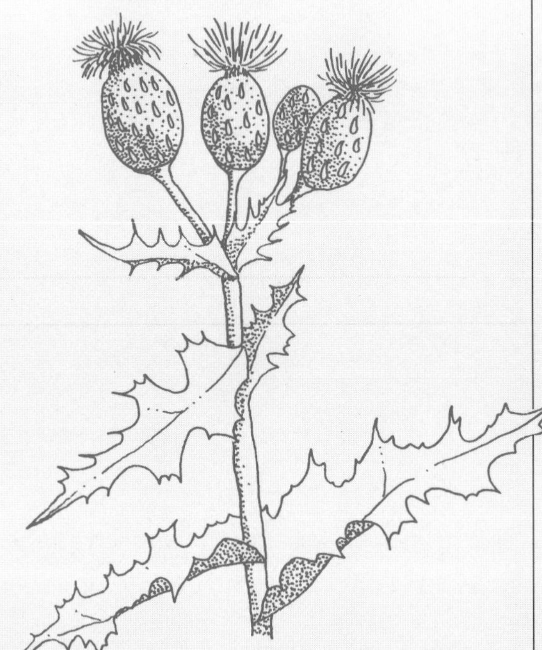

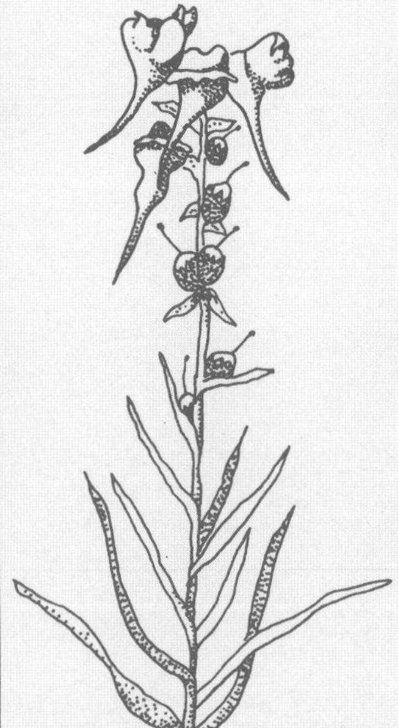

Butter and Eggs (Toadflax)

Butter and Eggs is a wild snapdragon with a very pretty flower. Dig out the rhizomes.

Carpet Weed

One plant can carpet an entire garden. Carpet Weed spreads by seeds. Pull it out, making sure you pick up all the stems.

Chickweed

This weed comes in two varieties, Common and Mouse-ear. It spreads by seeds. Pull it out or cut it off at the roots.

Clover

Clover, which spreads by seeds and natural soil layering of runners, is sometimes used as a ground cover and in lawn mixtures. Clover stays green when grass goes dormant. Controlling by hand is difficult because established plants develop a firm grip.

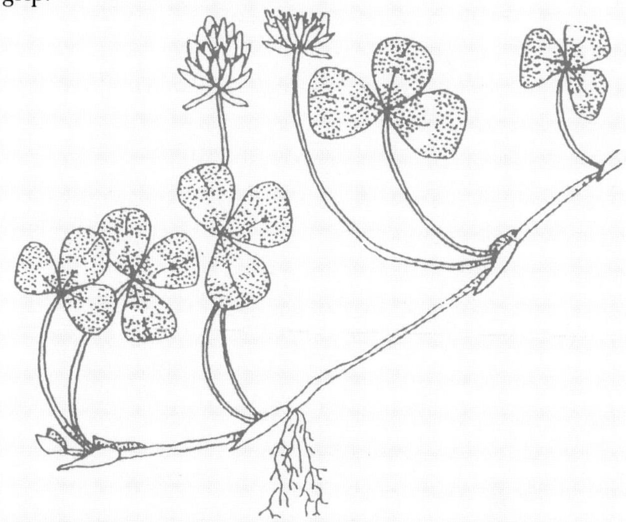

Chicory

Chicory is a pretty blue flower you might want to let grow against a split rail fence. It spreads by seeds. Pulling by hand is hard work since roots grip firmly. Likes hot, dry weather. Flowers in midsummer.

Common Purslane

The thick stems of Common Purslane make it easy to identify in lawns. It spreads by seeds. It can be pulled up quite easily, but it must be removed completely because it has an almost unbelievable ability to self-propagate.

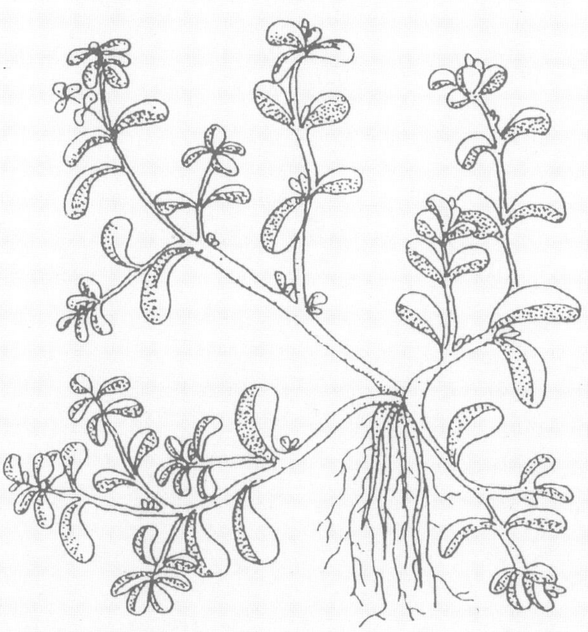

Crabgrass

Crabgrass flourishes in lawns which are under stress from lack of nutrients and improper seeding and watering. It's an annual which spreads by seed. If you have the patience, pick out the seeds. Annual overseeding with quality grass seed (including Perennial Ryegrass) will help to control Crabgrass in your lawn.

Common Yarrow

The fern-like leaves of Common Yarrow make it easy to identify before it flowers. It spreads by seeds and rhizomes. Dig up all the rhizomes.

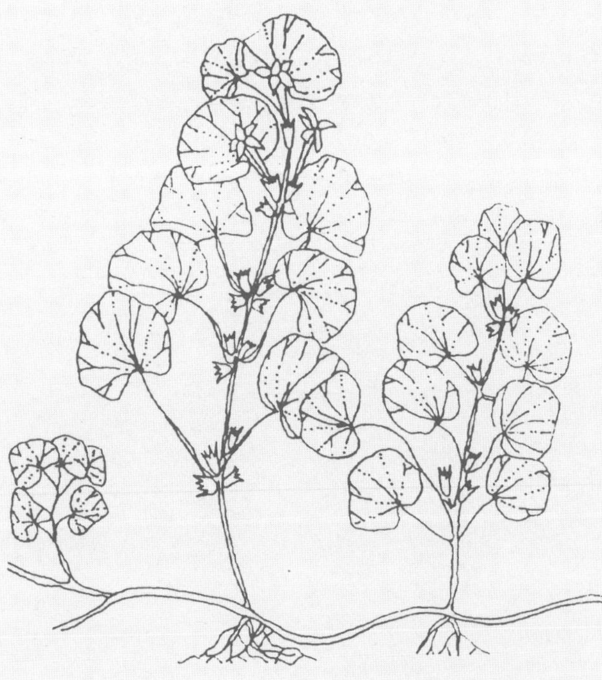

Devil's Paintbrush

Devil's Paintbrush spreads by seeds. In a meadow, the orange hawkweed flowers and red paintbrushes can be quite attractive, especially when combined with Daisies. Like most perennials, it's difficult to pull out by the roots.

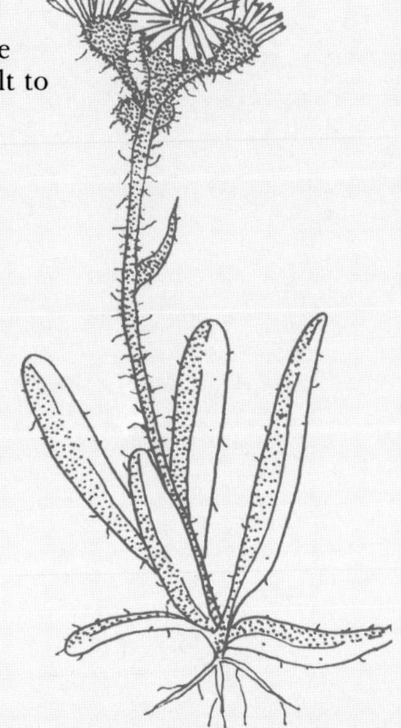

Creeping Charlie

Creeping Charlie, also known as Ground Ivy, spreads by seeds and natural soil layering of runners. It creeps very quickly, producing tiny violet flowers at leaf axils. With patience, you can dig it out.

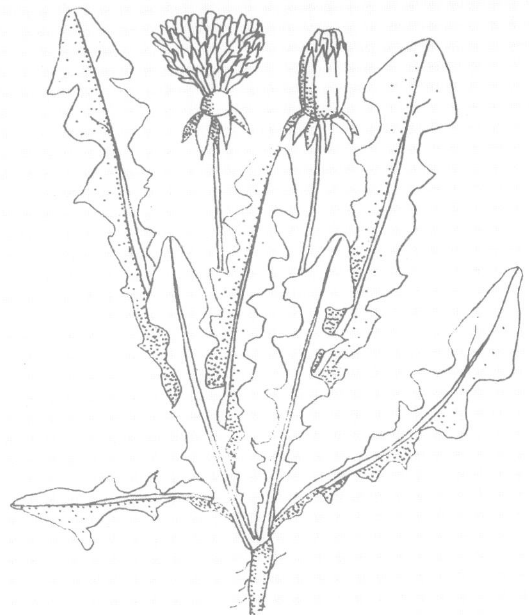

Dandelion

Dandelions spread by seeds, and sometimes by root division. Young leaves can be used in salads, and flowers can be used in wine. Dig out the entire root since new plants can grow from pieces left behind.

Field Bindweed

Field Bindweed spreads by seeds and rhizomes. Vines can cover a wide area, tying knots around many plants in the process. Separate from other plants, then dig up.

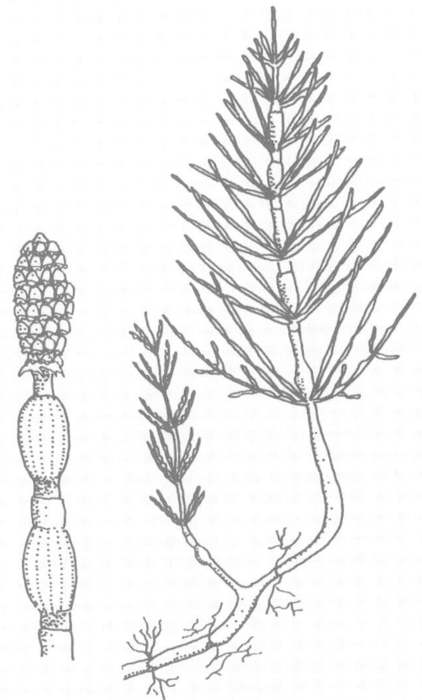

Horsetail

Horsetail spreads by spores and rhizomes. It's a very old plant, seen in prehistoric fossils. It's difficult to control manually. Be sure to dig up all the rhizomes. Usually an indication of acidic soils.

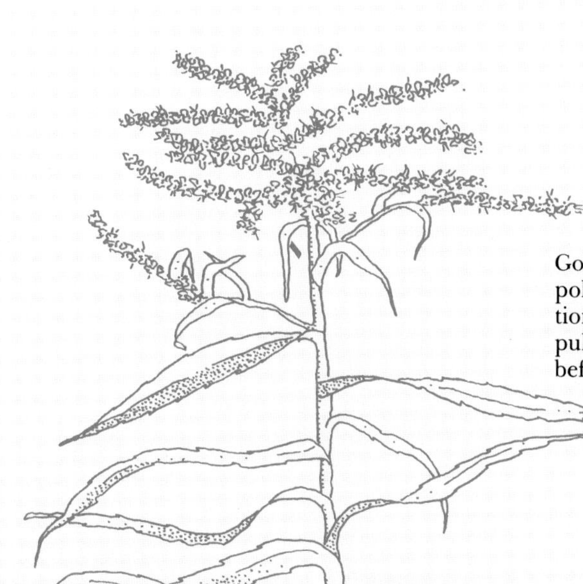

Goldenrod

Goldenrod spreads by seeds. Its pollen causes an allergic reaction in many people. It's easy to pull, and should be uprooted before its seeds mature.

Lamb's Quarters

Lamb's Quarters spreads by seeds. It's easy to pull up. Some folks cook and eat the young leaves, like Spinach.

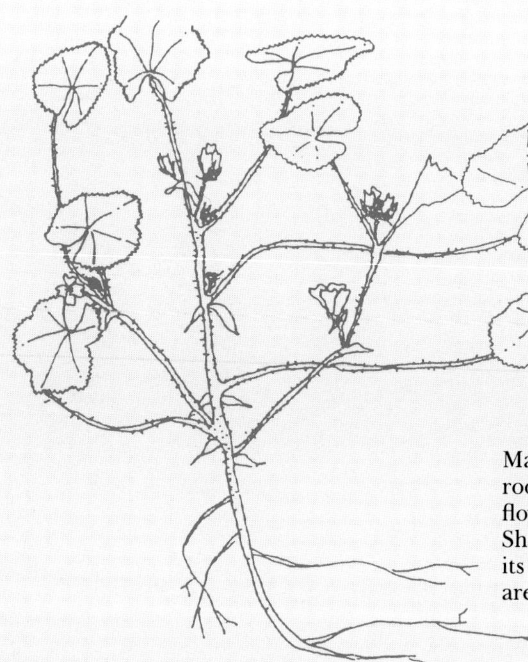

Mallow

Mallow spreads by seeds and root division. It has an attractive flower, similar to the Rose of Sharon. Like most perennials, its roots have a strong grip and are difficult to uproot.

Poison Ivy

Poison Ivy spreads by seeds and rhizomes. It can cause a severe allergic reaction. Even the smoke from burning plants affects some people. Manual control is not advisable unless you wear rubber gloves, boots, and a heavy rain coat. Always wash down your gear with soapy water before hanging it up. Avoid contact with Poison Ivy in the heat of late spring and early summer, when it is most potent.

Plantain

Plantain spreads by seeds. Its crushed leaves can relieve wasp and bee stings. It's usually easy to uproot manually, if soil is not compacted.

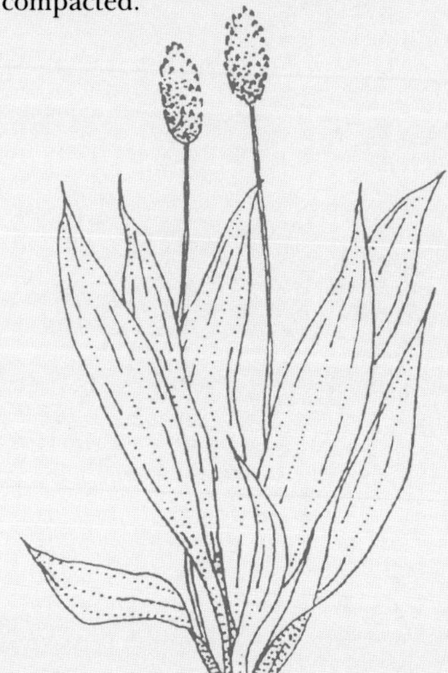

Quackgrass

Quackgrass, also well-known as Twitch Grass and Couch Grass, spreads by rhizomes, and sometimes by seed. It is a perennial troublemaker in a lawn, especially in its favourite location besides fences. It's coarse and unattractive, and grows faster than most other grasses, so it's visible the day after mowing. Re-seed trouble areas annually so healthy grass will push the Quackgrass out. Dig up all the rhizomes.

Ragweed

Ragweed is a particularly noxious weed which spreads by seed. It's hard to pull up, but can be controlled by hoeing early in the season.

Queen Anne's Lace

Queen Anne's Lace is a wild carrot which spreads by seeds. It's difficult to uproot in compacted soil, but be sure to cut off the top of the tap-root.

Sow Thistle

Sow Thistle has yellow flowers, as distinct from the pink flowers of the Canada Thistle. It spreads by seeds. The tap-root can be difficult to pull up, but hoeing is effective on young plants if you get the top of the root.

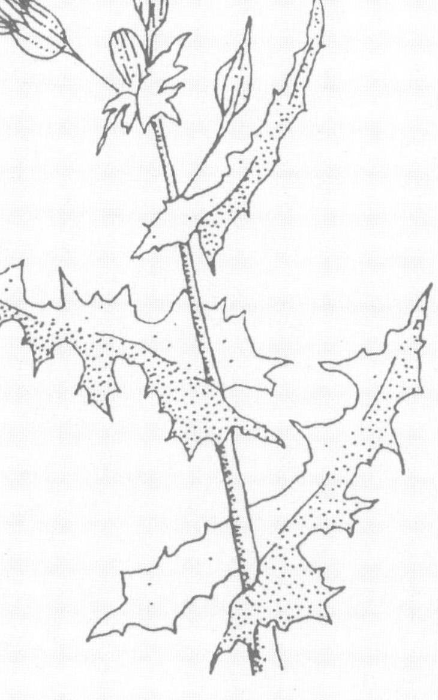

Redroot Pigweed

Redroot Pigweed, which spreads by seeds, is very prolific and should be stamped out immediately. It can be pulled up easily or cut off with a hoe or cultivator.

PESTS

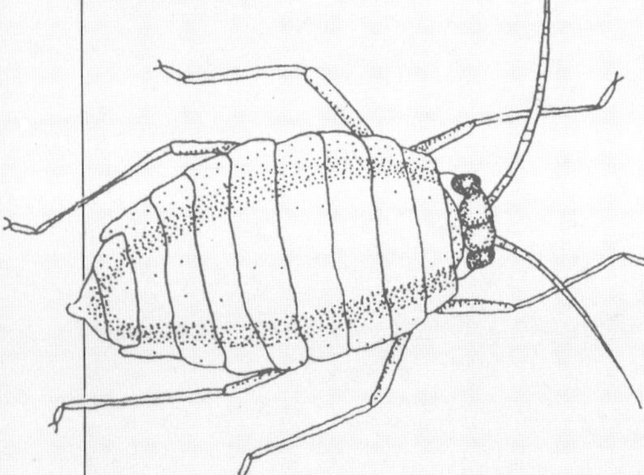

Aphids

Aphids attack almost all plants, including flowers, trees, vegetables, and fruits. Like chameleons, they often take on the colour of the plant they infest. They are most frequently found completely covering new growth, but sometimes they attack mature buds, leaves, and fruit. Garlic, Mint, Nasturtiums may repel aphids. Remove with a strong jet of water or insecticidal soap solution. Trap them with yellow sticky cards hung about the garden. You can also use rotenone or pyrethrum. Controlling aphids helps to control ants, which feed on the sticky secretions of this insect.

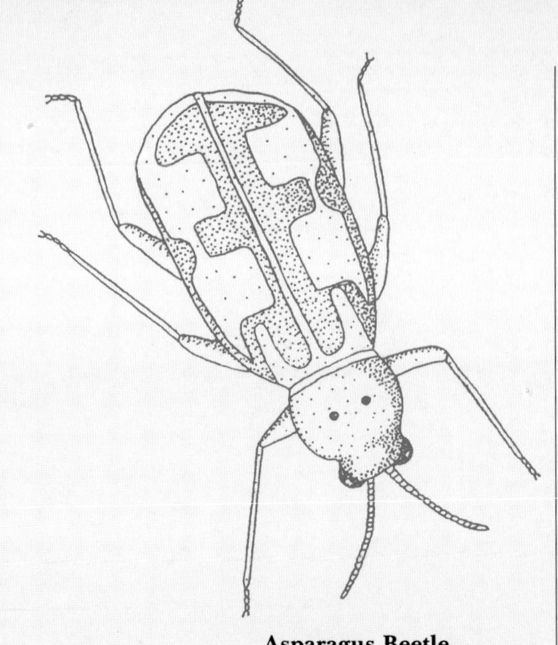

Asparagus Beetle

The larvae of the asparagus beetle attack Asparagus below ground. The adult attacks above ground, feeding on foliage. There are two types of asparagus beetle, one orange with black spots, the other striped. Pick them off by hand, and reduce infestations by carefully disposing of Asparagus tops when they turn brown in the fall. Apply pulverized lime or rotenone.

Cabbage Maggot

Cabbage maggot likes all members of the Cabbage family, including Broccoli, Cabbage, Cauliflower, and Brussels Sprouts. The maggot is the larva of a fly that lays its eggs at the base of the stem of plants in this family. Plant Mint, Rosemary, and Sage nearby to repel cabbage maggot. Spread wood ashes at the base of the plants or use a maggot mat. Hand pick, or hose off with water or insecticidal soap.

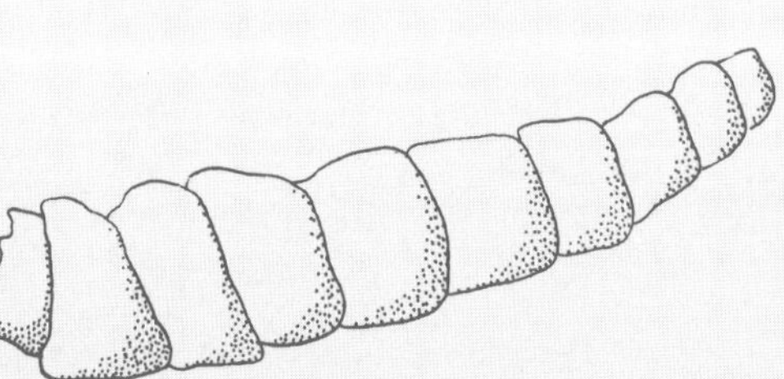

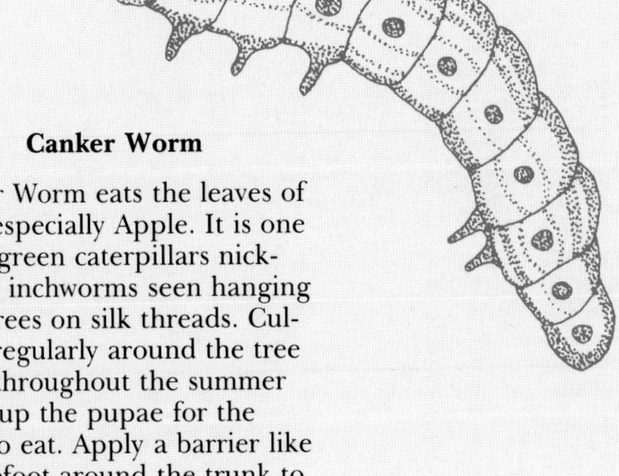

Canker Worm

Canker Worm eats the leaves of trees, especially Apple. It is one of the green caterpillars nicknamed inchworms seen hanging from trees on silk threads. Cultivate regularly around the tree trunk throughout the summer to dig up the pupae for the birds to eat. Apply a barrier like Tanglefoot around the trunk to keep the adult female from climbing into the branches to lay eggs (only the male has wings). Control with *B.t.* or rotenone.

Cabbage Worm

This is the larva of a small white moth seen fluttering over Cabbage, Broccoli, Cauliflower and Kale. Cabbage worm will also eat many other vegetables, including Celery, Lettuce, Peas, and Spinach. Repel by planting Thyme, Dill or Marigolds. Pick off a mild infestation. Capture the moth in a fish-net throughout the summer. Control by applying *B.t* or rotenone regularly every seven days.

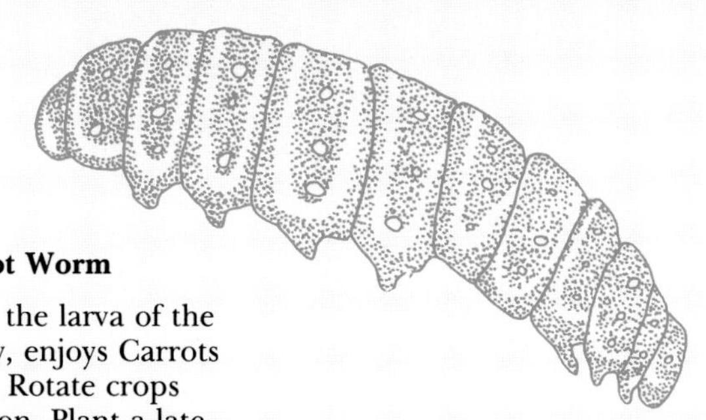

Carrot Worm

Carrot worm, the larva of the Carrot rust fly, enjoys Carrots and Parsnips. Rotate crops or skip a season. Plant a late-maturing crop to avoid mid-summer egg-laying.

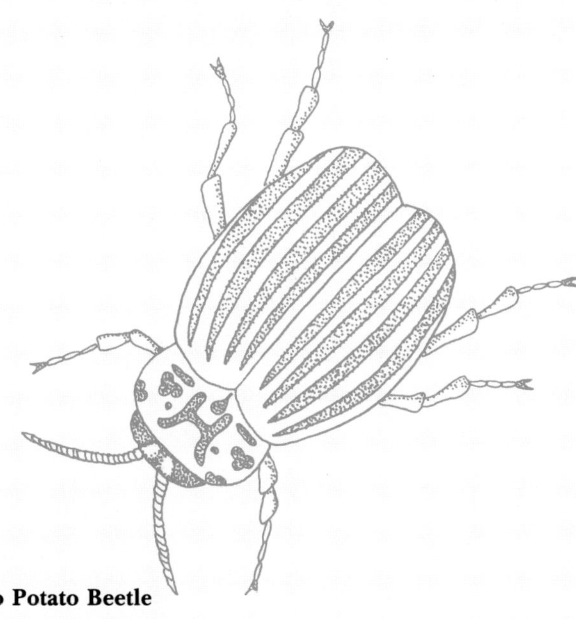

Corn Ear Worm

This larva of a common moth enters ears of Corn invisibly from the top. Clean up Corn stalks at the end of the growing season. Use Garlic or Onion sprays on larvae (see above). Apply 20 drops of mineral oil inside the tip of each ear after the silks have wilted. Control organically with *B.t.* or pyrethrum.

Colorado Potato Beetle

This beetle attacks all members of the Potato family, including Potato, Tomato, Eggplant, and Pepper. Both the orange larvae and the black-and-orange adult dine on foliage. Look for the bright orange egg clusters under leaves and pick them off by hand, usually in early summer. Pick off larvae or adults. Apply rotenone every seven days and after each rainfall.

Cucumber Beetle

The cucumber beetle attacks all gourds, including summer and winter Squash and Pumpkin as well as Cucumber. It eats the vegetable and helps to spread a bacterial wilt disease. Plant Radish on the hills to repel these beetles. Pick them off by hand. Control organically with rotenone.

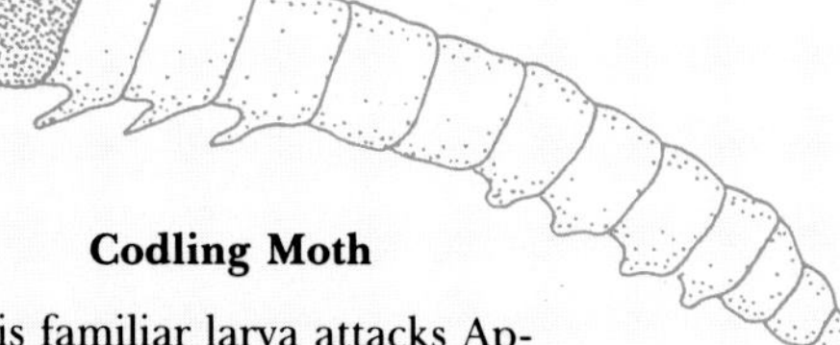

Codling Moth

This familiar larva attacks Apples and Pears, leaving a large hole in the skin surrounded by reddish-brown castings, which look like sawdust. Apply dormant oil and sulphur spray just prior to buds breaking in the spring.

Dipterous Flies

This group of insects includes the Onion maggot, the Cabbage maggot, and the Apple maggot – the worst pest of Apples in Eastern Canada. Apple maggot also loves Hawthorns and Blueberries. Clean up fallen Apples. Tangle Foot traps, using mock Apple, are known to be effective.

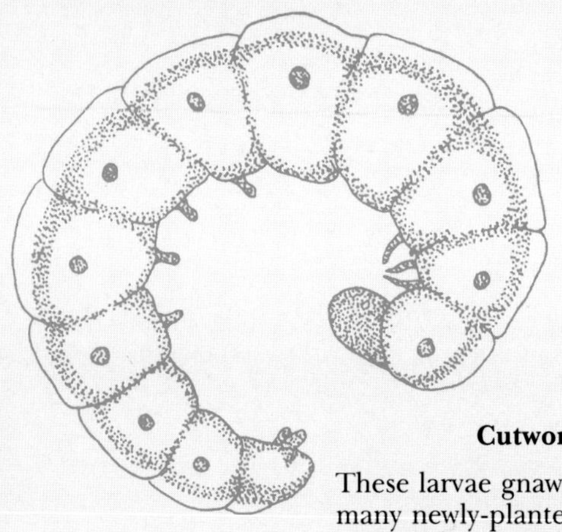

Cutworm

These larvae gnaw the stalks of many newly-planted seedlings, particularly Tomato, Cabbage, and Lettuce. Keep the garden weed- free in fall. Plant Tansy or Marigold as repellents. Use a cutworm collar. Circle plants with ashes or bran.

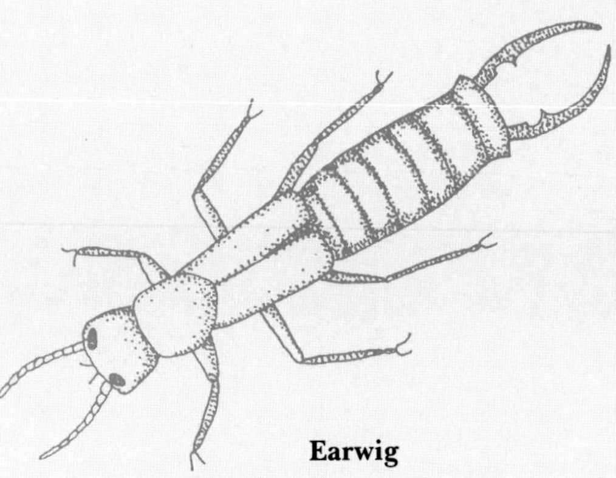

Earwig

The earwig may eat the leaves of tender flowers, creating irregularly shaped holes, but it does not do a great deal of damage to most plants, and it eats the larvae of harmful pests. If they are a problem they can be trapped in a short length of garden hose and drowned in soapy water. In areas of Canada where earwigs are an abundant problem, just about every experienced gardener has his or her own solution. Talk to your neighbours.

Flea Beetle

These tiny black beetles, which jump when disturbed, leave tiny holes in the leaves of plants in the Cabbage family, the Potato family, Radish, and Turnip. Young plants are particularly affected. Repel with garlic or garlic spray. Hand pick. Control with pyrethrum or rotenone.

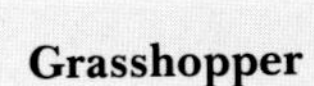

Grasshopper

This insect will eat almost anything green if there is competition for food. It enjoys grassy plants like corn, and can level entire wheat fields, but it seldom becomes a problem in the backyard. Repel with Nasturtium and Chrysanthemum. Control with pyrethrum or rotenone.

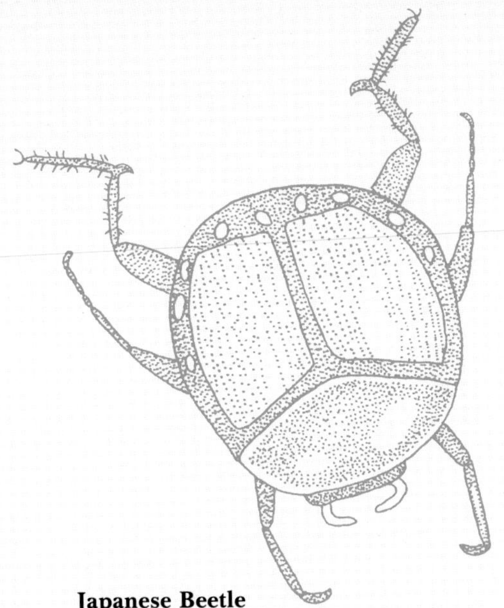

Leaf-Cutting Bee

This insect cuts neat circles and ovals from the edges of leaves of ornamental plants, particularly Roses, for use as nesting material. Damage is unsightly but control is seldom necessary.

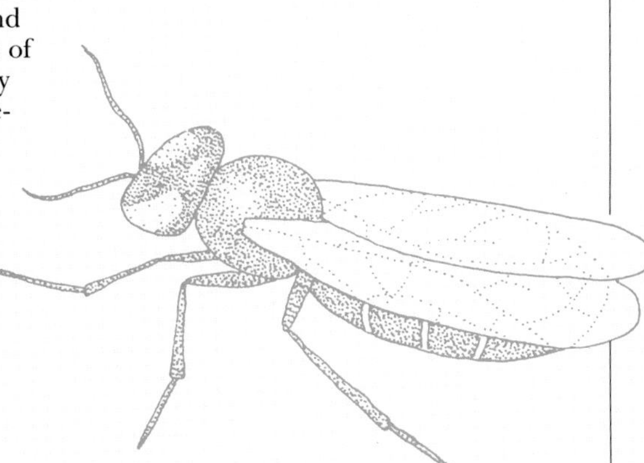

Japanese Beetle

Adults dine neatly and ravenously on the flesh between the veins of Grape leaves, Roses, Asparagus, Corn and Rhubarb. Strict controls are imposed on imports of soil, fruits and vegetables from abroad in an effort to exclude this insect. Grubs attack grass roots. Control with pyrethrum or rotenone. Fortunately, our winters seem to keep this insect under control.

Leafhopper

Serious infestations of this insect produce dead brown patches on the tops of leaves known as hopper burn. It can be found under the leaves of nearly every plant, and it can carry Potato viruses. Repel by planting Nasturtium and Marigold. Control with pyrethrum.

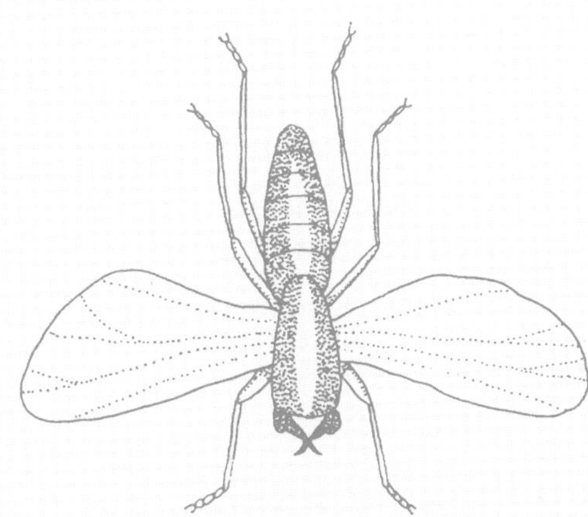

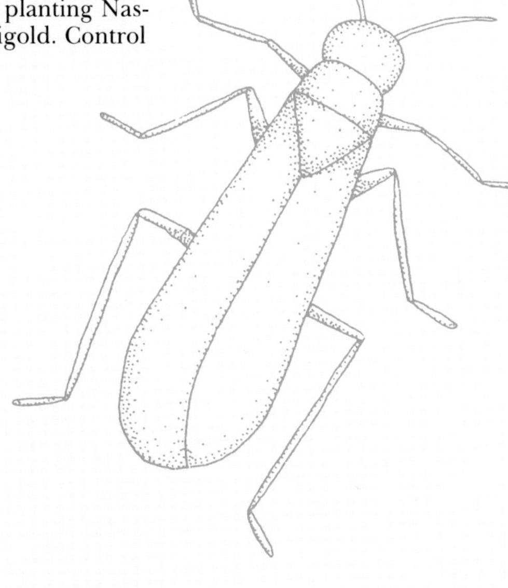

Leaf miner

There is a large family of miners, nearly one for every plant in the garden, but the damage is always the same: tiny meandering trails eaten on the leaves of Lilac, Chrysanthemum, Beet, Spinach and Chard. Birch leaf miners attack Birch trees exclusively. Remove infested leaves early, and weed regularly.

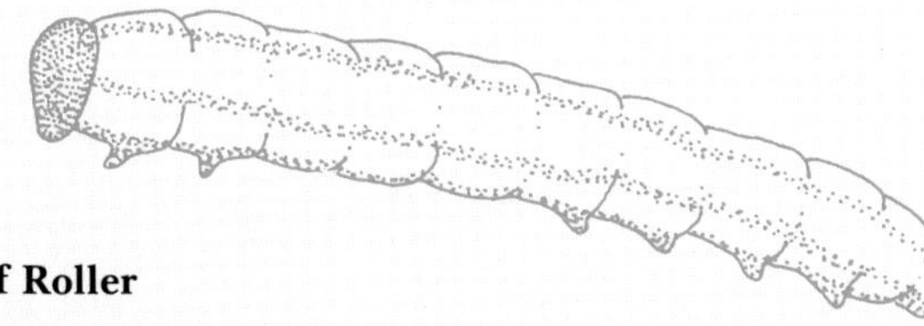

Leaf Roller

Leaf roller gnaws small holes in the leaves of fruit trees, Chrysanthemum and other plants. Larvae reside in the leaf, drawing it up with a web frequently found on dwarf and semi-dwarf trees. Hand pick larvae. Apply rotenone.

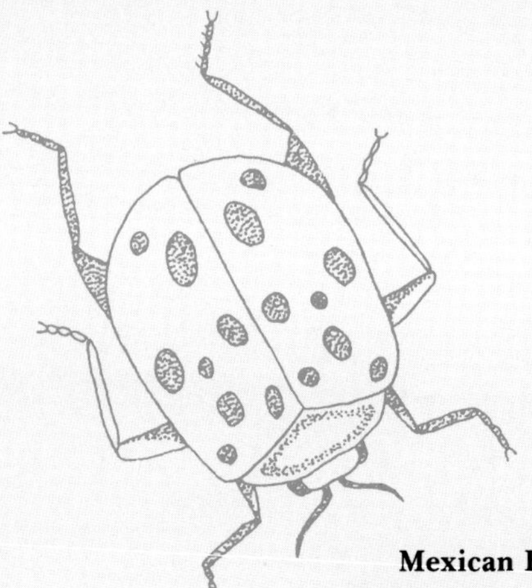

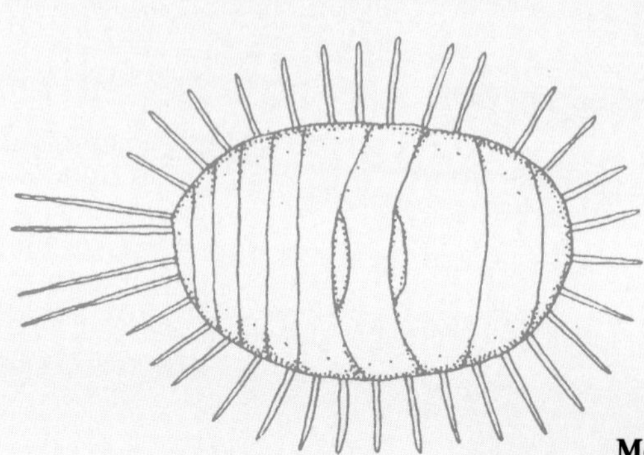

Mealy Bug

The mealy bug is usually found in a colony clustered around the leaf axils or under the leaves of many house plants, including Cactus and succulents, wrapped in a waxy silk. Hand pick, or paint using a Q-tip with 50 per cent strength rubbing alcohol.

Mexican Bean Beetle

This beetle, found on all Bean plants, is the black sheep of the ladybug family. It is copper-coloured with 16 black spots. It causes most damage in the larval stage, turning leaves into webs. Repel with Marigold and Rosemary. Hand pick. Apply rotenone. Clean up all plant debris in fall.

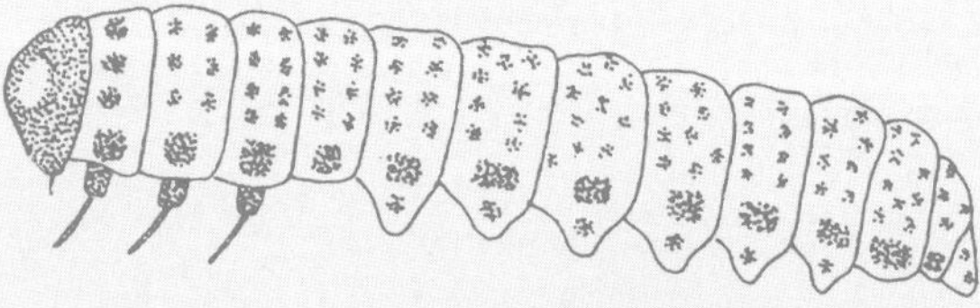

Sawfly

The sawfly family eats evergreens, Mountain Ash, fruit trees, and the leaves of Roses and Gooseberries. They vary in size from tiny leaf miners in Birch trees to large caterpillars such as the European pine sawfly. Spray with rotenone as soon as symptoms appear.

Rose Chafer

The adult is a light-brown, rounded beetle that eats the petals of Roses, Peonies, and other flowers. Grubs feed on grass roots. Repel with Onions. Keep a toad to eat the chafers. Keep grass out of your garden. Apply insecticidal soap or rotenone.

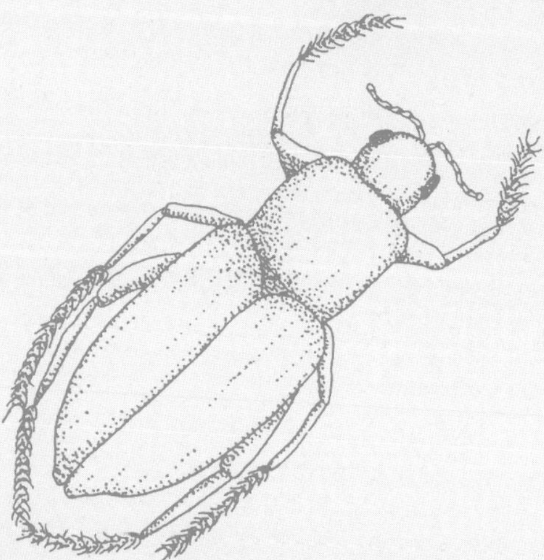

Scale

This is a family of very small insects which live under protective scales. They are usually found on the bark of trees, but also under the leaves of foliage plants, feeding on sap. On trees, spray with a mixture of dormant oil and lime sulphur in early April through early May. Repeat two or three times during the late dormant season, but do not spray when the plants are in full bloom.

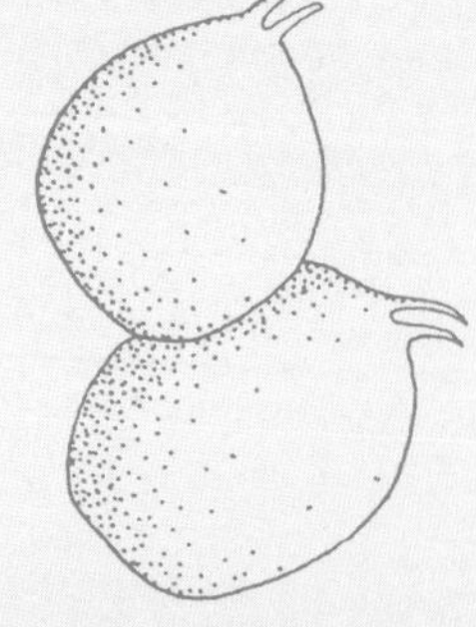

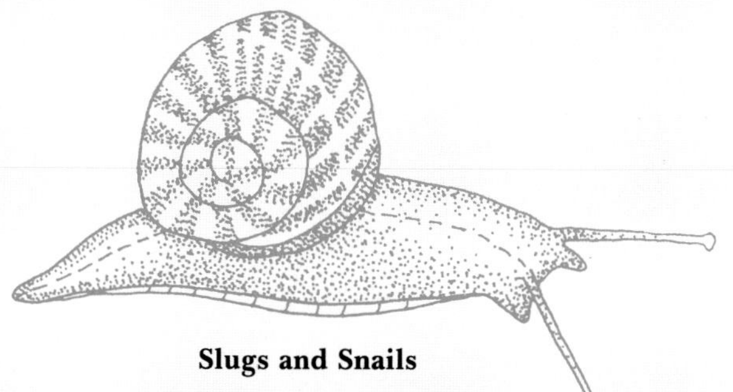

Slugs and Snails

These uglies leave behind trails of slime, and will eat anything, from Lettuce leaves to Chrysanthemum flowers. Hand pick at night and clean up garden debris. Set a saucer of stale beer on the ground to attract them and drown them. In my experience, regular beer is somewhat more effective than light beer. Trap under boards and remove each morning. Circle favourite plants with a ring of wood ashes or talc. Both dry the slimy film, which kills the slugs.

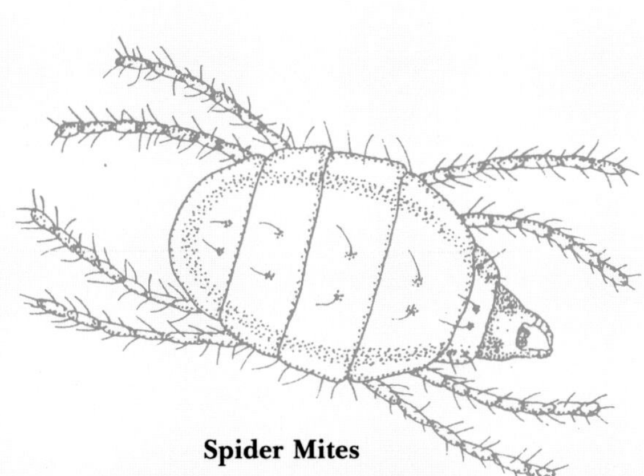

Spider Mites

Spider mites enjoy many plants, but are particularly fond of Fuschia, Peach, Rose, Strawberry, and Hibiscus. They are very small and hard to see, but may cause extensive damage because they reproduce very rapidly. They can cause mottling and eventually death of the affected area. Occasionally they spin very fine webs. Introduce lacewings and ladybugs, which eat spider mites. Plant Garlic near Tomato as a repellent. Wash off leaves with a jet of water during hot, dry weather, applying this stream during the heat of the day. Four or five weekly applications of insecticidal soap will bring mites under control. Concentrate on covering the underside of the leaves.

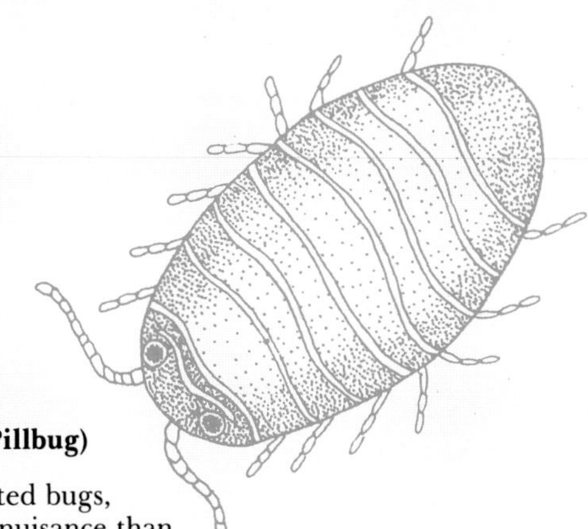

Sowbug (Pillbug)

These armour-plated bugs, which are more a nuisance than a pest, feed on surface roots and the shoots of newly sprouting plants. Improve drainage and air ventilation. They roll up in a ball when disturbed, and invade damp basements and cellar window wells. Hollow out Potato halves and lay them face down in the soil. Sowbugs attracted to this bait can be destroyed manually. Pour boiling water in cracks and crevices, especially if they are sand-filled, and clean up garden debris. Sowbugs are helpful too – they break down organic matter for use as plant food.

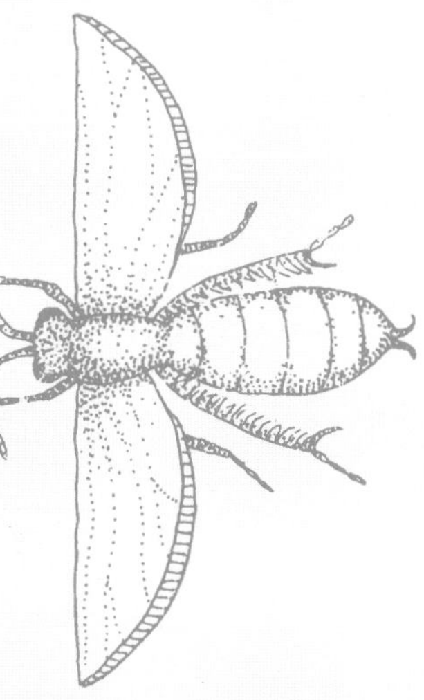

Squash Vine Borer

Larvae can be found on many plants, but favour vines of the Squash family. You know you've got Vine Borer when an entire vine wilts from one day to the next. Find the entry hole, often surrounded by green castings, then carefully slit the vine from the hole outward until you find the larva. Dig it out, or fish it out with a wire, and bury any part of the vine you opened. It should form more roots on the buried stems. Apply rotenone.

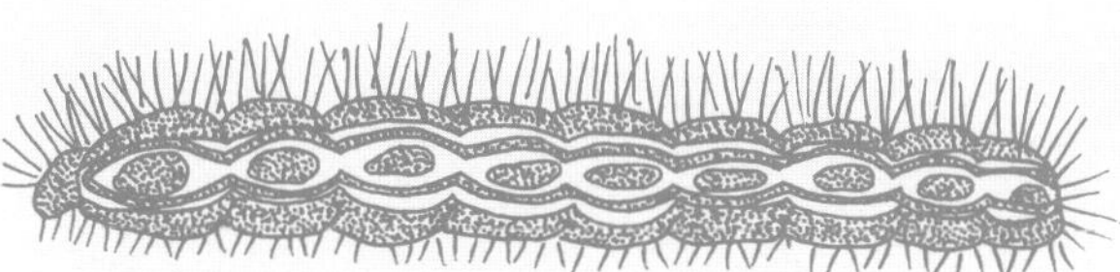

Tent Caterpillar

In a bad year, tent caterpillars can defoliate a tree. All trees may be afflicted. Remove tents manually at night, or cut off the infested branch and dispose carefully. Apply rotenone.

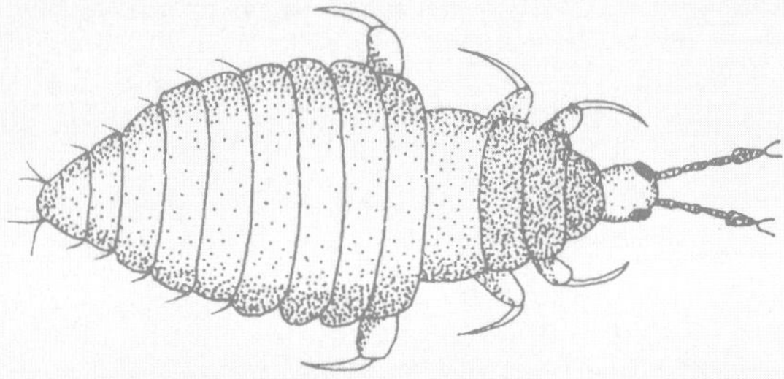

Tomato Hornworm

This is a very large caterpillar, 3 to 4 in. (7.5 to 10 cm) long, that masquerades as a Tomato vine while devouring the leaves, stems, and fruit of the Tomato. Hand pick. Apply *B.t.*.

Thrips

Thrips are very small, very active insects with piercing, sucking mouth parts. They suck plant juices, especially in hot, dry weather. They attack all plants, especially Gladiolus, leaving white strips on the leaves. Dust corms with sulphur dust before storing for the winter.

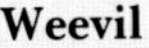

Weevil

The weevil eats the leaf edges of Bean and Pea plants, laying its eggs in Bean and Pea flowers. But it is not considered a serious problem in most Canadian vegetable gardens. Time plants so that Beans and Peas flower before the adult insects lay eggs. Ask your department of agriculture when weevils are due to propagate.

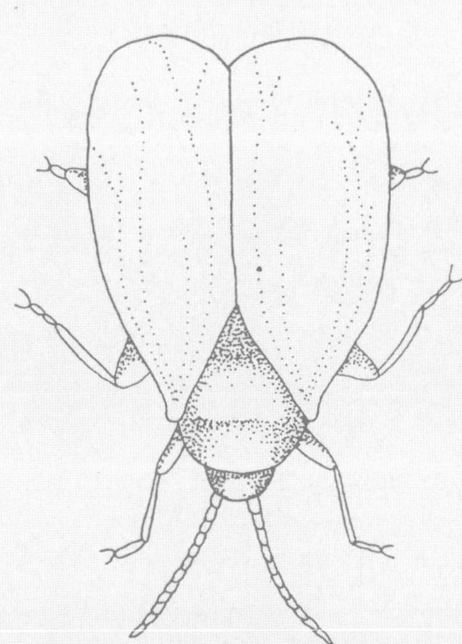

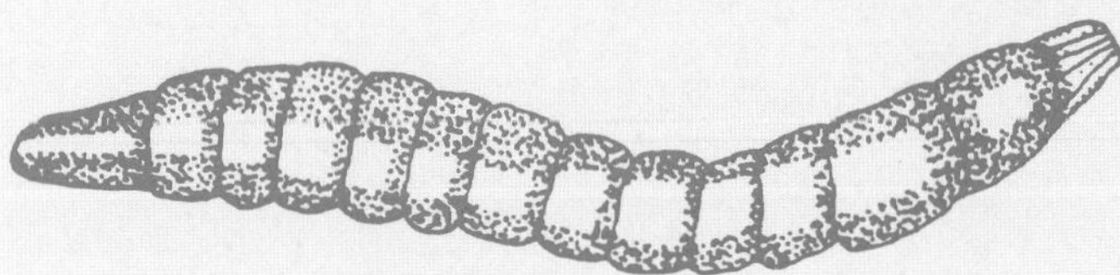

Wireworms

Wireworms eat the roots of Potato, Tomato, Carrot, Lettuce, and Chrysanthemum. By the time damage is noticeable it is too late to do anything for the infested plant until the following season. Regular cultivation keeps wireworms under control and they are seldom a problem in well-established gardens. Bury Potatoes around the garden, marked with stakes, and dig them up every two or three weeks. Discard and replace any that have attracted wireworms.

Whiteflies

These white insects gather beneath leaves. One good shake will produce a whole cloud of them from the leaves of Tomato, Fuschia, Chrysanthemum, Cucumber, Hibiscus, and many other tender juicy plants. Affected leaves will discolour, and eventually drop off. Nasturtium can attract whiteflies but stand up to considerable punishment from them. Marigold repels whiteflies. Hang a yellow ribbon coated with honey or maple syrup several feet above your crop to attract whiteflies and capture them like flypaper. (While on a recent rip to Disney's Epcot Centre in Florida, I visited the Land Pavilion, where this method was effectively used.) Apply rotenone or pyrethrum.

DISEASES

Anthracnose

Anthracnose, which appears as brown-black spots on leaves, affects many plants, especially Privet, Raspberry, and Ficus (Fig). On Beans, the pods are also affected. On Weeping Willow, the stems of new growth can show symptoms as well. Anthracnose is most prevalent in cool, wet growing seasons. Remove and discard any infected parts, but do not touch the leaves or harvest Beans if plants are wet. Rotate Bean crops, and use certified seed. Apply Bordeaux mixture. Apply a heavy dose of superphosphate, 1 lb/ 100 sq. ft.

Black Spot

This disease, which frequently affects Roses, appears as black spots on leaves, often surrounded by yellow. Remove all debris, especially fallen leaves and grass clippings, before protecting from winter weather. Spray with a mixture of lime sulphur and dormant oil spray in early spring. Boil Rhubarb leaves in water and spray solution on Rose leaves. A solution of garlic and warm water will help stop the spread of black spot fungus spores.

Blight

Blight begins as purple blotches on leaves of Potato and Tomato, which then turn brown and rot, causing vegetables to rot as well. Rotate crops annually, use disease-free stock, and control leafhoppers, which carry the disease. Apply Bordeaux mixture.

Blossom End Rot

Blossom End Rot appears as a brown concave section on the bottom of a Tomato. This usually happens when there is a prolonged dry spell, causing a calcium deficiency, followed by heavy rain or excessive watering. Water regularly so the roots never dry out. Lime soil to add calcium, or add a liquid calcium supplement. The crushed and dried shells of two or three eggs per plant will help. Do this early in spring.

Botrytis

Botrytis, also called grey mould, affects many plants in many different ways. On fruit (Bean, Strawberry, Tomato) it appears as a softening of the fruit under a powdery grey build-up. On flowers and leaves, it appears as brown spots followed by a powdery build-up and rotting (Lettuce, Chrysanthemum, Hydrangea, Peony). On stems, the grey mould covers brown rotting areas (Gooseberry, Magnolia, Rose). Botrytis can also affect tubers and root crops in storage (Tulip, Onion). Remove and discard any affected plants or parts, check humidity, and ensure proper ventilation by keeping weeds in check and spacing plants generously at planting time.

Clubroot

Clubroot affects all members of the Cabbage family (Cabbage, Broccoli, Brussels Sprouts, and Cauliflower). Roots become swollen and slimy, and their action is impaired. Leaves wilt and yellow. Infected soil must be kept crop-free for many years. Rotate crops, making sure soil pH does not drop below 7.0. Discard afflicted plants. Boil Rhubarb leaves in water and pour the solution into the hole before planting susceptible plants. Spread wood ash around the base of plants at planting time.

Crown Gall

Roses, Raspberry, and Blackberry are among the plants affected by this disease. A cluster of yellow-brown lumps called galls can grow to Cantaloupe size on the stems of affected plants. If possible, remove galls. Destroy severely afflicted plants. Paint galls with antibiotics (Bacticin, Streptomycin), available at a drug store, as soon as possible. Galls are caused by an irritation under the bark by small gnawing insects. Apply dormant oil in early spring to prevent insect problems.

Damping-Off Disease

Newly sprouted seedling or rooted cuttings with this disease weaken at soil level, eventually falling over and breaking off. Prevent damping-off disease by using sterilized soil mixture (or pasteurized soil, baked at a lower temperature) for propagation. Water and mist seedlings early in the day so the soil surface dries before evening. Leave 1 in. (2.5 cm) or more space between seedlings for air circulation. Improve air circulation around susceptible plants, using a room fan if necessary. Provide adequate sunshine or artificial light. Allow the surface of the soil to dry out somewhat between waterings, and remove afflicted seedlings.

Mildew (downy)

Downy mildew shows up early in the season, especially in wet weather, as yellow spots on the surface of vegetable leaves, accompanied by a white powdery build-up under the leaf. Lettuce, Cabbage, Cucumber, and Grapes are particularly susceptible. Rotate crops. Apply Bordeaux mixture on Grapes. Plant less susceptible cultivars.

Mildew (powdery)

Powdery mildew is a fine white dust on the leaves and new growth of Roses, Begonia, Lilac, and Grass. It also appears on the fruit and leaves of Apple and Strawberry when weather is wet and cool, particularly early and late in the season. Remove afflicted areas if possible. Reduce watering, and if mildew appears on the surface of the soil, add pulverized charcoal (the gardening variety, not the barbecue type). Control mildew on fruit with lime sulphur spray.

Rot

Rot is a general term applied to a group of diseases that usually affect plants at the soil level. Leaves weaken then topple. Rot particularly affects bulbs, corms, and tubers, and the crowns of some perennials. Provide good drainage and ventilation, control ground level pests such as slugs, and rotate crops. Remove and destroy afflicted plants, including fruit, and replace soil if the problem is widespread. Make sure bulbs, corms, and tubers are dry before they are stored, and place them in a dry storage medium such as peat moss. Check for rot during storage, remove afflicted specimens, and dust the remainder with sulphur.

Rust

Rust appears as powdery rust-coloured spots on leaves of grass, particularly Bluegrass, late in the growing season when the weather turns cool and wet. The problem often seems to be more serious in shaded areas. Overseed with rust-resistant grass strains, and apply nitrogen sparingly.

Snow Mould

Snow Mould appears in early spring as large dead patches in a lawn, covered with white web-like mould. All grasses can be affected. To control, rake area thoroughly, making grass blades stand up straight. Reduce applications of fast-release nitrogen in late summer growing season, and crop grass short at the end of the season.

Verticillium Wilt

Like fusarium wilt, this disease causes many plants to wilt from the ground up. Tomato is vulnerable, but Bean and Pea plants can also be afflicted. There is no cure. Select plant varieties resistant to fusarium and verticillium wilt, marked VF on the package. Rotate susceptible crops to different parts of the garden every year.

Virus Diseases

Virus diseases affect a variety of plants in ways resembling more common problems. Symptoms include yellowing of leaves, small irregular leaves, and stunted plants with weak flowers, small fruit, spindly steams or wilting. If you are sure there is no other cause, remove diseased parts and destroy them immediately. Always plant certified disease-free stock. Control insects that carry diseases, particularly aphids and leafhoppers.

INDEX

Page references in italic indicate illustrations

REFERENCES

Books

Hill, Lewis. *Cold Climate Gardening: How to Extend Your Growing Season by at Least 30 Days.* Vermont: Garden Way, 1987. Order from Storey Communications, Pownal, Vermont 05261.
Jeavons, John. *How to Grow More Vegetables Than You Ever Thought Possible On Less Land Than You Can Imagine.* Berkeley: Ten Speed Press, 1979. Order from Ten Speed Press, P.O. Box 7123, Berkeley, CA, 94707 USA.
Kourik, Robert. *Designing and Maintaining Your Edible Landscape Naturally.* Santa Rosa: Metamorphic Press, 1986. Order from the publisher, P.O. Box 1841, Santa Rosa, CA, 95402 USA.
Rodale, J.I. and staff. *Encyclopedia of Organic Gardening.* Emmaus: Rodale Press, 1970. Order from the publisher, Emmaus, PA, 18049 USA.
Smith, Miranda. *Greenhouse Gardening.* Emmaus: Rodale, 1985.
Yepsen, R.B.. *The Encyclopedia of Natural Insect and Disease Control.* Emmaus: Rodale, 1984.

Magazines

Organic Gardening, Rodale Press, Emmaus, PA, USA 18099-0003
Harrowsmith, 7 Queen Victoria Road, Camden East, Ontario K0K 1J0.
Gardens for All, Department 150A, 180 Flynn Ave., Burlington, VT, 04501 USA
Humus, 4545 Av. Pierre-de-Coubertin, C.P. 1000, Succ. M. Montreal, QC H1V 3R2 Canada

---

Photo Credits

Dieter Hessel	: 8, 20, 22, 23, 24-25, 26, 28, 29, 30, 31, 32, 37, 40, 41, 42, 51, 51, 65, 71, 81, 101-102, 128-129, 130-131, 132, 134, 138-139, 144, 145, 146, 148, 149, 158, 159, 160, 176-177, 180, 198, 200-201, 202.
Miller Services	: 10-11, 21, 45, 46-47, 49, 52, 55, 73, 75, 76, 79, 83, 85, 86, 90, 91, 92, 94, 96, 109, 126, 135, 140-141, 142-143, 147, 150, 151, 152, 154-155, 157, 161, 178-179, 183, 190, 194-195, 196-197, 199, 204, 205, 207.
Bulb Institute	: 42, 99, 100, 105, 111, 112, 113, 114, 115, 116-117, 118, 120, 121, 123.
Weall & Cullen Nurseries	: 18, 19, 25, 44, 50, 60-61, 67, 69, 87, 88, 153, 162, 163, 164, 165, 167, 168, 169, 170, 171, 173, 175, 181, 182, 186, 188, 189, 192.
Edward Mulsion	: 14-15, 25, 33, 36, 41, 53, 56, 59, 63, 111, 172, 177, 187.
Fred Bird	: 208.

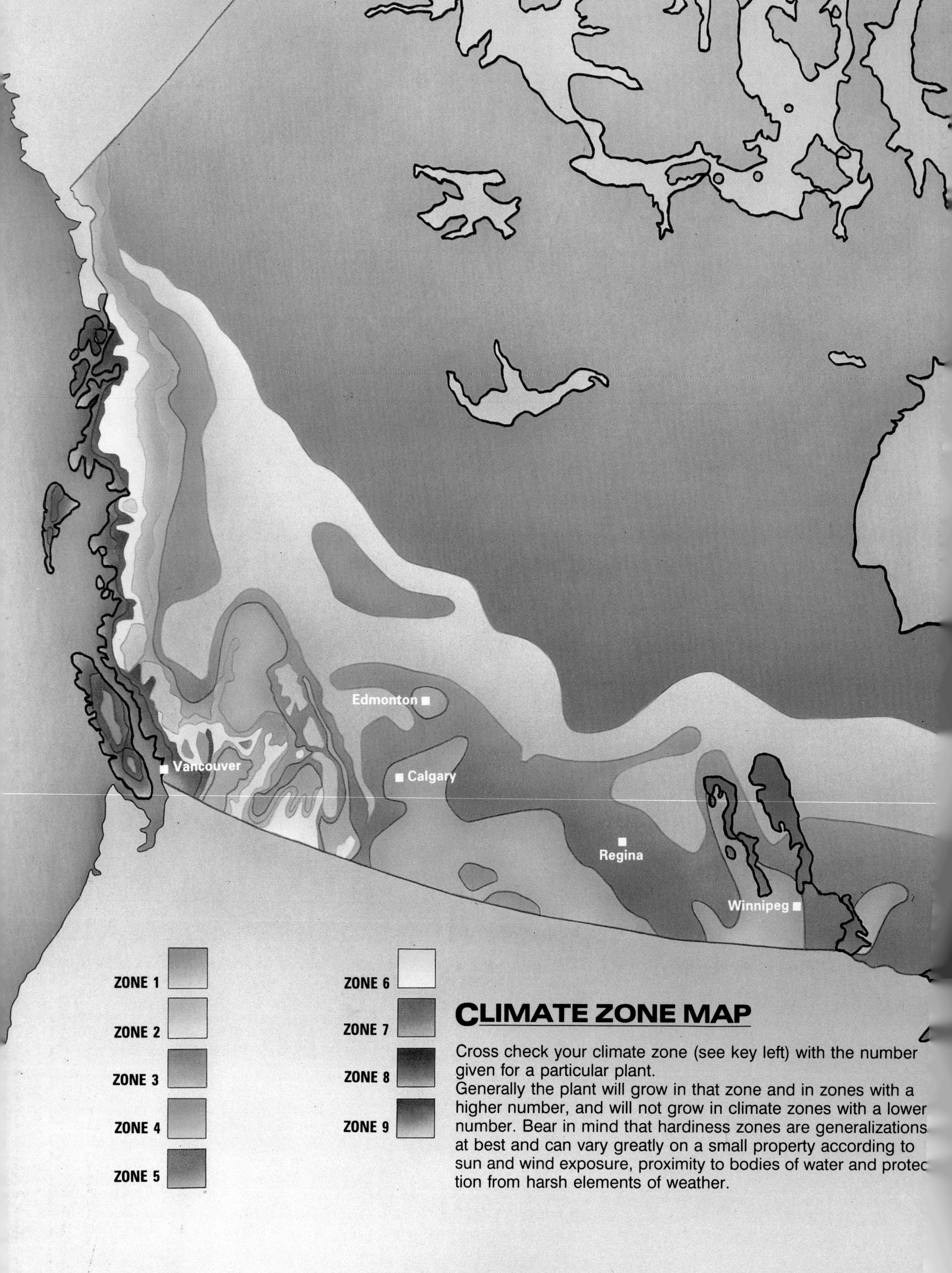
Edmonton
Vancouver
Calgary
Regina
Winnipeg
ZONE 1
ZONE 2
ZONE 3
ZONE 4
ZONE 5
ZONE 6
ZONE 7
ZONE 8
ZONE 9
CLIMATE ZONE MAP
Cross check your climate zone (see key left) with the number given for a particular plant.
Generally the plant will grow in that zone and in zones with a higher number, and will not grow in climate zones with a lower number. Bear in mind that hardiness zones are generalizations at best and can vary greatly on a small property according to sun and wind exposure, proximity to bodies of water and protec tion from harsh elements of weather.